Kenr

D1760082

GEOGRAPHY IN
BRITISH SCHOOLS, 1850–2000

Woburn Education Series
General Series Editor: Professor Peter Gordon

For over 20 years this series on the history, development and policy of education, under the distinguished editorship of Peter Gordon, has been evolving into a comprehensive and balanced survey of important trends in teaching and educational policy. The series is intended to reflect the changing nature of education in present-day society. The books are divided into four sections – educational policy studies, educational practice, the history of education and social history – and reflect the continuing interest in this area.

For a full series listing, please visit our website: www.woburnpress.com

GEOGRAPHY
in
BRITISH SCHOOLS
1850–2000

Making a World of Difference

REX WALFORD
University of Cambridge

WOBURN PRESS
LONDON • PORTLAND, OR

First published in 2001 in Great Britain by
WOBURN PRESS
Crown House, 47 Chase Side
Southgate, London N14 5BP

and in the United States of America by
WOBURN PRESS
c/o ISBS
5824 N.E. Hassalo Street
Portland, Oregon 97213-3644

Website: www.woburnpress.com

Copyright © 2001 Rex Walford

British Library Cataloguing in Publication Data:

Walford, Rex
    Geography in British schools, 1850–2000: making a world of
    difference. – (The Woburn education series)
    1. Geography – Study and teaching – Great Britain – History
    – 19th century. 2. Geography – Study and teaching – Great
    Britain – History – 20th century
    I. Title
    910.7′1041

ISBN 0-7130-0207-7 (cloth)
ISBN 0-7130-4027-0 (paper)
ISSN 1462-2076

Library of Congress Cataloging-in-Publication Data:

Walford, Rex.
    Geography in British schools, 1850–2000: making a world of difference /
    Rex Walford.
        p.   cm. – (Woburn education series)
    Includes bibliographical references and index.
    ISBN 0-7130-0207-7 (cloth) – ISBN 0-7130-4027-0 (paper)
        1. Geography – Study and teaching – Great Britain – History –
    19th century. 2. Geography – Study and teaching – Great Britain –
    History – 20th century. I. Title. II. Series.

G76.5.G7 W36 2000
910′.71041–dc21

00-049424

All rights reserved. No part of this publication may be reproduced, stored in or introduced into a retrieval system or transmitted, in any form or by any means, electronic, mechanical, photocopying, recording or otherwise, without the prior written permission of the publisher of this book.

Printed in Great Britain by
MPG Books Ltd, Bodmin, Cornwall

Contents

Figures and Tables

(First number represents the chapter in which figure is placed)

TABLES

Preface

There are a number of books which chronicle geography's development as an academic discipline, but none, as far as I know, about the history of geography in schools. Whilst working in teacher-education in England, I have often felt the need for such a text – not an exhaustive, definitive history, but one which outlines major themes and provides an introduction to personalities and trends. So this book is an attempt to fill the gap by providing both some information and some colour about the past.

Many of those who now come to train as teachers of geography have taken courses in 'geographical thought' or 'the history of geography' in their university degree. However, these courses usually make no mention of the way in which the subject has developed in schools: there is a relationship between the two histories but they are by no means in parallel. It would be misleading to predicate the character of school geography at any one time from contemporary preoccupations in the academic discipline or indeed to ignore the fact that sometimes change has permeated from the bottom of the well upwards rather than as a cascade downwards from the waters of academe.

I think it is important that all those who train to teach geography should gain some idea of the history of the subject in schools as well as a knowledge of its 'academic' territory, so that they can better appreciate the context in which they are going to operate. I also hope that the book may be of interest to three other audiences; those in higher education who are interested in the history of the geographical discipline as a whole; those educationalists interested in case-studies within curriculum history; and, probably most numerous, those who are already teaching geography but who have not previously explored the antecedents of their own work.

The book concentrates on the history of school geography in England and Wales, although there are some allusions to key events in Scotland along the way. The Scottish system has had over a century of separate organisation; the organisation of Welsh education has significantly diverged from the English only since the Education Act of 1988. These parts of Britain deserve their own chronicle from someone who is closer than I am to the fine-grain knowledge of their distinctive patterns.

In passing, I have tried to identify the major elements and landmarks in the history of education as a whole as well as those specific to geographical education. In trying to make the text readable, I have sought to avoid burdening it with great amounts of factual detail, though I have provided references and indicators for further study in the notes at the end of each chapter.

In seeking to tell the story, I decided that a straightforward chronological approach was best; however, the chapter headings indicate not only time periods, but particular emphases and themes prominent in the periods. It should not be deduced that these themes are circumscribed by the dates in the chapter headings: sometimes a particular aspect of geography's history in schools has been followed through over a longer period, but within a single chapter.

I am aware that some writers on education cast doubt on the whole conception of 'subjects' and believe them to be artificial constructions maintained by vested interests. I do not share that view and have sought to engage with the 'social constructivist' viewpoint briefly in the final chapter, but it should be made clear that this book is mainly concerned with accounting for past events in which 'subjects' have been part of the accepted curriculum landscape.

I recognise that, as Felix Driver has said, 'representing geography's past is inevitably an act of the present, however much we attempt to commune with the past'. Even if one has lived through and in a part of it, one sees the historical landscape from a contemporary perspective and a particular viewpoint. I cannot claim complete objectivity, nor should I wish to, but I hope there is some attempt at empathy with the views and the deeds of the past; in the current whirl of new initiatives, it is all too easy to be dismissive of the past, without looking at origins and contexts.

I have not attempted to be encyclopaedic, and some who might have expected to find their work recognised here may remain unidentified. Inevitably, in seeking to find a shape and meaning to history, some personalities prominent on the national scene become the focus of particular episodes or the exemplars to represent others. I do not intend, by that approach, to undervalue the debt that is owed to the many unsung heroes and heroines who have laboured in the geographical vineyard over the years.

I am very grateful to the many who have provided information and help along the way and who have offered me advice. I especially wish to thank my good friends in the world of geography education, Colin Conner, Matthew Judd, Bill Marsden, Angela Webster and David Wright, all of whom read some or all of the text in draft form and offered comment on it. My wife Wendy was, as ever, a relentless and invaluable critic of my intended coherence and my writing style, as well as a patient listener and adviser. Needless to say, those mentioned above bear no responsibilities for the selection of material I have made, the perspectives which I take, and the views on particular matters which I express.

Acknowledgements

The author and publisher wish to acknowledge the following, who have given permission for copyrighted material to be reproduced in this book.

The Geographical Association, for Figures 4.9, 4.10, 5.1, 5.2, 5.4, 6.1, 6.4, 6.9, 6.10, 9.3 and for extracts of text from *Geography and Teaching Geography*.

The Royal Geographical Society (with IBG), for Figure 1.1, an extract of text from the *Geographical Journal* and (from the RGS Photographic Collection) for Figures 4.5, 4.6 and 4.7.

The British Broadcasting Corporation, for Figure 6.2.

The Controller of Her Majesty's Stationery Office, for Figures 8.3, 8.4 and 11.1.

The London Metropolitan Archive, for Figures 3.2, 4.11 and photograph on jacket cover.

3D Education and Adventure Ltd, for photograph on jacket cover.

Arnold Publishers for Figure 7.4.

Oxford University Press, for Figure 8.7.

The *Cambridge Journal of Education*, for Figure 9.1.

Stanley Thornes, for Figure 11.2.

The Gernsheim Collection for Figure 3.1.

The Editors of the *Carthusian*, for the Obituary on p. 124.

Every effort has been made to find the present copyright holder of other substantial extracts published; the publisher will be glad to give credit in subsequent editions, if errors or omissions are brought to our attention.

I dedicate this book to:

the postgraduate students whom I have taught in the
University of Cambridge since 1973,
whose idealism about their vocation to teach geography
and belief in the educational value of what they are doing
has been a constantly heartening experience.

1

Introduction

Ginger began at once, 'I've found the head of 'em. He's a big fat man with a red face an' a white moustache an' he's sitting at a table lookin' at a map.'

'Well that proves it', said William, equally excited, 'that proves it. If he wasn't foreign he wun't need to be lookin' at a map, would he? If he was really English, like what they're pretendin' to be, he wun't need a map of England. He'd 've done England at school in geography.'[1]

William's belief that he had found spies was based on shaky supposition. But his view of school geography had greater certainty – informed by personal experience. He would already have 'done England' himself. William's geography teacher was presumably strong on having the class memorise facts.

William Brown's view is not untypical of that sometimes expressed by those who look back in middle and later life on their schooling. Geography lessons are usually recalled without fear or dislike but it is the resonance of the factual content – the so-called 'capes and bays' element – which is often remembered:

Anyone who had a reasonably good memory ... and could recite the capes and headlands from St Abb's Head to St Bees Head could escape trouble. The teachers were conscientious and hard-working and it never occurred to us or perhaps to them that education means more than committing facts to memory.[2]

[At the local Council school] ... I acquired a deep and knowledgeable passion for Geography. The subject was taught by a very keen master and a map of England hung permanently on the wall in front of my place. Soon I could reproduce that map from memory, naming all the headlands, and bays and rivers, marking the different types of agriculture, the various industries, the railway lines, the fishing areas. It was one way of coming to know the nature and story of England and to me it was not so much work as high romance.[3]

When I was but thirteen or so
I went into a golden land
Chimborazo, Cotopaxi
Took me by the hand

My father died, my brother too
They passed like fleeting dreams
I stood where Popacatapetl
In the sunlight gleams

I dimly heard the master's voice
And boys far off at play
Chimborazo, Cotopaxi
Had stolen me away.[4]

In my third year at secondary school I had a form teacher I was very fond of. Mr Macpherson was a large, burly, bearded Scot (who) switched me on to school, to golf and to geography, which, in between iron shots, he taught. I happily meandered through O-level and A-level learning the names of rivers and mountains, thrilling to the effects of glacial erosion, writing dissertations on deposition and trying to remember where and what Cotopaxi was. Geography appealed because it was fact-filled. You knew where you were ... Happy days.[5]

This portfolio of memories stretches from the turn of the century to the recent past. Alternatively a field-work experience or a vivid visual-aid may provide the substance of the recollection. Geography, on the whole, does not fare badly in school memories; but its image in such memories is revealing, especially when placed alongside accounts of what its practitioners were aspiring to do or thought that they were achieving.

For a long part of its history, geography was seen by many as a rather 'bread and butter' subject; it was recognised that a knowledge of its elements was needed by all as a part of general knowledge, but wasn't it mostly as a gazeteer of terrestrial bric-a-brac that could be safely dropped from study later? The view was similar to that held by one of Eric Linklater's characters in *The Wind on the Moon*, 'Geography is a good straightforward subject and would be quite easy if it were not so *big*.'[6] Indeed, geography was only rarely considered as an appropriate subject for high-ability pupils to study in the upper forms of secondary schools until about 30 years ago.

Today, geography has largely rid itself of a 'Cinderella' image in the hierarchy of subjects and stands strongly as a popular GCSE, A-level and university choice. The demands it makes on pupils are no less challenging than those of alternative subjects; but there are other concerns. Do children get the solid grounding in world knowledge that they once had? In its quest to grapple with issues, is it possible for geography to become a vehicle for propagandist teaching and indoctrination? What is geography's distinctive contribution to a curriculum which is increasingly grounded in 'basic skills'? Does the nation care as much about its children being educated geographically as it once did?

This book seeks to explore and explain some of the vicissitudes of the subject in schools, concentrating on its recent past and its place in English education since the years preceding the introduction of schooling for all (i.e., roughly the last 150 years).

This includes a deconstruction of some of the myths which have grown up about school geography's Victorian image; a consideration of its struggle for examination recognition in the early years of the twentieth century; an account of the periods when 'regional' and field-work emphases came to prominence; an analysis of the uncomfortable but stimulating revolution which transformed it in the 1960s and 1970s; an examination of some of the political and philosophical influences which have affected it; and, last but not least, the experience and the effect of the coming of a National Curriculum.

Though readers will bring their own predilections and perspectives to these matters, one thing will certainly become clear; geography in schools is (and, in the past, usually has been) something more than William Brown's image and recollection of it.

GOING BACK TO THE GREEKS

It is impossible to say when the first geography lesson took place, formal or informal, though, even in the Garden of Eden, Adam or Eve must have asked each other the way and talked of places and landscapes. The Twenty-Third Psalm speaks of shepherds, green pastures, and still waters, as well as 'the valley of the shadow'. The dimension of geography has been an inescapable part of human experience from the beginning of time; Descartes said, 'I think, therefore I am', but he might just as easily have completed the logic of his conclusion by adding 'I am, therefore I must be somewhere.'

The roots of geographical education lie in the natural curiosity that all of us have about places and ways of living other than our own. We know little about the origins of those roots in Asia and Africa, but as far as the European experience goes, it may be traced back with certainty to hundreds of years before the birth of Christ. Homer's *Odyssey* can be regarded as the first book to be mainly about travel, a prime stimulation to geographical study, if not strictly a formal geographical text.

From the days of Herodotus (*c.* 485–425 BC) onwards explorers and generals noted down their experiences and their knowledge for the use of their governments and of a wider circle of readers. The ancient Egyptians speculated about the nature of the world beyond the narrow confines of the eastern Mediterranean and had seminars about it. In the third century BC, Eratosthenes of Alexandria (276–194 BC) developed and refined the Greek view that the earth was a sphere, (though this insight did not survive through the 'Dark Ages', when beliefs about a flat earth returned).

The works of Strabo (whose life straddled the BC/AD time line) and of Ptolemy of Alexandria (AD 90–168)[7] were also considerable additions to the European and Middle Eastern knowledge of the ancient world. Strabo described various parts of the world in which he had been a traveller and his work marks the beginnings of descriptive place-linked geography. It also contains the first explicit written justification of the usefulness of geography:

> it has varied uses, not only for politics and war, but also in giving knowledge, both of the heavens and of things on land and sea, animals, plants, fruits, and of all that is to be seen in different regions.[8]

Strabo offered a salutary early warning, however, that the study of geography was more than just collecting knowledge and that no one should undertake to write about geography 'without the wide learning only possessed by the student of things human and divine, the knowledge of which men call philosophy'.

Ptolemy was more concerned with mathematical and cosmographical aspects of geography and he attempted to record the 'latitude and longitude' of over 8,000 places, though, as we know now, his calculations were based on imperfect evidence and were erroneous. Nevertheless he grappled with fundamental geographical issues and his books were acclaimed as great works of science in their period.[9]

But though there may have been some geographical education in the academies of that time, little survived as the 'Dark Ages' closed over Europe, as travel and exploration diminished and as the curriculum for the small minority who were educated in formal institutions became more narrowly circumscribed. What geographical knowledge was passed on related to the practicalities of living and the immediate surroundings – where water was likely to be found, what land was good for crops. The flame of wider geographical education in British schools was relatively dim until interest was renewed by the discoveries of sixteenth and seventeenth centuries and by the beginnings of Empire. The following chapters of this book take up in more detail the story from that time.

WHAT IS GEOGRAPHY?

Before that story can be told, it is important to consider a number of matters on which an understanding of the text depends; and the first of these is a question deceptive in its apparent simplicity – what is geography?

To some practitioners of the subject, navel-gazing about such an issue is seen as counter-productive. They take the view the great jazz pianist Fats Waller offered when asked, 'What, exactly, *is* rhythm?' by an eager musicologist. 'If you has to ask', replied Waller 'don't mess with it.' But, although 'geography' is a word easily understood and in current parlance everywhere, its exact meaning in relation to learning in schools is more problematic and has shifted through time.

'Geography is what geographers do' said Professor S. W. Wooldridge, when asked a question similar to that asked of Fats Waller. The strength of that enigmatic definition is that it can take into account changes of emphasis and direction in the subject over time; yet, few recount Wooldridge's aphorism without being aware of a feeling that it may be something of a cop-out.[10]

Some go more prosaically for definitions akin to those from the dictionary – 'Geographers study places and people'; 'Geography means, literally, the description of the earth' – often the kind of opening statements found in a secondary school pupil's exercise book, derived from a first lesson of the year in which the teacher is anxious to set the parameters of study. These definitions are safe but perhaps too simple; they indicate a large intellectual territory in a vague way but capture only the scope, and not the character or the essence of its study.

Though their words are not exactly couched as definitions, two of the most eminent of twentieth-century British geographers, Peter Haggett and David Stoddart, have, in recent times, provided thought-provoking and defining statements about the essence of the subject as they see it:

> The central and cherished aspects of geographical education are ; a love of landscape and of field exploration; a fascination with place; a wish to solve spatial conundrums posed by spatial configurations.[11]

> First we are concerned with earth's diversity ... second the use of maps ... third fieldwork ... I take these concerns as fundamental to our subject, at the elementary as well as the research level.[12]

An extended definition of geography appeared in 1998 in a significant publication from the Royal Geographical Society (see Figure 1.1). Though this requires close reading and considerable reflection to yield its full meaning , it is multi-faceted in its approach and does pick up many of the key themes and nuances of which students and teachers of geography become aware.

The views of graduates who have just completed geographical study provide a set of interesting, informed, contemporary viewpoints on the nature of the subject. Figures 1.2 and 1.3 represent some of the more distinctive of these, amongst over 250 gathered from students in the Postgraduate Certificate of Education geography course at the University of Cambridge between 1988 and 1998.[13]

Overall, the student definitions fall into four broad categories: those who emphasise the spatial aspects of the subject (spatialists); those whose main concern is for the linkage between physical and human environments (interactionists); those who stress geography's role in synthesising material from different disciplines (synthesisers); and those who describe geography mainly in terms of its study of places (placeists). Exemplifications of these are given in Figure 1.4.

WHAT IS GEOGRAPHY?

Geography is the integrated study of the earth's landscapes, peoples, places and environments. It is quite simply, about the world in which we live. It is unique in bridging the social sciences (human Geography) with its understanding of the dynamics of cultures, societies and economies, and the earth sciences (physical Geography) in the understanding of the dynamics of physical landscapes and environmental processes. Geography puts this understanding of social and physical processes within the essential context of places and regions – recognising the great differences in cultures, political systems, economies, landscapes and environments across the world, and the links between them. Understanding the causes of differences and inequalities between places and social groups underlie much of the newer developments in human Geography.

While each of the two broad areas of physical and human Geography exists in its own right, the subject also combines them to provide a much-needed capability to study and understand interactions in which they live and upon which they ultimately depend, both locally and globally. This is the core of Geography. In its role as an integrating discipline, Geography provides an ideal framework for relating other fields of knowledge. It is not surprising that those trained as geographers often contribute substantially to the applied management of resources and environments.

GEOGRAPHY IN ENVIRONMENTAL EDUCATION

The environment, both physical and social, is central to Geography. The compulsory elements of environmental education within the schools' National Curriculum in the United Kingdom is taught through Geography and through Science in roughly equal portions. In 1997 Geography was the sixth most popular GCSE subject, and indeed the most popular optional subject, and the fourth most popular A-level subject. At higher education level, Geography is the main provider of integrated environmental education and training. It equips young people with a wide range of cognitive skills and key skills including numeracy, literacy, problem-solving, research, team work, and IT. This is in addition to the subject specific knowledge, and specific skills such as field-work, map interpretation and laboratory analysis. The traditional language of Geography is the map, and in a world where over 75% of the data is referenced spatially to a location, this remains a vital skill. In recent years, traditional map work has been augmented by computer-based Geographical Information Systems and remote sensing from satellites and aerial photography.

GEOGRAPHY ENRICHING LIVES AND CITIZENSHIP

Geography is inherent in everyone's lives. It is all around us and it is capable of enriching even the most mundane of tasks, and instilling consideration for the world, its environments and its peoples. Geography, experienced from a young age through fieldwork and travel, often stimulates in people of all ages a life-long enthusiasm for the countryside, a respect and responsibility for conservation and cultural diversity, and an understanding of the interconnected nature of the world and the need for sustainable management of its resources. A country walk takes on new meaning when one has an understanding of the landscape, its age, how it formed, how it has been changed by human actions, and the threats it may face from soil erosion or nitrate pollution of streams. Behind each journey to work, so carefully recorded in the Census data, lies information matching work places to homes, on travel times and modes, on distances and fuel consumption and pollutant emissions, all of which are relevant to future planning of transport and sustainable cities. The manner and degree to which societies consume forest and fossil fuel resources will affect the local and global environment and climate, and every citizen should be aware of the impact of their lifestyle and how they can contribute to mitigating climate change. Increasing international travel serves to illustrate the interconnected nature of the world and associated globalisation and economic dependence. Understanding of such issues and responsibilities, together with awareness of the multi-cultural societies we live in, are necessary for citizens and employees of the future, and are central to Geography.

In short, Geography is, in the broadest sense, an education for life and for living. An understanding and enthusiasm for Geography, and the development of geographical knowledge, is essential for the 21st century in a world where population growth, rapid development, global environmental change, social and economic inequality and resource depletion threaten the very planet on which we live. These problems place increasing burdens on cultural tolerance, the sustainable management of societies, natural resources including bio-diversity, and landscapes. Geographers have a key role in understanding and helping to solve these issues.

Figure 1.1:
'What is geography?': a definition from the RGS–IBG Strategic Plan 1998–2005 (*Source:* RGS)

WHAT IS GEOGRAPHY?

(1)

Geography is a Pandora's box of study about the world and its people, of how the physical and social environments interact individually and collectively – it's more than just about maps!

(2)

Geography is beautiful; it is a cross-disciplinary, multiskill subject, concerning the spatial spread of physical, meteorological, social, political, biological and historical factors over time, and at all scales, both on and off the earth.

(3)

Geography is a subject whose teaching
Enjoys both a wide and varied briefing.
From glaciers to trade laws
And the geography of whores
It's a living study that'll take some beating.

(4)

Geography is understanding the earth and everything in, under, over and on it. It is reminders of yesterday, realities of today, and dreams of tomorrow.

(5)

Geography is the use of space to bridge intellectually imposed separations and thereby understand the world we live in better.

(6)

Geography ranges across global problems, international solutions, political chaos, river systems, city maps, house prices. It covers population, landforms, regions, environments. It asks Why? When? Where? What? and How?

(7)

Geography's value comes from its ability to provide an analysis that brings home to people the extent to which living itself is an intensely political act; an act that is usually reinforced by continuing global injustices on which our comfort rests. (The job of the geography teacher is to make children question this in the hope that the answers which they find will smash injustice and free the oppressed from the chains under which they live their lives.)

(8)

Geography is God's way of giving us mere mortals a chance of finding our way around this planet, and discovering what it all means.

(9)

Geography is, always has been, and always will be, what those who call themselves geographers choose to do.

(10)

Geography is a loom that enables us to pull together a plethora of threads concerning the world around us – its physical environment, human activity, and the interaction between the two – to systematically weave a pattern that helps us understand where we are, who we are and why we are.

Figure 1.2:
'What is geography?': some definitions of geography from Cambridge PGCE students
(*Source*: author)

7

Geography
Human, physical, political
Planning, fieldwork, glaciers, spatial,
Region, populations, land use, ecosystems, locality
Satellite images, soil, rocks, climate, trade, maps, development
Culture, environment, agriculture, urban, water, dynamic, global, place

Geography is so cool:
the most interesting lesson to learn in a school –
ranging from important matters of demographics and population
to the more obscure but nevertheless fascinating topics of denudation chronology and periglaciation

Figure 1.3:
'What is geography?': two definitions using shape and verse (*Source*: author)

A Classification of Responses

Spatialists (22%)
e.g. 'the scientific approach to the spatial distribution of phenomena in order to understand "what is where" and "why it is there"'
'the study of spatial interactions at a magnitude of scales over time'
'the differentiation of the content of space on the Earth's surface and the resultant analysis of space relations ...'

Interactionists (43%)
e.g. 'the constantly evolving study of the Earth, with special attention paid to the interaction within this environment'
'the study of the forces and processes of the natural world and of the interdependences and interaction between man and his environment and between nations, peoples and individuals'
'the observation, description and interpretation of people, spaces, places and processes, and the multivariate interactions achieved through natural response and/or pursuit of change'

Synthesisers (29%)
e.g. 'it is a subject which ties the loose ends of the disciplines together to explain how and why we come to the way we are and to fathom how such affecting processes and influences will shape the future'
'the great synthesiser; ... preparing global citizens for the task of planetary management in all its aspects'
'it has world vision; adopting a holistic approach it synthesises disciplines, examining both human and physical environments, their interactions in space and time and their expression within regional and national contexts'

Placeists (6%)
e.g. 'the study of the world around us – it leads from basic knowledge about the existence of continents and countries to the physical features which compose them and the human developments within them'
'literally speaking "writing the earth", describing and representing particular places and theorising about them'
'the essence of the subject is the development of a sense of place and of being able to answer sensitively the questions "what is it like here and why?"'

Figure 1.4:
An analysis of Cambridge student responses, 1988–98, to the question: 'What is geography?'
(*Source*: author)

Three of the four categories show links to a similar classification exercise undertaken by W. D. Pattison. Pattison suggested that in the writing and teaching of geography four traditions could be recurringly identified and linked these back to Greek origins:

> the earth-science tradition (illustrated by the writings of Aristotle)
> the area-studies tradition (illustrated by the writings of Strabo)
> the man-land tradition (illustrated by the writings of Hippocrates)
> the spatial tradition (illustrated by the writings of Ptolemy)[14]

It may be useful to consider the following chapters with these broad traditions in mind.

WHAT BRINGS PEOPLE TO GEOGRAPHY?

Quite apart from what geography is, it is also revealing and profitable to ask, what are the reasons that people like the subject and believe it to be important? What aspects of geographical study bring students (at all levels) stimulation, satisfaction and enjoyment – and a desire to carry their studies further when compulsion of study is removed?

Robert McNee suggested that six distinct value-systems could be identified amongst geographers:[15]

> globalism (the earth-as-a-whole view)
> localism (the interest to study small areas in situ)
> holism (a delight in geographic synthesis)
> map-love (maps as a source of aesthetic experience)
> earth-reverence (strong in conservation concern)
> geographic enquiry (the desire for exploration of new truths)

and that most who studied geography were more strongly motivated by one or two of the value-systems than by all six. (Indeed, the instincts of globalists and localists might be seen to be diametrically opposed.)

Stoddart's emphasis on love of maps and fieldwork can be identified in the fourth and fifth categories. Haggett's attachment to the solving of 'spatial conundrums' may be partly represented in the sixth category as well as in the first.

Over the years, the underlying value-systems held by teachers are likely to have been as important as the prevailing paradigms and images of the subject itself in determining what has been specified in syllabuses and examinations, as well as what has been taught in classrooms.

WHAT HAS BEEN THE JUSTIFICATION FOR TEACHING GEOGRAPHY IN SCHOOLS?

The understanding of the nature of geography and of the value-systems which dynamise its practitioners are, however, only preliminary to two other fundamental questions which need an answer in the context of this book. The first of these is to seek a justification of why geography should be taught at all. What priority has it claimed in the past (and can it claim now) over other things which might also wish to have a place in the school curriculum (astronomy or driver-education or fishing, for example)?

The aim of teaching geography cannot simply be justified by a wish or need 'to produce geographers' since only a tiny minority of students will find employment in such a professional capacity. In any case, all subjects can logically make the same case. Therefore, it must be asked, what more general educational objectives are involved? On what grounds can geography justify a place in a school curriculum when time allows pupils to study only a limited number of subjects or topics?

Geographers themselves have constantly sought to present a response to that question over the past 150 years and in Britain at least, have produced different answers at different times. The rising significance of scientific knowledge about the earth, the inspiration of Empire, the spur of war, the growth of leisure and mobility for all, the desire to solve international problems, the growing concern about how the planet will survive, have all been advanced as pressing auxiliary influences which strengthened the case at one time or another.

This may seem an overly pragmatic way to construct a justification for an area of educational study. Yet, if it had been left to geographical knowledge and ideas to demonstrate their value to others by their own self-evident virtues and simply by a dispassionate appeal to reason, would it have been enough? The politics of the curriculum are a jungle. As the following pages show, from an unpromising position of little influence, geographers developed the merits of their case with a growing realisation of how it needed to be packaged and presented effectively in order to win the approbation of those who were initially not disposed to accept it. As perceptions of the world changed and expanded, a resultant appreciation of geography's potential accompanied the change.

For this to happen geographers have had to engage critically and deeply with major educational ideas and philosophies. They have had to realise that what is offered in schools needs not only interest and colour, academic sinew and coherence, but also a fundamental relevance to the needs of the whole person. Those who teach geography in school, in the last resort, are not aiming to produce mini-geographers (except in exceptional circumstances on occasion) but are making a contribution to the general education of a future citizen.

The possibility of geographical knowledge, ideas and insights being transmitted through other disciplines was mooted as far back as the 1870s. Various alternative formulations which encompass some or all of geography (social studies, environmental science, humanities) have been seen as a possible option for schools from time to time.

But from the days of Halford Mackinder, Scott Keltie and Douglas Freshfield onwards, the community of geographical scholars has proved to be a surprisingly durable and coherent force. An examination of history suggests that geography as a discipline has gained rather than lost a sense of community over most of the century – though, as we enter the twenty-first century, signs of specialist preoccupation leading to fragmentation within the subject in higher education may threaten that situation.

In the best of all possible worlds, it would be the inherent virtues of the case, rather than the political skills of presentation which have been responsible for advancing geography to parity with other longer-established subjects in the school curriculum. But in the end who can be sure?

The struggle for parity lasted for over a century. As late as 1967 E. C. Marchant HMI, Chief Inspector of Schools in Geography, would say in his Presidential Address to the Geographical Association:

> we have a vital responsibility to ensure that our subject is not superficial but is intellectually rigorous. Geography is at last attaining to intellectual respectability in the academic streams of our secondary schools. But the battle is not quite over.[16]

The journey was completed and confirmed in the second half of the twentieth century. The convenient 'twinning' of geography with history began to be a feature of secondary school timetables after the Second World War and the two were seen as of equal importance when a National Curriculum was specified for the first time in 1987. The high-water mark was the implementation of geography lessons for all pupils in schools in England and Wales from 5 years to 16 years in the years immediately following. The tide has ebbed a little since then.

WHAT OUGHT GEOGRAPHY TO BE LIKE IN SCHOOLS?

The consideration of how and why geography in schools has been justified over the last 150 years leads inevitably to a consequent question – what *is* this geography that should be taught in formal education if it is to be relevant and useful for pupils? Is its nature the same for pupils of different ages? What, in essence, ought school geography to be like?

The answer is unlikely to be found in a definitive once-and-for-all-time statement; the dynamic of change has been a feature of existence since the Industrial Revolution and continues unabated. If education is to be relevant it must evolve and adapt to the changing nature and needs of society. There is a salutary message in the story of the tribe who continued to base their curriculum on learning the traditional skills of how to hunt sabre-tooth tigers, as the Ice Age closed around them and the tigers stole away to warmer climes. Yet the alternative is not to embrace a relativist (or post-modern) view uncritically. Most teachers would not have any inclination to go to school day after day if they did not believe in some eternal verities.

As long ago as 1885, Prince Peter Kropotkin had a clear answer about the possible virtues of learning geography. In a review article for a general periodical called *The Nineteenth Century*, he commented on the

'Report on the State of Geographical Education' commissioned by the Royal Geographical Society and presented by J. Scott Keltie, under the title 'What geography ought to be':

> The task of geography (in early childhood) is to interest the child in the great phenomena of nature, to waken the desire of knowing and explaining them. Geography must render, moreover, another far more important service. It must teach us, from our earliest childhood that we are all brethren, whatever our nationality ... it must show that each nationality brings its own precious building-stone for the development of the commonwealth ... it has to enforce on the minds of children that all nationalities are valuable to one another ...
>
> There is a third task ... that of dissipating the prejudices in which we are reared with regard to the so-called 'lower races' and this precisely at an epoch when everything makes us forsee that we shall soon be brought into a much closer contact with them than ever.[17]

These sentiments may be thought surprising in a time of high Victorian pomp, when thoughts of empire-building and colonisation were dominant. Avril Maddrell and other authors have shown how many of the geography textbooks of this time reflected the imperial cast of mind[18] and also the general extent of Anglo-centrism and of the dominance of masculine images and roles.[19]

But there is also evidence that not all geography teachers were entirely absorbed by jingoistic sentiments. Fairgrieve and Young, two of the most successful and influential school textbook writers of the early twentieth century, conclude the final chapter, on 'The British Empire', in one of their best-selling texts with these words:

> We sometimes hear it said that Canada or New Zealand or some other country is 'ours', or that it 'belongs' to Britain. This is not true, even if we are thinking of the land called Canada, and it is even less true if we understand that the Empire is not made up of land but of people. It is made up of the people of Britain and Canada and India and Australia and the rest. The Empire is not 'ours' but 'us'. And what keeps us together? Good will and knowledge. That is one reason why we learn geography.[20]

This predates by some 30 years the British Empire's transformation into a Commonwealth of equals. A relatively enlightened internationalism infused Imperial sentiments for a good proportion of geography teachers, though some were, inevitably, prisoners of the prevailing mood of their time.

At other stages in the twentieth century, changing national and world circumstances (already outlined) have materially affected the nature of what teachers and other educators thought school geography 'ought to be'. The high aspirations of Kropotkin have not always been reached, nor perhaps even glimpsed at. The prosaic purveying of material has sometimes been characterised by T. S. Eliot's pithy lament 'Where is the knowledge we have lost in information?'[21]

But even so, there can be discerned recurring elements in the everyday traffic of geography classrooms – the attempt to pass on a hard core of world knowledge is usually suffused by the teaching of understandings and insights about places and spaces, landscapes and settlements, and the interaction of human beings and their environment. A humane approach to societies and a sensitive approach to environments is usually the base. Lessons are almost always serviced by a plentiful use of maps and visual aids, and often supplemented by work in the field.

The Charter on Geographical Education formulated and accepted by the International Geographical Congress of 1992[22] was carefully devised to be in accordance with the modern principles of the United Nations, the World Declaration of Human Rights and the Rights of Children, and UNESCO recommendations about the need for education in cross-national understanding, co-operation and peace. Yet, in essence, its underlying ideas and attitudes derive not from painstaking bureaucracy but from the practical example of countless geography teachers through the century.

WHAT IS SCHOOL GEOGRAPHY TODAY?

So, before progressing with the story, it may be a useful bench-mark to try and assess what the role of geography has come to be (or what, it aspires to be) for practitioners in today's school classrooms as it links its own subject material with wider educational goals.

On the human side, perceptive teachers know that it is more necessary than it ever was for geographical studies to help in giving pupils some sense of their own *identity* – to help them understand their own community and nation and its multiple heritage as a prelude to other matters. Geography also has a major role in revealing and explaining the *diversity* of the world's peoples and cultures – showing that the world is a world of difference but not one in which people should regard each other with feelings of superiority and inferiority. The ultimate aim (beyond all the factual knowledge and consideration of particular issues) is to bring these two building-brick concepts together, so that pupils have some sense of *universality* – some sense of human brotherhood and sisterhood which may lead them to want to make the world a happier and more stable place.

On the physical side, many teachers seek to lead pupils towards informed *observation and appreciation* of the natural world – to develop a sensitivity to the wonder and beauty of different kinds of landscape, and not confine this merely to a few spectacular tourist landmarks. As well as 'seeing' landscapes, there is a need to develop a *technical understanding* of them – to learn how they are formed and how they have changed over time. Beyond that, as we move into the new millenium, one of the ultimate aims of geography in schools (and of schooling itself) must surely be to develop an awareness of the need for *conservation* of the physical landscape, rather than to acquiesce in its continuing destruction – to encourage, in other words, a sense of stewardship for the environment.

All this needs to be carried out in an environment of intellectual challenge and stimulation. If competently and imaginatively taught, the varied physical and human geography of the modern world should surely have enough richness to interest learners and to retain their goodwill.

To this author at least, these contemporary objectives, held consciously by some and demonstrated unconsciously by others, show a clear link to Kropotkin's thoughts of over a century ago. The story that unfolded in between is told in the pages that follow.

NOTES

1. An extract from Richmal Crompton, *William the Good* (George Newnes, London, 1942), p. 77.
2. James Callaghan, *Time and Chance: An Autobiography* (Collins, London, 1987), p. 26.
3. Sir Alan Cobham, *A Time to Fly* (Shepheard-Walwyn, London, 1978), p. 7.
4. W. J. Turner, *Selected Poems 1919–1936* (Oxford University Press, Oxford, 1939). The verses are an extract from 'Romance'.
5. Stephen Moss, 'Off the map', *Guardian*, 4 May 1999.
6. Eric Linklater, *The Wind on the Moon* (Macmillan, London, 1944).
7. Strabo wrote a seventeen-volume *Geographica*; see Strabo, *The Geography of Strabo*, trans. H. L. James (Harvard University Press, Cambridge, MA, 1967). Ptolemy wrote an eight-volume *Geography*; see Ptolemy, *The Geography*, trans. E. L. Stevenson (Dover, New York, 1991).
8. Quoted by E. W. Gilbert, from Strabo's *Geographica*, Vol. I, p. 1 (trans. Sir Richard Livingstone) in his inaugural lecture as Professor of Geography to the University of Oxford (*Geography as a Humane Study*, Oxford University Press, Oxford, 1955).
9. This period is well documented in A. Holt-Jensen, *Geography: History and Concepts* (Sage, London, 1999, 3rd edn), a book which provides a clear perspective on the 'academic history of geography' and helps illuminate educational contexts in general.
10. See, for instance, J. H. Paterson 'Some dimensions of geography', *Geography*, 64(4) pp. 268–9. 'I do a great deal of examining students, in the course of which I routinely ask them for their understanding of what geography is. And I am frankly tired of having my question answered by a fatuous grin and the response "Oh, that's a very difficult question; it's hard to say." I am almost equally tired of being told that geography is what geographers do; or that I really should not bother about these purely academic definitions. I am sorry to be a nuisance, but I *do* bother and I happen to think that *anybody* should bother who earns any sort of living from a subject which, apparently, no one feels it necessary to define.'
11. P. Haggett, in E. Rawling and R. Daugherty (eds), *Geography into the Twenty-First Century* (Wiley, Chichester, 1996), p. 17
12. D. R. Stoddart, *On Geography and its History* (Blackwell, Oxford, 1986), pp. 55–6.
13. R. Walford, 'What is geography?: An analysis of definitions provided by intending teachers of geography', *International Research in Geographical and Environmental Education*, 5 (1), (1996), pp. 69–76.
14. W. D. Pattison 'The four traditions of geography', *Journal of Geography*, 63 (1964), pp. 211–16; also reprinted in J. Bale, N. J. Graves and R. Walford (eds), *Perspectives in Geographical Education* (Oliver & Boyd, Edinburgh, 1973), pp. 2–11.
15. R. B. McNee, 'The geographic value-system', *New Approaches in Introductory College Geography Courses* (Association of American Geographers, Washington, DC, 1967).
16. E. C. Marchant, 'Some responsibilities of the teacher of geography', *Geography*, 53 (2) (April 1968), pp. 129–44.

17. P. A. Kropotkin, 'What geography ought to be', *The Nineteenth Century*, December (1885), pp. 940–56.

18. A. Maddrell, 'Empire, emigration and school geography: changing discourses of Imperial citizenship', *Journal of Historical Geography*, 22 (1996), pp. 373–87. T. Lilley, 'The black African in Southern Africa: images in British school textbooks', in J. A. Mangan (ed.), *The Imperial Classroom* (Routledge, London, 1996), pp. 40–53. D. R. Wright, 'Visual images in geography textbooks: The case of Africa', *Geography*, 64 (3) (July 1979), pp. 205–10.

19. A. Maddrell, 'Discourses of race and gender and the comparative method in geography school texts 1830–1918', *Environment and Planning*, D 16 (1) (1998), pp. 81–104.

20. J. Fairgrieve and E. Young, *Human Geography: The World* (George Philip, London, 1920), p. 224. The book went through 15 editions and remained in print for almost 30 years.

21. T. S. Eliot, *The Rock* (Faber & Faber, 1934). The chorus of which this is a part is also to be found in Eliot's *Collected Poems* (Faber & Faber, London, 1954).

22. The Charter is reprinted in *Teaching Geography*, 20 (2) (April 1995), pp. 95–9.

2

Travellers' Tales and Cosmography before 1850

Peter Heylyn, a seventeenth-century academic, records in a book published in 1649 that he was one day walking between Westminster and Whitehall in London when a 'tall big gentleman' thrust him roughly against a wall, looked scornfully over his shoulder at him, and said hoarsely, 'Geographie is better than divinitie', before passing on.[1]

Since Heylyn had delivered lectures on 'cosmography' at Magdalen College, Oxford in 1618, but turned mainly to theological writing in later life, the context of the confrontation can be deconstructed, but this curious event, more akin to a Morecambe and Wise sketch than to a genuine intellectual encounter, is nevertheless, one of the few pieces of evidence we have to suggest that 'geography' was significant as a term for a codified subject of study or general adult discourse in that period.

Before the nineteenth and twentieth centuries, not many people in Britain had the benefit of anything other than rudimentary schooling, in an uneven patchwork of elementary schools; most of that elementary education was concerned with learning to read, write and count at a simple level. Beyond this, in schools of secondary type (taking pupils at 11 or 13 years of age), the education provided was designed for those who would be the men of influence (priests, officials) and leaders of the British nation and for the aristocracy.

It derived in essence from mediaeval constructions of the curriculum – the *trivium*, which consisted of (Latin) grammar, rhetoric and dialectic; and the *quadrivium*, consisting of arithmetic, geometry, music and astronomy.[2] Of these, geometry and astronomy were, in practice, given least emphasis.

Even when new 'grammar schools' were founded, their curriculum was tied to traditional structures by the statutes which set them up. Only in the small minority of schools known as 'dissenting academies', institutions for the children of non-conformists to the Anglican faith (i.e. the Free Churches), were newer subjects such as history, science and modern languages encouraged. Some geography was taught in these academies in the later part of the seventeenth and the eighteenth centuries,[3] but it was mainly of the 'mathematical kind', which showed how longitude and latitude were derived and how map projections were constructed. This developed in essence from the growth of scientific ideas associated with the 'Enlightenment' and the 'Age of Reason' in the mid 1700s.

In 1797 the governors of Leeds Grammar School put forward a scheme to extend the curriculum of their school, beyond Latin and Greek, to include mathematics and modern languages; but Lord Eldon, in a famous judgement, ruled in 1805 that, by the terms of its foundation deeds, the school was only for 'teaching grammatically the learned languages'. Therefore it was bound, went the reasoning of the judgement, to teach a literal fulfilment of its name.[4] Many other grammar schools and independent schools had been founded under similar terms and had a similar classically oriented curriculum. Not until an Act of 1840 were the Grammar Schools freed from such constraints and able to introduce 'modern' subjects, such as elementary mathematics, English language and literature, French, German, history and geography.

The independent fee-paying (or, as they are confusingly known by tradition, 'public') schools were not bound by the 1840 Act and so the influence of 'modern' subjects was sometimes delayed even later. Of the 'modern' subjects considered in the nineteenth century for introduction into the curriculum of secondary schools, geography was amongst the least influential and least developed. Some of the most prestigious independent schools did not encourage geography as a serious academic study in their upper forms until the 1960s (see Chapter 8).

Yet centuries earlier, through the influence of the Renaissance and later the growth of exploration and developing trade, the teaching of some geography gained at least a toe-hold in the lower reaches of the British educational system because of the increasingly perceived utility of basic locational knowledge and the belief that school pupils should at least know the rudiments of how the seasons and day and night originated. If these were not known, there might be practical disadvantages in later life. The great English poet, John Milton (1608–74) regarded geography as 'both profitable and delightful'. 'I do perceive that I am very short in my business through not knowing the geographical part of my business', lamented Samuel Pepys (1633–1703), referring to his work as a senior clerk at the Admiralty.

MARINERS AND TRAVELLERS

Following the discovery that there were New Worlds beyond the oceans as well as an Old World based on Europe and the Mediterranean, it was not surprising that some of this exciting and revolutionary new knowledge and its implications was passed on to children in schools. The fact that many British seafarers and traders played a leading part in this global expansion in Elizabethan times added impact. The earlier adventures of John and Sebastian Cabot, and the contemporary exploits of national heroes such as Francis Drake and Sir Walter Raleigh were recounted in addition to those of Christopher Columbus, Vasco da Gama and Ferdinand Magellan. Later the travels and adventures of Captain James Cook and other pioneer explorers would add to the canon of exciting stories which would thrill young children and inspire some of them to dream of exploring the world themselves and visiting 'foreign parts'. From Hakluyt's 'Voyages'[5] onwards these 'travellers' tales', as we have come to call them, demanded imagination in response to narrative rather than intellectual appreciation – the later image of geography as an undemanding, 'stories of other lands', subject was nascent in this.

The other usual part of elementary geographical education in schools in the seventeenth and eighteenth centuries was the consideration of the globe (it was not so long before that theories of a flat earth had been discarded) and the demonstration of how day and night and the seasons occurred, and why some parts of the earth's surface were climatically different from others. This simple 'cosmography' was usually done in a practical way; an early indication of the way in which artefacts and visual-aids have been an essential part of the effective teaching of the subject. Erasmus (1466–1536), the Dutch scholar, had advocated geography as an important part of education, as had the French satirist Rabelais (1494–1553).

It is almost impossible to locate descriptions of geography lessons from this period in any meaningful detail, but it seems from more general accounts that the teacher would, as J. A. Comenius, the Czech educational writer (1592–1670), advocated, 'stand on a dais so that all the pupils might look at him' and do the reading or teaching in a didactic mode. Pupils might learn rhymes or mnemonics and repeat back to the teacher certain key facts to be learnt; there would be regular testing of locational knowledge, often through the teacher pointing to a map or globe and having children name the places which were indicated.

Comenius's *Orbis Sensualium Pictus* (Visible World), 'for the use of young Latin scholars', was one of the first printed textbooks to include illustrations; a version of it was translated into English by Charles Hoole in 1672.[6] The book contained many wood-cut sketches with constituent parts annotated by numbers, and these were identified on each accompanying page (see Figure 2.1). The illustrations of 'the city' and the 'the inward parts of a city' (see Figure 2.2) are perhaps two of the first illustrated urban geography models.

Another of the early geographical school textbooks is William Pemble's, *A Brief Introduction to Geography, containing a description of the grounds and general part thereof very necessary for young students in that science*;[7] this was a popular textbook for elementary schools and also almost certainly for individual tutors who taught children at home. There are relatively few textbooks still extant from the eighteenth century, though we know of Richard Turner's, *View of the Earth* (1762) and William Guthrie's, *New Geographical Historical and Commercial Grammar*.[8] The latter was read (in *Vanity Fair*) by Becky Sharp at Miss Pinkerton's Academy for Young Ladies as preparation for finding a rich husband, though maybe not by Becky's friend Amelia Sedley, since Miss Pinkerton's final report home about Amelia said that, 'In geography,

(20)

IX.

Terra.

The Earth.

(21)

In the Earth	In *Terrâ*
are	funt
high Mountains 1.	*Montes* 1. altî,
Deep Valleys, 2.	*Valles* 2. profundæ,
Hills Rifing, 3.	*Colles* 3. elevati,
Hollow Caves, 4.	*Spelunca* 4. cavæ,
Plain Fields, 5.	*Campi* 5. plani,
Shady Woods. 6.	*Sylvæ* 6. opacæ.

31

C 3   *Terra.*

Figure 2.1:
Page from Comenius' *Orbis Sensualium Pictus* (reduced in size)

(250)

CXXIII.

The inward parts of a City.   *Interiora Urbis.*

Within a City	Intra Urbem
are Streets, 1.	funt *Plateæ* (Vici) 1.
paved with ftones;	lapidibus ftratæ :
Market-places, 2.	*Fora*, 2.
(in fome places	(alicubi
with Galleries) 3.	cum *Porticibus*) 3.
and narrow Lanes, 4.	& *Angiportus*.
The publick buildings	*Publica ædificia funt*
are in the middle of the	in medio Urbis,
the Church, 5. (City,	*Templum*, 5.
the School, 6.	*Schola*, 6.
the Guild-hall, 7.	*Curia*, 7.
the Exchange. 8.	*Domus Mercaturæ* : 8.
	About

(251)

About the walls,	Circa Mænia,
and the Gates,	& Portas,
are the Magazine, 9.	*Armamentarium*, 9.
the Granary, 10.	*Granarium*, 10.
Innes,	*Diverforia*,
Ale-houfes,	*Popinæ*,
Cooks-fhops, 11	& *Caupone*, 11.
the Play-houfe, 12.	*Theatrum*, 12.
and the Spittle ; 13.	*Nofodochium* ; 13.
In the by-places	In receffibus,
are houfes of office, 14.	*Forica* (Cloacæ) 14.
and the Prifon. 15.	& *Cuftodia* (Carcer)15.
In the chief Steeple	In Turre primariâ
is the Clock, 16.	eft *Horologium*, 16.
and the Watchmens	& habitacio
dwelling. 17.	*Vigilum*. 17.
In the Streets	In Plateis
are Wells. 18.	funt *Putei*. 18.
The River 19.	*Fluvius*, 19.
or Beck	vel *Rivus*,
runing about the City,	Urbem interfluens,
ferveth	infervit
to wafh away the filth.	*fordibus* eluendis.
The Tower 10.	*Arx* 20.
ftandeth in the higheft	exftat
part of the City.	in fummo Urbis.

Judge-

Figure 2.2:
Early urban model: page from *Orbis Sensualium Pictus* (reduced in size)

there is still much to be desired."[9] In general, textbooks from the period substantiate an impression that, at least, suggestions about teaching methods in geography were developing in interesting ways, even if most teachers remained conservative in their actual classroom approaches.

A LATE EIGHTEENTH-CENTURY TEXTBOOK

A school textbook called *Geography and History* (1790)[10] includes a preface by 'E.R.', interesting enough to reproduce in whole (adapted and reformulated here, to make easier reading) as an example of such development:

> The following pages were originally intended solely for the use of my own children, and would never have been presented to the public eye if I had not myself experienced an inconvenience from the manuscript; for though the first sheets were purposely written in a large and distinct hand, I found (the children) read them with a difficulty that retarded their progress; and this first gave me the idea of putting it into print.

> I have selected from different authors such matters as appeared to me the most necessary for the improvement of young minds; and have, as much as possible divided them into small sections, and endeavoured to throw such headings together, as I thought would best assist the memory.

> Children that are accustomed to learn things by question and answer, very frequently 'get' them by rote, in the same words that are before them, without attending to the sense; and if the question be put in any other form, it throws them out and they are totally at a loss for an answer. To obviate this I have placed each different subject in a detatched sentence, which will give the teacher the opportunity of varying the mode of the question at (their) pleasure.

> We are, in general, too apt to under-rate the capacities of children; but I believe experience will evince that they are just as capable of learning something that may be useful (provided a proper method be taken to render it agreeable to them) as they are of repeating the little tales that are frequently told them for their amusement; and as Geography and History enlarge the mind more than any other studies, they cannot be begun too early.

> Geography is by no means a dry and irksome task to children; on the contrary they have a pleasure in looking over a map, and are rejoiced if they happen to discover any place they have ever heard of. They are naturally inquisitive and by judicious management may be easily led on by every object that surrounds them; and when once their curiosity is excited, and they begin to enquire, how such a thing is made? or where it comes from? they may every day

acquire some useful knowledge; and will often be delighted if you refer them to the maps and show them the place of country where the object of their enquiry is produced.

I would begin with a dissected map of England, merely as a toy, when you chose to be at leisure to play with (a child); and at first give (him) the county he lives in, with a few of the adjacent ones; point out to him his own town; explain to him that it appears but a speck because the map is little and takes in a great many places; then throw him any other towns that are familiar to his ear, where any of his acquaintances come from, and etc.

When he can readily join these, and remember them by name, add a few countries more and so on, till he gets pretty well through England. In the meantime, if he can read well enough you may sometimes, as an indulgence, allow him to look over some of the 'sections' (chapters) on England and make him find out the places on his map of whatever he reads.

When they have gone through England in this manner (which if they begin at five or six years old may perhaps take up a twelvemonth) they should then begin with the divisions of the earth, and proceed regularly.

It is a good method to let them read over any new section, or a part of it, every day for a week or more, accompanied by a map, before you give it them to 'get' by heart; by which means it makes a deeper impression on their minds, and comes much easier to them, as they have half-learnt it before they consider it as a lesson. And by frequently reading the historical part, during the period taken up in getting the rest, they generally remember it quite sufficiently without obliging them to repeat it word for word.

To prevent them from forgetting any thing they have learnt, it is proper that they should have a general repetition of all they have gone through after every new country; this may appear a tedious process, but will turn to account in the end, as every such repetition will impress it more strongly and they will not forget anything very essential while their memory is thus constantly exercised.

By the time they have made the tour of the Globe according to this plan, they will be fit to begin a regular course of History. (In that part) I have presumed to mention such as seemed the most concise, and for that reason best adapted to youth; and would have the Geography of every country gone through anew, with its History. (pp. iii–iv)

There then follow 105 sections (or chapters), the overwhelming number of them to do with geography. The first three are 'Of the world in general' and then there are no less than 96 chapters which deal systematically with different continents and countries of the world. The chapters begin with factual information concerning the principal towns, rivers, lakes, etc., and descriptions of topography and climate but go on to offer views and opinions which make startling and controversial reading to readers of the twenty-first century.

In the chapter on Arabia for instance, following some factual information, the following paragraphs occur:

> The Arabian horses are much admired.

> The Arabians are of middle stature, thin and of a swarthy complexion, with black hair and black eyes. They are swift of foot, excellent horsemen, expert at the bow and lance, good marksmen and are said to be a very brave people. The inhabitants of the inland country live in tents, and remove from place to place with their flocks and herds, as they have done ever since they became a nation.

> The Arabians are in general such thieves, that travellers and pilgrims, who are led thither from all parts through motives of devotion or curiosity, are struck with terror on their approach towards the deserts. Those robbers, headed by a captain, traverse the country in considerable troops on horseback, and assault and plunder the caravans. On the sea-coasts they are mere pirates and make prize of every vessel they can master, of whatever nation.

> The Arabs are descended from Ishmael, of whose posterity it was foretold, that they should be invincible 'Have their hand against every man and every man's hand against them.' They are at present, and have remained from the remotest ages, a convincing proof of the truth of this prediction. (pp. 157–60)

This description appears to mix fearless reporting with breathtaking judgementalism, and goes on to castigate Mahomet as a 'deceitful hypocrite' – hardly an enlightened multi-cultural approach – but it must be seen in the context of its time. At this stage in history, all nations saw each other in terms of distinct 'other-ness' and 'strangeness' and it makes limited sense to apply indiscriminately a twenty-first century set of values in an instinctive vilification of these remarks. Rather, the comments need to be explored for their origins and some understanding given of how they came to be made: they show how insular people generally were, how little they knew of each other and how far away the world was from being a 'global village' at this time.

As an example of the coverage of British geography, Cambridge is noted briefly as 'one of the chief towns of Cambridgeshire' in a recital of information about counties. The only descriptive information added is that it is 'on the Cam' and 'celebrated for an university'. Newmarket (now in Suffolk) is also listed as a Cambridgeshire town at this time and said to be 'remarkable for horse-races and sharpers'.

Later chapters in the book include a cosmographical set:

Of the voyages that have been made round the world
Of the Globes
Of the Circles delineated on the Surface of the Globe and their various uses
Of the Circumference of the Earth, Latitude, Longitude, Zones and Climates

A set of 'tables' in the book reflect the recent advances made in navigation and reveal how 'longitude expressed in the degrees, minutes and seconds, may be reduced to hours, minutes and seconds', an oddly prescient glimpse of time-distance formulations of modern geographers. There is also a chapter which is written in a question and answer framework, showing how various questions about day and night can be solved by reference to the movement of the earth.

Tables of the world's population (still computed as less than a billion at this time), a chronological table of Remarkable Events (listing the date of the creation of the world as 4004 BC by Bishop Usher's pre-Darwinian computations), and tables of 'men of learning and genius amongst the Ancients' (no women are deemed worthy of inclusion) are the final elements of the book.

Despite the risibility of the latter elements to modern eyes the preface itself bears some reflection. There is a clear preoccupation with factual material as the basis of a geographical education – an issue which was to bedevil the subject for the next two hundred years – but the author (E.R.) questions the automatic rote of memorisation of material (paragraph 3) and envisages the use of maps and objects (paragraphs 5 and 6) as basic visual aids. Something more demanding than 'little tales' is required (paragraph 4) and the author offers an early warning about the dangers of underestimating the abilities of pupils.

There is a strategy proposed for progression – moving from that of local to that of more distant places – essentially from the known to the unknown. Perhaps more significantly the author sees the learning of geography as a forerunner to the learning of history. Seen in one light that is an encouraging statement of the basic importance of the subject; but seen in another it presages a dangerous relegation of geography to the antechambers of serious learning.

It was the latter view of geography which was to prevail in high places in the coming years, as education for all became a nearer prospect.

THE REVEREND WAS AN ALIAS

The most prolific geography textbook writer of the first half of the nineteenth century was the 'Rev. J. Goldsmith',[11] one of the nom-de-plumes assumed by the tireless Sir Richard Phillips (1767–1840), who produced school-books on a number of subjects, following his varied career as schoolmaster, hosier, stationer, publisher, bookseller and patent medicine vendor.[12]

Goldsmith's 'An easy grammar of geography for schools and young persons' ran into over 50 editions, as a sequel to his ' Geography on a popular plan'. It was of pocket size (see Figure 2.3) and included some small fold-out maps of the major continents because, as the author stressed, 'though they add to the expense nothing can be more absurd than to attempt to teach geography without them'.

The 'easy grammar' began with 60 pages of factual material divided into sections on each of the major continents, and summarised in two pages of 'General facts worthy to be remembered'. Then followed a cosmographic section in which ways of using the terrestrial and celestial globes were given prominence (see Figure 2.4), reflecting the adult world's interest and enthusiasm of the times both for navigation (now in process of becoming much more accurate through Harrison's invention of the chronometer).[13]

Goldsmith then embarks on an extensive set of questions and exercises to which the answers are given in a separate publication called 'The tutor's key'. The questions and exercises (there are 692 of them) recapitulate on the information in the first-half of the book and are clearly designed to be a methodological prop for teachers and tutors. They are an early example of 'activity work'.

A flavour of them may be gained from the following section, chosen at random:

334. What was the ancient name of Asiatic Russia?
335. What is the general description of Arabia?
336. How is Lapland divided?
337. Upon what government is Norway dependent?
338. What is meant by the Universe?
339. What part of the world does Turkey comprehend?
340. What is the population of Prussia estimated at?
341. What is the chief city of the Austrian dominions and under what title is the Emperor ranked there?
342. How are the Birmans separated from Hindoostan?
343. Which are the nearest fixed stars?
344. Repeat Gay's description of the palmetto?
345. How is the eastern Archipelago divided?

These questions mix historical geography (334) with political geography (336), astronomy (343) with demography (340), government (337) with biogeography (344). The scope and breadth of this small set of questions (and, note, they are set in deliberate juxtaposition with each other) is an indication of the way in which geography, as taught in schools, was already being seen as a synthesising subject, drawing material from many different sources, in order to describe and explain the earth's surface and its peoples.

This potential strength bore the seeds of its own weakness, however, as demonstrated by Goldsmith. Searching questions such as 335, 'What is the general description of Arabia?', and 338, 'What is meant by the

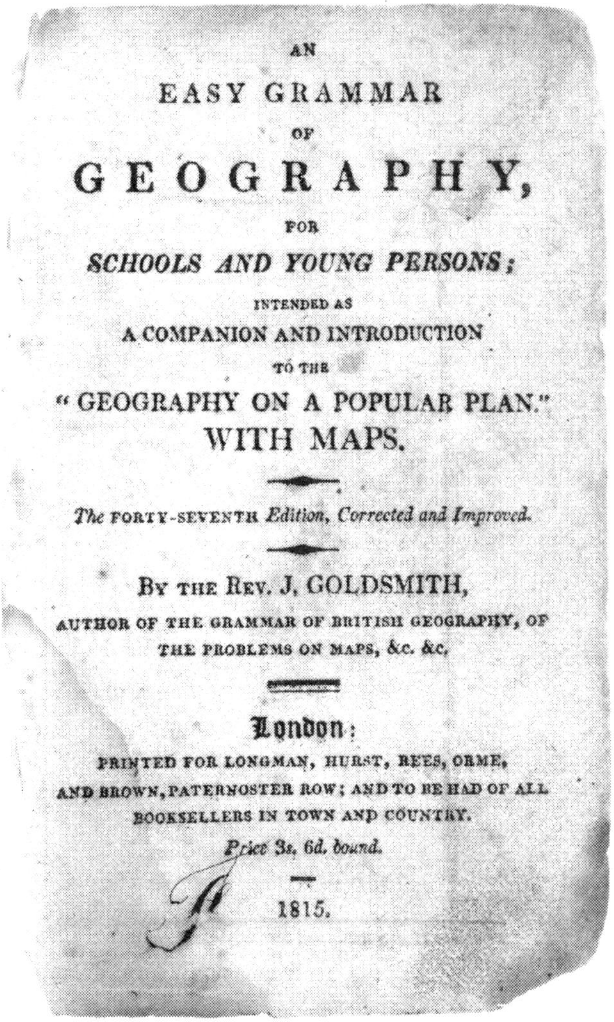
AN
EASY GRAMMAR
OF
GEOGRAPHY,
FOR
SCHOOLS AND YOUNG PERSONS;
INTENDED AS
A COMPANION AND INTRODUCTION
TO THE
"GEOGRAPHY ON A POPULAR PLAN."
WITH MAPS.

The FORTY-SEVENTH *Edition, Corrected and Improved.*

BY THE REV. J. GOLDSMITH,
AUTHOR OF THE GRAMMAR OF BRITISH GEOGRAPHY, OF
THE PROBLEMS ON MAPS, &c. &c.

London:
PRINTED FOR LONGMAN, HURST, REES, ORME,
AND BROWN, PATERNOSTER ROW; AND TO BE HAD OF ALL
BOOKSELLERS IN TOWN AND COUNTRY.
Price 3s. 6d. bound.

1815.

Figure 2.3:
Title page of Rev. J. Goldsmith's *Easy Grammar of Geography* (1815)
(actual size)

Universe?', were deemed susceptible to memorised one-sentence answers in the same way as such straightforward factual material such as 341, 'What is the chief city in the Austrian dominions?'. It was a short step from here to seeing geography as essentially a purveyor of terrestrial bric-a-brac and a mediator of the world at a very superficial level; the study of which might be useful as a base of information at a junior level, but which had little or no place in more demanding contexts.

The question and answer approach suggested in Goldsmith's books did, however, show that geography teaching and learning of the period was not entirely a one-way process with the teacher solely an expositor. There are other indications (see below) that methodology was lively, even where intellectual challenge was rather mild.

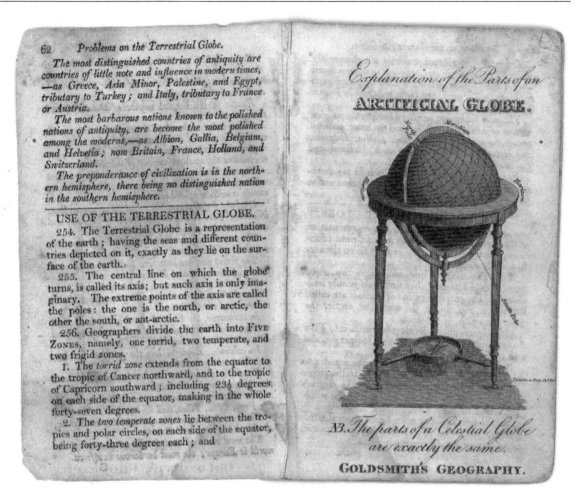

Figure 2.4:
Double-page of text and picture from *Easy Grammar of Geography* (slightly reduced in size)

EARLY GEOGRAPHICAL GAMES

The Abbe Aloisius Edouard Camille Gaultier (1746?–1818) came to London after the French Revolution to set up a school for the education of children of other French refugees. In 1817, as a result of his experiences, he published *A Complete Course of Geography by Means of Games Invented by the Abbe Gaultier*.[14] His major game prefigured the late twentieth-century phenomenon of Trivial Pursuit in that players moved round a board and were given counters in exchange for correct answers. Though this was not a simulation game, it was an early example of the motivation of play and leisure pursuits being harnessed for the benefit of education. In the nineteenth century, domestic game playing of various kinds was a regular and popular pastime in many families.[15]

Gaultier's admonition to those intending to use his approach had a modern late twentieth-century ring to it: 'The first rule of the game is that the instructor shall be the friend of his pupils and lay aside all magisterial authority, menaces and reprimand.' Such an approach was typical of that advocated by the influential Plowden Report on Primary Education (1967) and by the advocates of 'progressive' approaches to education throughout the twentieth century. It was replicated as one of the pedagogical justifications for the use of simulation games in geography teaching, a movement which gained considerable support amongst teachers in the 1970s and 1980s (see Chapter 8).

A similar approach was taken in the Rev. Robert Bullock's *Geography Epitomised*,[16] where pupils used a spinner to determine which question they would answer – Mr Bullock provided 820 of them and thoughtfully also gave the answers in a separate tutor's book.

The vogue for card games and jigsaws was also harnessed in the service of teaching geography. Many children of this period learnt their rudiments of world geography by such methods, as well as by the more stereotypical image of rote-learning. It was said of Thomas Arnold, (1795–1842) later to be Headmaster of Rugby School that ' at the age of three he used to sit at his aunt's table, arranging his geographical cards and recognising by their shape at a glance the different counties of the dissected map of England'.[17]

A footnote to a factual section in *Geography and History* (1790) observes:

> It is a very amusing exercise to children, and at the same time very instructive, to let them make an imaginary voyage through all the seas and straits of Europe; let them, for instance, embark on the Sea of Asoph, sail through the Straits of Caffa, and, crossing the Black Sea, enter the Bosphorus, which is the passage into the Sea of Marmora, and etc.

Another way of stimulating interest was by the recounting of real or imaginary journeys, a method likely to attract much more interest then than it would to a modern generation made blasé by multiple images of the world from the media. A glimpse of the colour and life of the world overseas could be seen for the first time through such accounts, and it captured the imagination of young pupils especially if it included the experiences or the adventures of children as well as adults.

One successful author in this sphere was Priscilla Wakefield (1751–1832), a Quaker philanthropist with a keen interest in education. Her work is perhaps the earliest example of a major contribution to geographic educational writing by a woman. Women played many other significant roles in the early history of the teaching of geography in schools and their prominence in early geographical education was in sharp contrast to the way in which women fared in academic geography until the middle of the twentieth century (see Chapter 4).

Mrs Wakefield's first book was called *The Juvenile Travellers*, 'containing the remarks of a family through the principal states and kingdoms of Europe' and described what she and her family (acknowledged by her as favoured by birth and financial circumstance) saw on their travels.[18] She recorded usefully not only the descriptions of places, but also the views and feelings of herself and her children.

A later book of hers, *A Family Tour through the British Empire*,[19] had a sub-title which accurately described both its coverage and its style. It contained 'some account of its manufactures, natural and artifical curiosities, history and antiquities; interspersed with biographical anecdotes, particularly adapted to the amusement and instruction of youth'. Priscilla Wakefield's children are reported to have shown an abhorrence of slavery and of 'the buying and selling of their fellow-creatures' but were not so concerned about the practice of the use of juvenile labour in cotton mills, where, it was recorded, they observed 'children employed usefully'.

Other books provided stories about the environment of other lands for British children to enjoy. One popular one (quoted later by Rudyard Kipling) was Mrs Sherwood's story of 'Little Henry and his beaver' (1815),[20] another was Thomas Bingley's 'Tales about travellers: their perils, adventures and discoveries' (1840).[21]

INFLUENCE OF THE CHURCH

In the days before state education for all, the Church of England played a key role in the education of the nation, as the survival of many church-linked village primary schools demonstrates. Even today a third of all English schools are church linked. Not surprisingly, some of the earliest geography taught in schools related to imparting a better understanding of the lands of the Bible, as well as to the home country.

The Records of the Board of Governors of St Luke's College, Exeter, a Church of England foundation, report that in 1838 the Board pronounced themselves as against the teaching of geography since they regarded it as 'unnecessary and likely to produce dangerous ideas'. In particular they thought that it was unnecessary to teach the geography of Europe, though they grudgingly conceded that 'it is necessary to teach the Geography of Palestine for (the students) cannot understand the Bible without it'. Not all the Governors were in agreement with this traditionalist view, however, and one of the more progressive described it as 'insulated religious geography'.

Church influence was not always as obscurantist as this, but the emphasis on key Biblical events led to the pre-eminence of the study of the Middle East region and a preoccupation with the identification of locations such as The Garden of Eden and Mount Ararat, the supposed haven of Noah's Ark in the Great Flood.

Before 1850, physical geography and the origins of rocks and landforms were taught in a pre-Darwinian frame, as indeed were all other subjects. In most cases, small elements of geography were taught as adjuncts of other disciplines. The more prestigious secondary grammar schools and the public schools (most of them church foundations) might allow some geography of the Eastern Mediterranean to buttress both classical and religious studies but were unlikely to adopt it as a separate subject.

There is some evidence to suggest that geography was studied more by girls than boys, as it was seen as a 'polite' subject and therefore suitable for female education. William Butler, in his preface to *Geographical and Biographical Exercises Designed for the Use of Young Ladies* (1801) asserted, 'The utility of geography has been universally admitted and that science now forms an essential branch of female tuition.'[22] The gender-specific comment is interesting and possibly significant, though it may be no more than an author seeking to justify the terms of reference for his title.

Indeed, one of the difficulties in seeking to assess the state of geographical education in the early nineteenth century is the absence of detailed and specific accounts of what actually happened in classrooms where teachers taught or in the studies of country houses where tutors worked. These are needed to put the realism of everyday teaching life alongside the optimistic and enlightened prefaces quoted above. The rhetoric of authors and publishers is always likely to be a little in advance of actual classroom practice and so there were no doubt many ways in which the ideas contained in the texts of Goldsmith, Gaultier and Wakefield *et al.*, could be reduced to unimaginative ways of teaching and learning.

AN ATLAS FOR COUNTRY SCHOOLMASTERS

Given the preponderance (almost total dominance) of church schools, and the strength of the Sunday School movement in the period before 1850, it was not surprising that the Society for Promoting Christian Knowledge (SPCK) should, through its publishing operations, be involved in the production of geography texts and atlases.

Their *Atlas of Educational Maps for the Use of Schoolmasters* published in 1847 is a fascinating example of the state of both geography and cartography of the period.[23] The chief object of the atlas was said to be 'to furnish the Country Schoolmaster with such outlines as shall enable him to use the Maps which he may happen to possess, to greater advantage in imparting a knowledge of Geography to his Scholars'. Other references make it clear that it was designed to be used in the 'National Schools', the elementary schools run by the Church of England in many parts of England.

The authors of the atlas (uncredited) were in no doubt about the best method of teaching geography: 'no instruction should be given excepting with the map before the eyes of the scholars that they may understand the picture which is explained to them by the instruction given', and that 'instruction in geography is best conveyed in this order – Geometrical Geography, Physical Geography, Historical Geography'.

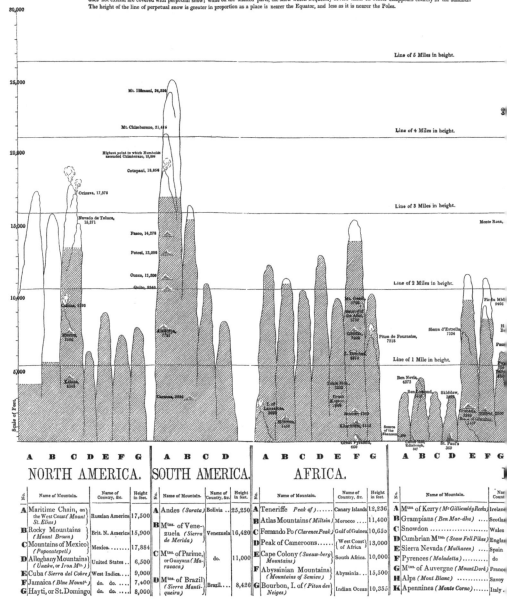

Figure 2.5:
Early piece of innovative cartography: principal mountains of the world from *Educational Maps for the Use of Schoolmasters* (1847) (reduced in size)

30

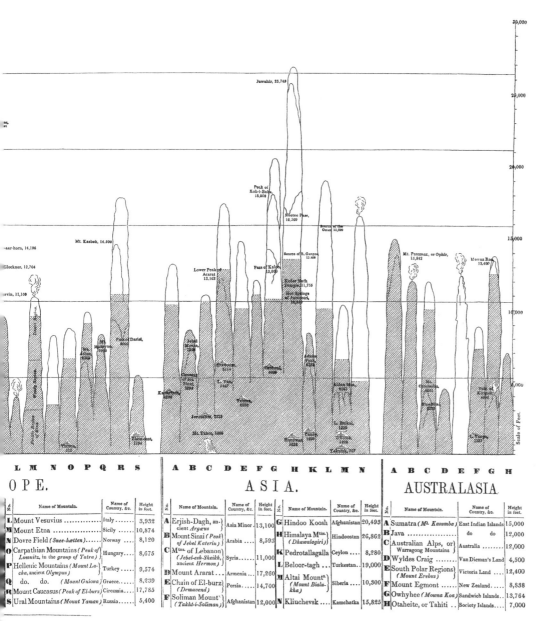

L M N O P Q R S

O P E.

No.	Name of Mountain.	Name of Country, &c.	Height in feet.
L.	Mount Vesuvius	Italy	3,932
M.	Mount Etna	Sicily	10,874
N.	Dovre Field (*Snee-hætten*)......	Norway	8,120
O.	Carpathian Mountains (*Peak of Lomnitz*, in the group of *Tatra*)	Hungary	8,675
P.	Hellenic Mountains (*Mount La-cha*, ancient *Olympus*)	Turkey	9,574
Q.	do. do. (*Mount Guiona*)	Greece......	8,239
R.	Mount Caucasus (*Peak of El-burz*)	Circassia....	17,785
S.	Ural Mountains (*Mount Yaman*)	Russia.......	5,400

A B C D E F G H K L M N

A S I A.

No.	Name of Mountain.	Name of Country, &c.	Height in feet.	No.	Name of Mountain.	Name of Country, &c.	Height in feet.
A	Erjish-Dagh, ancient *Argæus*	Asia Minor	13,100	G	Hindoo Koosh	Afghanistan	20,493
B	Mount Sinai (*Peak of Jebel Kateriu*)	Arabia	8,593	H	Himalaya M^{tns.} (*Dhawalagiri*)	Hindoostan	26,862
C	M^{tns.} of Lebanon (*Jebel-esh-Sheikh*, ancient *Hermon*)	Syria......	11,000	K	Pedrotallagalla	Ceylon	8,280
D	Mount Ararat ...	Armenia ...	17,260	L	Beloor-tagh ...	Turkestan..	19,000
E	Chain of El-burz (*Demavend*)	Persia	14,700	M	Altai Mount^{s.} (*Mount Bialu-kha*)	Siberia	10,300
F	Soliman Mount (*Takht-i-Soliman*)	Afghanistan	12,000	N	Kliuchevsk	Kamchatka	15,825

A B C D E F G H

AUSTRALASIA

No.	Name of Mountain.	Name of Country, &c.	Height in feet.
A	Sumatra (*Mt. Kasumba*)	East Indian Islands	15,000
B	Java	do do	12,000
C	Australian Alps, or Warragong Mountains	Australia	12,000
D	Wyldes Craig	Van Dieman's Land	4,500
E	South Polar Regions (*Mount Erebus*)	Victoria Land ...	12,400
F	Mount Egmont	New Zealand.....	8,838
G	Owhyhee (*Mowna Koa*)	Sandwich Islands..	13,764
H	Otaheite, or Tahiti ..	Society Islands....	7,000

Education, appointed by the Society for Promoting Christian Knowledge.

GREAT QUEEN STREET, LINCOLN'S INN FIELDS.

31

What is meant by 'Geometrical Geography' is the inculcation of basic ideas about longitude and latitude and the relative scales of maps. This is seen as an essential preliminary to the other two aspects of the subject. Less easy for us to fathom as educationally appropriate is the substantial section on map projections which then follows (pp. 7–14), and which would be likely to tax the understanding of a professor of geography (of which there were none at the time) as much as that of a country schoolmaster or his pupils. However, the drawbacks of Mercator's projection (that it showed true direction but distorted land areas) are carefully pointed out and the advantages and disadvantages of other projections encompassed in a lengthy discourse on this topic. If this material was indeed passed on to pupils in national schools, then geography at this time was far from being a subject concerned with superficial facts.

The textual section on physical geography is also considerable, though it gives a description of the landforms of the earth rather than any explanation of them. The level of instruction may be judged by extracts from the following paragraph about Mountains:

> Mountains possess great varieties of shape and appearance; some rise with a gradual slope and have rounded summits, or form a level plain at the top. Others have a steep and rugged ascent, sometimes almost perpendicular, with sharp and broken peaks in their highest parts.
>
> Some mountains are at intervals burst open at the top or the sides by the action of subterranean fire; these are called Volcanoes and the occurence of such an event is called an Eruption, in the course of which smoke, ashes, pieces of rock, and various other substances are ejected from them.
>
> In some countries the mountains consist of detached or isolated elevations, while in others they are connected in various ways, forming in some cases groups or mountain-knots, and in others mountain-chains or ranges. (p. 17)

No indication is given of the difference between fold or block mountains, or any speculation made about their origins. The paragraph about volcanoes might have been written at the time of the covering of Pompeii. There is little in the section which goes beyond topographical description of a superficial kind. This is in contrast to the detailed calculations and diagrams in the preceding section of map projections.

There is, however, some innovative cartography which shows (with the aid of large hand-coloured double-page diagrams) the relative sizes of lakes, oceans and countries, the relative heights of mountains (see Figure 2.5) and the relative lengths of rivers.

Then follows an index map of the world 'exhibiting principal physical features' but no political divisions: a world isothermal map and a map showing the influence of climate on vegetation. The major set of maps are labelled 'historical' and show respectively the maximum extent of the Assyrian, Persian, Macedonian, Roman, Christian and Mahometan Empires.

The final map shows 'The Christian Empire at the present time' and it is revealing to see huge areas of blank space in the USA west of the Mississippi, central South America and almost all of Africa, as well as in the more remote and little-inhabited parts of the earth.

A rubric to the map reminds both teachers and pupils that this map 'gives the strongest argument in favour of more extended and judicious exertions in the Missionary cause'. It is a graphic reminder in both map and text of the context in which most geographical education was conducted at this time.

A concluding paragraph in the physical geography section makes this point eloquently clear in another way. It also indicates that, far from being a mere catalogue of inert facts, there was a clear agenda of value-transmission underlying the teaching proposed:

> we would direct attention to the variety of subjects which even the above brief and imperfect sketch of physical geography brings under the student's notice and to the abundant manner in which the diversities of external nature – the ocean in its vastness and ever-changing magnificence, the desert in its gloomy solitude, the mountain in its towering grandeur, and the cultivated plain in its fertility and the evidences of human industry which it exhibits – testify to the greatness and the glory of God ...

> ... all the features of outward nature serve their purpose as parts of a vast whole. Rivers point out the locality where man fixes his abode, and the oceans constitute the great highways upon which the commercial intercourse of nations is pursued. And, in a still higher degree, the productions of the vegetable and animal world, in their surpassing beauty, their infinite diversity, and the numberless evidences of design which they exhibit, bear enduring testimony to the wisdom and goodness of an omnipotent Creator.

NOTES

1. P. Heylyn, *Cosmographia* (1649). Recounted in the Preface.
2. For a fuller description of this curriculum, see W. K. Richmond *The School Curriculum* (Methuen, London, 1971).
3. H. Robinson 'Geography in the Dissenting Academies', *Geography*, 36(3) (1951), pp.179–86. Robinson estimates that between 1662 and 1691, 3 out of 17 academies taught some geography; between 1691 and 1750, 7 out of 35; between 1750 and 1800, 11 out of 23.
4. R. S. Thompson 'The Leeds Grammar School case of 1805', *Journal of Educational Administration and History*, 3 (1) (December 1970), pp. 1–6.
5. Richard Hakluyt, *The Principal Navigations, Voyages and Discoveries of the English Nation Made by Sea or Over Land* (?1582). Hakluyt (?1552–1616) seems to have given some

lectures on geography in Oxford in the 1580s; he was predated in this by Baldwin Norton, who was paid by Magdalen College as a lecturer in geography in 1540–41. For more detail on the biographies of these pioneers and on the early history of the subject in general, see J. N. L. Baker, *The History of Geography* (Blackwell, Oxford, 1963).

6. J. A. Comenius, *Orbis Sensualium Pictus*, trans. by C. Hoole (S. Mearne, London, 1672).

7. W. Pemble, *A Brief Introduction to Geography*, 6th edn (Lichfield, Oxford, 1685).

8. R. Turner, *View of the Earth: Being a Short But Comprehensive System of Modern Geography* (1762). W. Guthrie, *New Geographical, Historical and Commercial Grammar* (c. 1790).

9. W. M. Thackeray, *Vanity Fair* (Bradbury & Evans, 1848; Penguin English Library, London, 1968). The curriculum of Miss Pinkerton's Academy seems to have been weighted towards the practical: the other subjects of study mentioned in Amelia's report are music, dancing, orthography, embroidery and needlework.

10. Author unknown, *Geography and History* (B. Law, London, 1790).

11. A. Maddrell, 'Discourses of race and gender and the comparative method in geography school texts 1830–1918', *Environment and Planning*, D16 (1) (1998) thinks that Phillips' taking of a clerical nom-de-plume for his geographical textbook writing 'suggests the legitimating role of the church for popular education in general and geography in particular' at this time.

12. J. E. Vaughan, 'Aspects of teaching geography in England in the early nineteenth century', *Paedagogica Historica*, 12 (1984), pp. 128–42.

13. The story is brilliantly told in D. Sobel, *Latitude* (Hodder & Stoughton, London, 1997).

14. A. E. C. Gaultier, *A Complete Course of Geography by Means of Games Invented by the Abbe Gaultier* (Harris, London, 1817).

15. B. Love (ed.), *Great Board Games* (Ebury Press and Michael Joseph, London, 1979).

16. R. Bullock, *Geography Epitomised* (or 'A companion to the atlas: comprising a series of lessons, proper for a first course of geographical instruction in schools') (Author, Wigan, 1810).

17. A. P. Stanley, *Life of Thomas Arnold* (John Murray, London, 1901), p. 4.

18. Priscilla Wakefield, *The Juvenile Travellers* (Darton & Harvey, London, 1802).

19. Priscilla Wakefield, *A Family Tour through the British Empire* (Darton & Harvey, London, 1805).

20. M. M. Sherwood, *An Introduction to Geography, Intended for Little Children* (Houlston, London, 1815).

21. T. Bingley, *Tales about Travellers* (publisher unknown, 1840).

22. W. Butler, *Geographical and Biographical Exercises Designed for the Use of Young Ladies* (Harris, London, 1801).

23. Anon, *Atlas of Educational Maps for the Use of Schoolmasters* (Society for Promoting Christian Knowledge, London, 1847).

3

Capes and Bays – Millstones or Milestones? 1850–80

Though Mary Somerville (1780–1872) could remember from her schooling in Burntisland that 'it seemed that half the world was incognita', the increase of factual material available to the teachers and tutors who purveyed lessons in geography was considerable by the time her significant book on *Physical Geography*[1] was published in mid-century.

The romance of a largely uncharted world had an undoubted attraction for those who gazed at large blank spaces on the maps which hung from classroom walls, but the educational spirit of the time was becoming more pedestrian. The matter was not helped either by the theories (if they can be called such) of educational development which were current or by the growing desire to make schools more comparable and accountable and thus to seek ways of testing their effectiveness.

THE MOVE TO 'FACTS'

Dickens characterised (and indeed caricatured) contemporary approaches to teaching and learning in several of his novels, and Mr Gradgrind in *Hard Times* stands as chillingly representative:

> Now what I want is Facts. Teach these boys and girls nothing but Facts. Facts alone are wanted in life. Plan nothing else and root out everything else … Stick to Facts Sir![2]

Gradgrind's philosophy, as explained to Mr M'Choakumchild, lately trained in one of the earliest of the nation's teacher-training colleges, was that children's minds were akin to empty vessels. M'Choakumchild obediently followed Gradgrind's precepts and poured gallons of facts into the waiting receptacles. The growth of factual information about the world – the names of towns, the lengths of rivers, the heights of mountains – was convenient grist to the mill for such teachers. It could (using the Gradgrind philosophy) be easily taught, recited, memorised and tested.

Figure 3.1:
Stereo-daguerreotype, c. 1850,
'A Family Geography Lesson'
by A. Claudet
(*Source*: Gernsheim Collection)

Other events conspired to make this an attractive proposition. The Reform Act of 1832 had widened the franchise and soon afterwards the government had taken its first halting steps towards intervention in the nation's education, by providing money for grants to schools. Previous Parliamentary Committees of investigation (1834 and 1838) had produced little direct result, but in 1858 a Commission, under the chairmanship of the Duke of Newcastle, was set up to 'inquire into the present state of Popular Education in England and to consider and report what Measures, if any, are required for the extension of sound and cheap elementary instruction to all classes of the people'.

The Report, presented three years later, found that the state of elementary education was unsatisfactory. The churches (through their educational arms, the National Society and the British and Foreign

Schools Society) were not able to keep up the provision of enough schools for the growing population (especially in the rapidly developing urban areas)[3]: not more than a quarter of pupils in the elementary schools that did exist were receiving 'a good education' : more time and care was spent on the education of older pupils than younger ones.

Then came the fateful paragraph:

> There is only one way of securing this (desired) result, which is to institute a searching examination by competent authority of every child in every school to which grants are to be paid, with the view of ascertaining whether these indispensable elements of knowledge are thoroughly acquired, and to make the prospects and position of the teacher dependent, to a considerable extent, on the results of this examination.[4]

(Government thinking and strategy at the end of the twentieth century – the introduction of protracted inspections, publication of league tables of examination and test results, a plan for teachers to be rewarded differentially through the application of 'performance criteria' – echoes this mid-nineteenth-century pronouncement in an eerie way...)

'The Revised Code' of 1862, drafted by the Education Committee of the Privy Council, laid down conditions for grants, and guidelines for inspections and curriculum. Grants were to be paid to elementary schools, and were to be related to the success rate achieved in an annual examination of all children, starting from the age of 6. This was the beginning of 'payment by results' and it lasted until nearly the end of the century.

The 'Code' initally emphasised reading, writing and arithmetic (a trio of subjects which have curiously and ironically become misnamed and misspelt as the 'Three Rs' in popular parlance ever since) and was revised periodically. By 1867 it had been widened so that a school received extra grants if it included at least one 'extra' subject to the major trio.

Thus geography became one of the subjects frequently included in the inspection and 'payment by results' mechanism linked to elementary schools. It is not difficult to understand how a geography dominated by a learning of 'capes and bays' was further encouraged in these conditions. The level of elementary school teacher-training (and, by its products, the level of subject understanding) was, at the time, often rudimentary; knowledge about the world was becoming more easily available and therefore more extensive; the teaching of factual information and the testing of it provided a convenient vehicle for the demonstration of 'achievement'. The writings and musings of Ritter and von Humboldt, as well as of Mary Somerville, about the nature of geography in this period were literally a world apart from most schoolteachers.[5]

Robert Lowe, responsible for introducing the Revised Code, later commented, memorably, when Chancellor of the Exchequer, that, 'We must educate our masters.'[6] His well-intentioned desire to introduce an overall set of educational standards for the working classes was, however, partly nullified by the fact that, in seeking to meet them, pedagogical imagination and pupil motivation was often significantly diminished. H. G. Wells saw it as educating 'the lower classes for employment on lower-class lines and with specially trained inferior teachers'.[7] The informational tendencies which were encouraged by 'payment by results' in turn influenced the kinds of textbooks produced and used, as well as having an indirect effect on the curriculum of the independent school sector. Douglas Freshfield (1854–1934), at preparatory school in the 1860s, before going on to Eton, remembered that:

> In my day there were many boys at public schools who acted consistently and not altogether unsuccessfully, on the principle that whatever was not a city in Asia Minor, was an island in the Aegean Sea …[8]

J. R. Green, writing in the Introduction for a *Short Geography of the British Islands*, a book published in the early 1880s,[9] looked back on the previous 30 years with some disfavour:

> No drearier task can be set for the worst of criminals than that of studying a set of geographical textbooks, such as the children in our schools are doomed to use.

Yet the 'capes and bays' approach was neither adopted universally, nor taken on uncritically. Instructions to Her Majesty's Inspectors of Schools in 1885 reflected awareness of the problem and concern about the state of affairs which the Revised Code was developing:

> Geography teaching is sometimes too much restricted to the pointing out of places on the map, and to the enumeration of such details as the names of rivers, towns, capes and political divisions. It is hardly necessary to say that geography, if taught to good purpose, includes also a description of the physical aspects of the countries and seeks to establish some association between the names of places and those historical, social or industrial facts which alone makes the names of places worth remembering.

In other words, if judiciously taught, the 'capes and bays' could be milestones rather than millstones.

MORE ENLIGHTENED APPROACHES

Not all schools subsided into the caricature of perpetual rote-learning that is sometimes drawn by uncritical condemnations of the period. Teresa Ploszajska's recent detailed research has shown how London Board schools had, post-1870, many imaginative teaching strategies for geography lessons, and how the use of maps and models was encouraged, as well as the frequent use of visual illustration and outdoor practical exercises in the playgrounds of schools even in the most deprived urban slum areas.[10]

Elizabeth Baigent has observed that:

> Many nineteenth-century educationalists saw that geography in nineteenth-century schools could be used to buttress the Imperial cast of mind and also could stimulate children to learn from their surroundings. Either motive or both led to the use of surprisingly progressive methods. Colourful wall maps were the focal point of otherwise severe classrooms whilst 'object lessons' which taught children to learn and observe from everyday articles often had a geographical emphasis.[11]

Charlotte Yonge's immensely popular novel of the time, *The Clever Woman of the Family*, written in 1863, has the enthusiastic young teacher Rachel Curtis teaching an 'object lesson' to a group of lace-makers.[12] Artefacts such as a lump of coal or a piece of cloth were displayed at the start of lessons to start productive trains of thought and encourage genuine classroom discussion and interaction between teachers and their pupils.

Neither is it altogether necessary to decry 'capes and bays' geography and 'rote-learning' as misguided episodes on the path to a Holy Grail of geographical education entirely conducted by enquiry or discovery learning. The Victorians no doubt became aware of the situation which later psychological studies have confirmed – that the gathering of facts is an activity positively enjoyed by children at a certain stage of mental development and that there is sound reason to include an element of this in the curriculum of upper elementary and lower secondary schools.[13]

Facts have practical use in establishing a basic framework of knowledge for later work, and are grist to the mill of the intellectually acquisitive child. If no steps are taken to inculcate such a framework the pupil does not (as optimists have hoped) acquire it by osmosis in later life. Strange and serious lapses of geographical knowledge about simple matters become apparent when an adult.

What was disliked (by Dickens and HMI alike) was the unthinking application of rote-learning to all situations and its dominance in many classroom activities. To the teacher with little training it was an attractive but dangerous raft on which to cling in the midst of pedagogical storms, and its perpetration as an exclusive method of teaching inhibited the development of an intellectual (as distinct from a content) framework on which to base the subject.

Through the middle years of the twentieth century, a mounting (though often inaccurate) criticism was levelled against geography lessons dominated by 'capes and bays' teaching by those who drew selectively from experiences of their own youth. The pendulum swung so violently against the routine purveyal of such factual learning in the 1960s, 1970s and 1980s that subsequent surveys showed that a generation of children (and adults) had little substantive geographic knowledge of any kind.[14]

Starting with the Report of the Government's National Curriculum Working Group on Geography in 1987 (see also Chapter 10), there has been a rehabilitation of the idea of learning the names of places.[15] The Group suggested that a core knowledge of locations and areas (e.g. the names of major cities, continents, rivers, oceans and mountain ranges), needed to be actively taught in schools and produced maps to indicate these core facts. A more balanced view about the need to have some framework of knowledge as a basis for studying important geography themes and concepts now appears to prevail.

A REPRESENTATIVE TEXTBOOK OF THE PERIOD

A major secondary school textbook of the period, *Clyde's School Geography*, reflected on the increasing availability of information to teachers and the problems caused in the preface to the tenth edition, published in 1866.[16]

> Now-a-days there exists a plethora of matter; and the duty of the compiler is not so much to find materials, as to select from the immense mass of them competing for admission into his manual the more important and suggestive facts and to exhibit these in their mutual natural bearings so that they shall express a unity.

> The author's objective ... is not to dissect the several countries of the world and then label their dead limbs, but to depict each country, as made by God and modified by man, so that the relations between the country and its inhabitants – in other words the present geographical life of the country – may appear.

James Clyde was described on the title page as 'one of the classical masters in the Edinburgh Academy' but he seems to have profited well from his geographical sideline, since the book remained in print for 40 years and went to its 24th edition in 1890, substantially unchanged, though with the addition of fold-out maps.

Clyde felt that 'the amount of matter in a schoolbook should not be determined by the maximum retentive power of the memory', but nevertheless his two main principles of inclusion were 'Is this matter rememberable?' and 'Is this matter examinable?', a rather Puritan diet for prospective readers. There was, however, a genuine desire for pupils to move beyond the rote-learning of knowledge:

> When principles are traced in facts, and facts are referred back again to principles, Geography, besides enriching the memory, disciplines the understanding and even the heart.

The Athanaeum, an influential periodical of the period, which reviewed the book, offered something of a back-handed compliment:

> We have been struck with the ability and value of this work which is a great advance on previous geographic manuals... Almost for the first time, we have here met with a school geography that is quite a readable book – one that, being intended for advanced pupils, is well adapted to make them study the subject with a degree of interest they have never yet felt in it.

The chapters of the book are indeed written in reasonably fluent prose, though there are no 'activities' of any kind suggested to the pupil readers. A set of statistics begins each of the chapters of the book on a particular country and these chapters form the major part of the book, over 400 pages of them.

Prefacing them are chapters titled 'Mathematical geography' (dealing with the globe, latitude and longitude, the seasons, etc.), and 'Physical and political geography' (in which a contrast is made between the old and new worlds). At the end of the book are chapters on 'Physical Geography' (with sections on Crust, Winds, Currents, Climate, the Distribution of Plants, the Distribution of Animals, Man) and a 'Technological Appendix' (a dictionary of terms).

In 1866, as in 1790, the same willingness of the author to chance his arm in unflattering descriptions of other nations and races remains. In the section on Iberia, Clyde comments, 'The same indolence clings to the Portuguese as to the Spaniard; and if the former wants the pride of the latter, neither is he so manly.'

Of Arabia, he notes:

> The people are ruled by a severe hereditary despotism, no distinction being recognised under the sovereign, except that of mollah or spiritual guide. The doctrine taught is unmitigated election and reprobation; and the offences most carefully punished are quasi-ecclesiastical. Riadh is the present capital of this strange community.

In the section on Arabia, there are other paragraphs on: configuration and climate: government; Turkish provinces; the Central Kingdom; maritime districts; and islands. This pattern is followed in other country-based chapters.

A comparison of a British location with the 1790 text, quoted in Chapter 2, reveals that the description of Cambridge has expanded a little and becomes of more colourful human interest:

> The whole valley of the Cam is occupied by dairy farms, and Cambridge butter, which at Cambridge is sold by the inch for the convenience of students, is famous in the London market.

FORSTER'S EDUCATION ACT OF 1870

Fuelled in mid-century by a mixture of national prosperity and idealism, the clamour grew for the government to introduce a system of elementary education to cover the whole of England and Wales. The feeling against any interference by the state into people's lives was still very strong in some quarters, and the church regarded such a scheme warily. But its own resources could not cope with the demand. Some in the higher echelons of society were worried for a different reason – having the thought that increasing levels of education might make the 'lower orders' restless and discontented. But W. E. Forster, Vice-President of the Council and unofficial minister for education in Gladstone's renowned 1868–74 government, was determined to grasp the nettle.

The scheme which he devised was one which incorporated, rather than supplanted the work of the church schools, and was a patchwork on an existing foundation, rather than a fresh start. Voluntary (church) schools would continue and receive increased grants, as long as they were well-conducted; the church was given another year to build new schools; after that the government would build new schools wherever they were needed and these would be managed by locally elected school boards.

New Codes of Instruction were drawn up in 1871 and 1875 (with geography included as one of the basic subjects to be taught, though only as a third tier of importance), provision was made for the training of thousands of new teachers, and plans for new buildings were prepared. The results of the Forster Act can still be seen today: many village primary schools remain church-linked, the descendants of the schools given a new lease of life by Forster's successful pragmatic approach.

At the secondary level, a system of grants, dependent on inspections, was also set up for the endowed grammar schools (most of which had been founded by private benefactors in past centuries) by the Endowed Schools Act, which followed the deliberations of the Taunton Commission (1868).[17] The Commissioners sought to modernise the curriculum of these schools, but geography was seen as a minor subject at this level and had little prominence in the revisions suggested. The leading schools, most of whom had a predominantly classical curriculum, were urged by the Taunton Commission to include elements of political economy, modern languages, mathematics and the natural sciences as a proper preparation for pupils who might go on to university. Other grammar schools had less lofty ambitions for their pupils and now prepared them for the professions, for commerce and for the armed forces, but were urged to adopt a broadly similar curriculum.

GEOGRAPHY IN THE PUBLIC SCHOOLS

A third strand of education in this period is represented by the 'public' schools. Some of these, such as Eton, Harrow, Winchester and King's School, Canterbury, were ancient foundations, but many new ones were founded in the middle of the century, as the prosperity of the era created a new class of wealthy industrialists and merchants who wanted their children (perhaps more accurately, their sons, at least) to have the benefits of a 'proper education'.

The curriculum of these schools was determined independently, with heads such as Edward Thring (at Uppingham) and Thomas Arnold (at Rugby) wielding immense power. Some heads, Arnold amongst them, broadened their curriculum beyond the emphasis on classical studies, and geography might feature as an optional subject in the lower schools of such institutions, though invariably it was in the hands of masters who taught it from interest rather than from academic training.

Some geography was made compulsory at Eton in the lower school, following the 1864 Clarendon Report[18] (the recommendations of a a Royal Commission set up to enquire into the quality of education at nine of the nation's leading public schools), though it was within the realm of the Classical Masters, and the atlases produced reflected a strong preoccupation with the lands of the Eastern Mediterranean and little else. It was not until 1961 that the first specialist geography master was appointed at Eton.[19]

At Harrow, geography was given a filip by the institution of the Strangford prizes in 1876. It was a happy accident that a former pupil, Percy Smythe, later Viscount Strangford, became 'an earnest student of political and physical geography' and married the daughter of Admiral Beaufort, the mariner who invented a scale for measuring the wind force, subsequently known to thousands of those taught in the geography classrooms of Britain. On her husband's early death, Viscountess Strangford instituted three prizes 'for the encouragement of the study of geography'. Harrow thus became probably the first individual secondary school in Britain to recognise geography as a subject worthy of annual awards for senior pupils.[20]

THE ROYAL GEOGRAPHICAL SOCIETY MEDALS SCHEME

There had been an earlier but unsuccessful attempt from an outside source to make such awards in an effort to increase the visibility and importance of geography in the 'public' schools. The Royal Geographical Society (RGS) had been founded in 1830 to promote 'that most important and entertaining branch of knowledge – geography' but its initial objectives did not include specifically educational ones. In its early years, the RGS functioned mainly as a forum for explorers and travellers, a provider of popular talks and lectures, and a gatherer of books, and 'instruments as are useful to the compendious stock of a traveller.'[21] However its very presence and growing prestige in the early Victorian era benefited the status of school geography indirectly and it was not long before it made its first excursion into specifically educational territory.

Prompted by Francis Galton, Honorary Secretary of the RGS between 1857 and 1863, and a man of many parts,[22] the RGS set up a scheme in

1869 whereby medals were to be awarded to the pupils who did best in annual geography examination papers which they set. In response to the expressed wishes of some schools, it was decided that the scheme should offer the boys a chance to 'follow their favourite studies' and this led to a separation of prizes for physical and political geography.

However, only a few schools were persuaded to enter for the medals and two institutions, Liverpool College (where Galton's brother-in-law was the headmaster) and Dulwich College won almost half the medals awarded in the 15 years that the scheme was run. The Headmaster of Dulwich argued that the failure of the scheme resulted from awarding only a limited number of prizes and for not widening the incentive by publishing a longer list of those who had done well or rewarding more pupils. But more crushingly, the Headmaster of Bath College was reported as saying that two of his own students who had been awarded medals 'were boys of singular inaptitude for studies of a nobler sort and he could not but think ... that he had been indulging them...in a weakness that he ought to have corrected'.[23]

Though Galton himself claimed to be an 'integrationist' as far as geography was concerned, the RGS scheme, unwittingly or not, perpetuated and accentuated a growing divide between physical and human geography by offering separate medals in these areas. This was much to the dislike of William Hughes (1817–76), then Professor of Geography at King's College, London, who fought to maintain a view of the subject as one covering both physical and human environments.

> Every page of history bears evidence of the large extent to which the great actors in the domain of public life have been guided (often controlled) by the circumstances of surrounding locality...by the geography or topography of a particular region. The statesman and the warrior are alike students of geography or find their schemes miscarry.[24]

Hughes is an interesting, though somewhat ill-defined figure, and appears to have been one of the first people distinguished with the title of 'professor of geography' in a university, though a Captain James Maconachie, RN, held such a title briefly at University College, London between 1833 and 1836.[25] Hughes had earlier taught at St. John's College (the latter-day College of St Mark and St John, now removed from London to Plymouth) and at Battersea Training College. His duties at King's seem to have been related to the teaching of specific courses rather than to the creation of coherent programmes of study in which geography was dominant. He was the author of several important geography school textbooks of the period and emphasised the importance of pupils understanding rather than memorising geographical material, though his own books were as indigestible as anything that had gone before. He also produced maps for schools, and was an active writer of articles and a frequent lecturer.

Besides giving courses at King's Hughes had teaching duties at Queens College, (in spite of its name, not a comparable institution but a central

London academy for the training of governesses) and so he bridged both school and university spheres. But despite his assiduous work, his courses at Kings were peripheral, though well-regarded, and he was not replaced upon his death.[26] The establishment of the first geography degree courses and departments of geography in universities did not come until almost 50 years later (see Chapter 5/6).

Perhaps the one significant positive outcome to emerge from the abortive medals scheme was a letter to Galton from the Provost of Eton, the Rev. Edwin Hale, who suggested that the RGS might be better advised to give priority to establishing geography in the universities, and that this would in turn stimulate the subject in the public schools.[27] In the wake of the Keltie Report, this would be an initiative to which the RGS would return within only a few years (see Chapter 4).

TENSIONS WITH GEOLOGY

Another to see the potential of geography and to advocate its importance and its role as an integrating science, linking both physical and human environments, was Archibald Geikie, one of the most eminent earth-scientists of the time. Geikie was Director of the Scottish branch of the Geological Survey from 1867 (and later Director of the Geological Survey itelf) but he was also a man of broader interests, who was passionate in seeing science and geography extended in schools, and active in writing for and about geographical education.[28]

Speaking to the RGS in 1879, Geikie commended geography as a subject which:

> ever looks for a connection between scattered facts, tries to ascertain the relations which subsist between the different parts of the globe, their reactions on each other and the general economy of the whole... It traces how man, alike unconsciously and knowingly, has changed the face of nature and how, on the other hand, the conditions of his geographical environment have moulded his progress. With these broad aims, geography comes frankly for assistance to many different branches of science.[29]

But, as the infant geographical science began to grow in influence in schools, geographers were having their first experience of the politics which curriculum debate could engender. The broad integrationist stance advocated by Geikie was falling out of favour, especially with those who had supported the development of scientific modes of geographical study but who regarded it as primarily a sub-science of geology. There was a growing feeling among the earth scientists that, whereas there was a place for 'above-ground' geomorphological and topographical studies of the physical environment to supplement 'below-ground' geological work, as long as they were carried out with due rigour (as in Mary Somerville's, *Physical Geography*), there was much less to be said intellectually for the

Figure 3.2:
An early photograph of modelling in geography at a London Board School
(*Source*: London Metropolitan Archive)

work being presented as human and political geography. It seemed to lack hard scientific rigour and, given the evidence of what was going on in schools, it was little more than a recitation of lists.

Sir Roderick Murchison, one of Britain's greatest nineteenth-century geologists had been President of the Royal Geographical Society four times between 1850 and 1870 when the marriage between geography and geology had been firm. Divorce loomed as other eminent geologists fell out with the Society over its espousing of an 'integrated' (i.e. physical and human) approach to geography in the mid-1870s.

In time Geikie, also, despite his belief in the value of geography, would cross swords with the RGS as it sought to promote the cause of geography as an independent subject in the universities. He wished geography to remain as a part of geology. Stoddart ascribes this attitude of geologists to them experiencing a loss of confidence about their subject at this time. Geological Survey staff numbers were being cut back in the 1870s; the days of the great pioneering field geologists and their expeditions were over. 'When the geographers began to press their claims, particularly to the science of landforms, it was seen by the geologists as a yet further assault on an already beleaguered position and, as a result, was almost universally opposed.'[30]

Douglas Freshfield was later to point the finger at geologists as 'perhaps the most forward of the would-be "chuckers-out" of geography from the Hall of Education'.[31] But that is a story which takes its place amidst more significant educational developments in the following chapter.

NOTES

1. Mary Somerville, *Physical Geography* (Murray, London, 1848). For biographical detail on Somerville see Marguerita Oughton, 'Mary Somerville', in T. W. Freeman and P. Pinchemel (eds), *Geographers: Biobibliographical Studies*, No.2 (Mansell, London, 1978), pp. 109–11.
2. Charles Dickens, *Hard Times* (Penguin, London, 1972), p. 1.
3. Historians of the period generally agree that in the 1860s barely a third of the nation's children were getting any schooling worth the name.
4. Report of the Commissioners appointed to enquire into the state of Popular Education in England, 1861 (Newcastle Commission), p. 157.
5. See A. von Humboldt, *Sketch of a Physical Description of the Universe*, trans. E. Sabine (Longman, London, 1847); K. Ritter, *Die Erdkunde* (19 vols) (Reimer, Berlin, 1822–59).
6. Quoted by Robert M. Rayner, *Recent Times* (Longman, London, 1949), p. 42.
7. H. G. Wells, *Experiment in Autobiography* (Gollancz, London, 1934), p. 93.
8. D. Freshfield, 'The place of geography in education', *Proceedings of the Royal Geographical Society*, 8(11) (1886), pp. 698–718.
9. J. R. Green and A. S. Green, *A Short Geography of the British Islands* (Macmillan, London, 1880).
10. T. Ploszajska 'Geographical education in London schools 1870–1944', unpublished PhD thesis, 1997. (The thesis can be consulted in the University of London Senate House Library.) Some of the chapters of this excellent thesis have formed the basis of subsequent published articles by Ploszajska, e.g., 'Constructing the subject; geographical models in English schools, 1870–1944', *Journal of Historical Geography*, 22 (1996), pp. 388–98; 'Cloud cuckoo land?: fact and fantasy in geographical readers, 1870–1944', *Paradigm*, 21 (1996), pp. 2–13; 'Down to earth?: geography fieldwork in English schools', *Environment and Planning: Society and Space*, 16 (1998), pp. 757–74.
11. E. Baigent, 'Recreating our past: geography and the re-writing of the *Dictionary of National Biography*', *Transactions of the Institute of British Geographers*, 19 (2) (1994), pp. 225–7.
12. Charlotte M. Yonge, *The Clever Woman of the Family* (1863; repr. Virago Press, London, 1986). Yonge's novels were as popular as those of Dickens and Thackeray in her time, though she has been neglected by literary critics until recently. For a sympathetic assessment of her life and work, see Alethea Hayter, *Charlotte Yonge* (Northcote House, London, 1996). See also D. Frew, *Object Lessons in Geography and Science* (Blackie, London, 1900); V. J. Murche, *The Teachers Manual of Object Lessons in Geography* (Macmillan, London 1902).
13. See, especially, Keiran Egan, *Educational Development* (Oxford University Press, Oxford, 1984).
14. This issue is further explored in Chapter 12. See especially note 10.
15. L. Fielding *et al., Geography for Ages 5 to 16* (HMSO, London, 1987), especially Sections 6.11–15.
16. J. E. Clyde, *Clyde's School Geography*, 10th edn (Oliver & Boyd, Edinburgh, 1866).
17. Report of the Schools Inquiry Commission (Taunton Commission), 1867–68.
18. Report of the Commissioners appointed to inquire into the revenues and management of certain schools and the studies pursued and the instruction given therein (Clarendon Commission), 1864.
19. At Eton, in the early nineteenth century, geography was only an 'extra' for the fifth form, but by the 1880s, geography and history were given 'one hour a week and an exercise' in the lower school. A small class of boys learnt history 'as volunteers' in the upper school. There is evidence that geography was taught in some form even in the eighteenth century at Eton. Thomas James, a pupil at Eton, who later became a Head of Rugby, wrote in 1776, 'Once arithmetic has been mastered in the Fifth Form, it will not be amiss if, for about half a year they spend this time on a whole holyday in learning geography' (from P. S. H.

Lawrence, *The Encouragement of Learning* (Michael Russell, London, 1980). The Eton College Library holds a copy of *Geography Questions and Answers* dated 1800 and a gazeteer compiled by A. Arrowsmith and published in 1831, *A Compendium of Ancient and Modern Geography for the Use of Eton School*. I am grateful for the help of Kevin Stannard in unearthing much of this and other information about geography at Eton.

20. E. W. Howson and G. T. Warner, *Harrow School* (Edward Arnold, London, 1898). I am grateful for the help of David Elleray in enlightening me about this and other aspects of geography at Harrow.

21. Ian Cameron, *To the Farthest Ends of the Earth: The History of the Royal Geographical Society 1830–1980* (Macdonald, London, 1980), pp. 16–17.

22. F. Galton, *Memories of My Life* (Methuen, London, 1908). One of Galton's most innovative projects was a 'geographical study of the distribution of pulchritude in Britain'. Another of his statistical papers concerned the best way to divide a fruitcake.

23. D. R. Stoddart, 'The RGS and the "New Geography": changing aims and changing roles in nineteenth century science', *Geographical Journal*, 146 (2) (July 1980), pp. 190–202.

24. Quoted by T. W. Freeman, *A Hundred Years of Geography* (Methuen, London, 1965), p. 40.

25. H. R. Mill, 'The first London professor of geography', *Geographical Journal*, 81 (1933), p. 538.

26. For more on Hughes' life see J. E. Vaughan, 'W. E. Hughes as geographical educationist', in W. E. Marsden (ed.), *Historical Perspectives in Education* (University of London Institute of Education, London, 1980), pp. 66–75; J. E. Vaughan, 'William Hughes', in T. W. Freeman and P. Pinchemel (eds), *Geographers: Biobibliographical Studies*, vol.IX (Mansell, London, 1985), pp. 47–54.

27. As quoted in W. E. Marsden, 'The Royal Geographical Society and geography in secondary education', in M. Price (ed.), *The Development of the Secondary Curriculum* (Croom Helm, London, 1986), Chapter 7, pp. 182–213.

28. See W. E. Marsden, 'Archibald Geikie 1835–1924', in T. W. Freeman and P. Pinchemel (eds), *Geographers: Biobibliographical Studies*, vol. III (Mansell, London, 1979), pp. 39–52. Geikie wrote *The Teaching of Geography* (Macmillan, London, 1887), but it was criticised by Mackinder and others for its supposed deficiencies on the human side.

29. The address is reprinted in *Proceedings of the Royal Geographical Society*, (new series) 1 (7), 1879, pp. 422–43.

30. D. R. Stoddart, *On Geography and Its History* (Blackwell, Oxford, 1986), p. 43.

31. Freshfield, 'The place of geography in education'.

4

Imperial Imperatives,
1880–1900

AN EMPIRE EMERGES

The introduction of universal elementary education through the Forster Education Act (and the increasing consciousness of the importance of education for all to continue the nation's well-being) benefited geographical study. In many of the new elementary schools built in the years subsequent to 1870, the teaching of some geography was seen by teachers, the officials of the new School Boards and by Government Inspectors as an acceptable adjunct (and handmaiden) to the teaching of reading and writing. The Codes of Regulations were revised on a regular basis (see Figures 4.1 and 4.2) to take account of this. In this respect the view was more enlightened than that of a hundred years later when the 1997 Labour Government's crusade for improved literacy and numeracy seemed unimaginatively to be unaware of the potential of other subjects to assist such a cause.

In this period, the subject had no developed 'shape' to speak of, only sporadic presence in secondary schools, no teachers yet trained specifically to teach it, nor any coherent form in the universities (though some geologists and historians included geographical elements in their courses) (see Figure 4.3). Yet, in elementary schools, the study of the surface of the earth, its physical form and its peoples (sometimes combined but, at most times, taught separately) developed strength, and was seen by most pupils as a useful area of learning in the context of the society in which they were being brought up.

The reasons for this are not difficult to understand. The later Victorians basked in the unprecedented expansion and growing influence of the British Empire. The map was quickly being 'coloured red' as trade and settlement followed the flag and merchants and emigrants followed British explorers to all parts of the globe. Canada and Australia experienced unprecedented population growth from British migrants in mid-century; the British Raj in India was being formed as a powerful unifying force over many smaller fiefdoms; the 'scramble for Africa' resulted in European powers making many territorial acquisitions in that continent with the British and French the leading colonial powers amongst them.

Article 109.f [There will be]... a grant, on examination of class subjects, amounting to one shilling or two shillings for each subject, if the inspector's report on the examination in class subjects is fair or good.

Rules of Examination:

(i) The recognised class subjects are:-
1. English
2. Geography
3. Elementary science
4. History
5. Needlework , for girls in mixed schools (according to Schedule 3)

(ii) For the purpose of examination in class subjects, a school is considered as made up of two divisions

(iii) The lower division must contain the scholars presented for examination in the elementary subjects in the Standards below the fourth, and the upper division those in the Standards above the fourth. The managers may place in either division the scholars in Standard IV.

(iv) No more than two class subjects, one of which must always be English, may be taken by either division. The same number of class subjects must be taken throughout the school.

(v) If two class subjects are taken, the second must be, in the lower division, either geography or elementary science: in the upper division, geography, elementary science or history. If the scholars in Standard IV are placed in the upper division, that division will be limited in the same manner as the lower division.

Figure 4.1:
Code of Regulations for Elementary Schools, 1882

PREFACE.

THIS series of Geographical Readers is intended to meet the requirements of the New Education Code 1884, as interpreted by the circular to Her Majesty's Inspectors.*

The work of the several Standards is divided as follows :—

Standard I.—To explain a plan of the school and play-ground. The four cardinal points. The meaning and use of a map.

Standard II.—The size and shape of the world. Geographical terms simply explained, and illustrated by reference to the map of England. Physical geography of hills and rivers.

Standard III.—Physical and political geography of England, with special knowledge of the district in which the school is situated.

Standard IV.—Physical and political geography of the British Isles; and either British North America or Australasia, with knowledge of their productions.

Standard V.—Geography of Europe, physical and political. Latitude and longitude. Day and night. The seasons.

Standard VI.—Geography of the world generally, and especially of the British colonies and dependencies. Interchange of productions. Circumstances which determine climate.

Standard VII.—The ocean. Currents and tides. General arrangement of the planetary system. Phases of the moon.

[In Standards V., VI., and VII. maps and diagrams may be required to illustrate the answers given.]

The object of these Readers is to give geographical ideas, and not merely a list of geographical facts; for this purpose pictures and maps have been freely interspersed with the descriptions.

W. G. B.

* Circular No. 228.—In reading-books, 40 lessons and not less than 80 pages of small octavo text should be required in Standards I. and II., and not less than 60 lessons and 120 pages in higher Standards.

Figure 4.2:
Extract from the preface of Baker's *Geographical Reader,* 1884

The Changing Place of Geography in the School Curriculum of England and Wales 1870–1930

| Sporadic Presence | Significant Presence | Strong Presence |

1885 - Scott Keltie Report to RGS & Exhibition
1887 - RGS helps to fund Oxbridge lectureships

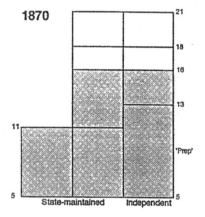

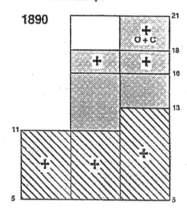

1893 - Founding of the GA
1902 - Education Act
1905 - 'Regulations for the teaching of geography' (statutory)

Post 1918 - Tide of post-war 'Internationalism'
1922 - Board of Education Regulations include geography as an Advanced Course

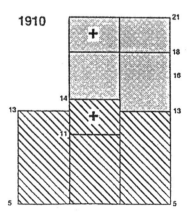

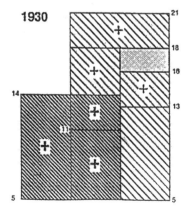

Figure 4.3:
The changing place of geography in British schools
(*Source*: author)

This expansion of influence overseas was accomplished in a period of increasing mobility, as railways and iron ships developed and made travel more universally possible. The genius of Brunel and the Stephensons, of Telford and Brassey, inspired many other engineers; allied to the entrepreneurial skills of men like George Hudson and Sir Edward Watkin, major transport systems were created in Britain within a few years. Thomas Cook's first excursions were railway trips in the Midlands, but his business quickly prospered as the idea of visiting countries overseas became a practical reality and desired objective for others besides explorers, high government officials and armies.

Wordsworth might bemoan, 'Is there no nook of English ground secure from rash assault?' as the Kendal and Windermere Railway was driven through his beloved Lake District, and Ruskin thunder 'Now every fool in Buxton can be in Bakewell in half an hour and every fool in Bakewell at Buxton; which you think a lucrative process of exchange – you Fools everywhere!' but they were in a minority. Dr Arnold of Rugby, – he who had played with his shapes of English counties as a child and encouraged geography on to the curriculum at Rugby – rejoiced at the liberation he saw through the opening of the London and Birmingham Railway – 'to think that feudality has gone for ever'.

His comment had an interesting resonance in relation to railways overseas, since the building of railways by British engineers was often the cement which bound together the disparate communities of new colonial possessions. 'The idea of a Cape-to-Cairo railway, though it remained an idea, was conceived by Cecil Rhodes as the high-water mark of later nineteenth century British imperialism.'[1] The same railways which allowed administrators, doctors, teachers, and law-enforcers to travel between widely spaced locations also brought a greater freedom of travel to the inhabitants who previously might not have stirred many miles from their own village. Both flows contributed to an emergence of new nationhood.

The nineteenth-century revolution in transportation was the catalyst for the creation of the British Empire – or at least for its transformation into a place which was reachable by ordinary folk; where they might visit or perhaps go to serve a humanitarian or missionary cause for some years, or migrate and carve out a new life for themselves.[2]

IMPERIAL ECHOES IN THE CURRICULUM

In 1893 an editorial about the school curriculum in the *Daily Graphic*, one of the popular newspapers of the time, put the point succinctly:

> The Royal Colonial Institute is again calling the attention of headmasters to the importance of colonial geography and history as subjects of instruction in schools. It certainly does seem odd that so little should be done in British schools to give boys and girls and adequate idea of the development and resources of the various parts of the Empire. If the French or the Germans had an Empire of equal

extent and splendour, then we may be sure that they would take good care that justice was done to it in their national system of education...

Properly taught, the leading facts relating to India and the colonies would greatly interest young people and in many cases the knowledge obtained at school would be of practical service in later life. Moreover the study could not fail to encourage the growth of a wholesome patriotism.[3]

Thus the impulse for a greater prominence for geography in schools largely came from the belief that all Britons should have an interest in the world because of the newly acquired possessions of their nation and that young citizens of the Empire should certainly be aware of the rudiments of the places to which they might go. This national mood is sometimes portrayed by commentators as a collective villainy in an unscrupulous past, the results of which were wholly malign. But the matter is much more complex than that. In some regards, it was a staging-post to a concept of global citizenship.

Victorian society was certainly gripped with a sense of its own social superiority and some of its outpourings about 'natives' and 'savages' sit curiously with professed Christian ideals and the supposed benificence of the ruling colonial classes. Yet there was also much altruism and idealism mixed with these attitudes, and probably as many migrants gave 'service' to their fellow human-beings in Empire (for instance, by improving health and educational standards) as oppressed them, or 'destroyed' their culture, knowingly or otherwise.

A significant educational characteristic at this time in Britain was that the geography of other countries continued to be presented in terms of strangeness and wonderment, even after colonists and settlers had supplanted the first pioneers and explorers. The basis of attitudes towards people in other continents was entirely Anglocentric. This was hardly surprising, given the freshness of perception of places and peoples hitherto unknown to Europeans or only previously glimpsed through myth and legend.

The gulf between lifestyles which had experienced agricultural, industrial and transport revolutions and those which had not could scarcely fail to be remarkable to both. The awe and curiosity of early travellers was captured by these other places, made interesting by the intensity of their 'otherness'. Similarly, in the classroom, because this was such an absorbing and motivating approach for almost a century, much geography in schools emphasised a world of 'difference', with the differences often exaggerated. The 'educational' revolution had still to come.

Free from any higher academic educational scrutiny at this period, the teaching of geography in elementary schools took on uncritically the pride in Empire of most of society and played its part in the development of young citizens who would accept it and support it. The imperial imperative was clearly dominant as the major sub-text of geographical learning in the schools of the latter part of the nineteenth century.

THE STRENGTH OF ELEMENTARY SCHOOL GEOGRAPHY

The 'payments by results' initiative and the dominance of the teaching of 'capes and bays' was only a relatively short chapter in the history of geography teaching in schools, and the representation of it as a widespread and long-term educational blight is a misrepresentation of the evidence. Though Keltie's report is often cited as a wholesale condemnation of geography teaching of the early 1880s (see below), it is the prominence of particular comments about *secondary* education in the document which has created this impression. Such a reading ignores the fact that the report was complimentary about what was going on in the *elementary* schools of the nation. Keltie repeats, in several places, his admiration for what teachers of geography were doing in elementary schools; there was strength at the base of the educational pyramid, even if the subject had, as yet, to hoist a flag at the peak.

Within a few years of elementary education being available for all, Government and School Board Inspectors were pointing out the shortcomings of exclusively factual teaching. In his general report for 1877, a London General Inspector, Mr Barrington-Ward, made his feelings clear:

> What am I to say of teachers who make the weary scholars learn by heart tedious strings of mere names and numbers, who are content with mechanical instruction and stereotyped sets of words, who work as if they and their scholars were machines and not reasonable beings? It is unpardonable for a child, a year under instruction, to have no vivid idea of the meanings of the terms taught to him, and no fund of information regarding the land specifically studied.[4]

Many inspectors urged schools to supplement factual manuals with texts which provided stories and descriptions of places. With the birth of photography as an art, and with increasing technology allowing the cheap representation of wood-block sketches as supplements to text, the possibility of illustrations in classroom books became a real possibility.

THE RISE OF THE GEOGRAPHICAL 'READER'

Thus, in the context of a developing market for geography publications at the elementary level, the individual geographical 'reader' became prominent – a book with large type and simple narratives. This was just as likely to be avidly read by the keen pupil in a private reading time, as followed word by word in a session of class reading. Many teachers found the geographical reader an ideal way of stimulating basic literacy, precisely because of the intrinsic interest of the stories and descriptions within its pages.

The readers, of course, presented the world in terms of Empire. One such example was the series of *Alternative Geography Readers* (authors not credited) published by Collins. At crown quarto size (nearly 10″ by 8″: 250 mm × 203 mm) these were clearly designed for pupil reading and were twice as large as many of the earlier factually oriented texts.

Book 3 *The British Empire* published in the 1890s (for Standards VI and VII – i.e. for scholars of 11, 12 and 13 years of age at the top of the elementary school) proudly claimed it had '67 coloured photographs, 16 coloured maps and numerous illustrations'.[5]

The section on Australia (pp. 97–126) begins with a chapter on 'Settlers and Explorers' and a practical, colonial perspective immediately emerges:

> Cook made Great Britain a present of an almost unpeopled continent and therefore the next thing to be decided was the use to which it should be put.

The internal and coastal explorations of Bass, Flinders, Sturt, Mitchell, Eyre, Leichardt, Kennedy and Burke and Wills are each chronicled with a paragraph of description, and then follows:

> 15. In 1873, Colonel Warburton, with thirty camels, succeeded in reaching the western coast from the centre of Australia. The journey occupied eight months.

> Describing the natives of Western Australia, Warburton says: 'They are the very lowest in the scale of humanity, and I cannot conceive how anything could fall much lower. They do not even take the trouble to put a few bushes up to shelter themselves from the sun or the rain – when it does rain, though I don't know when, for I didn't see it; the sun is hot enough.' (p. 99)

These comments are, presumably, injected by the author(s) of the Reader to bring a personal and topical perspective to the evocation of the area. Did the young scholars (and teachers) take Warburton's from-the-hip observations with uncritical admiration, with horror, or with a pinch of salt?

The evidence of the text alone is, alas, not enough to reveal the way in which the topic might have been handled in the classroom but one hopes, at least, that not all the stories and the opinions of the explorer-raconteurs were swallowed whole... Perhaps an astute pupil or teacher would be aware of the curious irony in the large coloured sketch accompanying this paragraph (almost certainly not originated by Warburton himself): three white explorers (one still mounted on his camel) seem to be having the grace to accept directions from an almost

Figure 4.4:
Illustration from Collins'
Alternative Geography Reader,
1891 (reduced in size)

unclad Aboriginal, who is giving them the benefit of his superior local knowledge by pointing the way forward for them (see Figure 4.4).

Not all 'native peoples' were regarded with disfavour, however. In another section, the author(s) assert that:

> The Maoris, or natives of New Zealand, are a much superior race to the natives of Australia. They are intelligent, brave and daring, and capable of civilisation.

A CRUCIAL SPUR TO IMPROVEMENT

To someone writing in one period, the events of previous times often parade themselves in somewhat undifferentiated perspective. Different events are highlighted, and invested with significance depending on the line being taken or the point of view being propounded. Within the history of geographical education, however, there is almost universal agreement that the Keltie Report of 1886 represents a key moment in the discipline. It was an event which generated many others and which has been perceived as the start of geography's journey to both recognised stature and intellectual coherence within the educational world.

The genesis and consequences of the Report link together the lives of three key figures in the history of geographical education: Douglas Freshfield (1845–1934), activist, enthusiast, shrewd operator;[6] Scott Keltie (1840–1927), writer, investigator, man of judgement;[7] Halford Mackinder (1861–1947) scholar, prophet, politician.[8] These three can lay claim to be the dominant nineteenth-century personalities of geographical education on the national scene if words are to be matched by deeds as measure of their importance (see Figures 4.5, 4.6 and 4.7).

Freshfield had been a supporter of Francis Galton's plan to offer RGS Medals to schools, but was aware of its relative failure (see Chapter 3). In January 1884 the RGS voted to discontinue the scheme but also to consider 'whether any and what encouragement to geographical study should be substituted'. Its line of sight lay towards the secondary, rather than the elementary sector.

Three ideas emerged. Clements Markham, one of the joint Honorary Secretaries, a gradualist by nature, re-presented a scheme which he had put forward five years earlier. This suggested the Society's next move should be to offer instruction to intending travellers in survey techniques and mapping, and to provide regular courses of lectures about other subjects closely connected with geography. He thought the RGS Council should give encouragement to better teaching in the 'ordinary schools' of the country, but his ideas were tentative in this sphere, though he did suggest the possible arrangement of lectures for schoolteachers.[9]

Francis Galton, the instigator of the Medals scheme, had a more sharply focused proposal. It was that the RGS should finance and appoint a Professor of Geography for a limited term who would apprise himself of the state of geographical education at home and abroad, and give lectures in London and at schools and universities. Markham was against this since he thought that 'there was no one in England possessed of enough acquaintance with all the different branches of geographical knowledge'.

Freshfield saw the merits of Galton's scheme but thought that a Society-appointed figure, who would mainly lecture at the RGS, would be of limited value and credibility. Freshfield worked diplomatically to keep Markham's goodwill, whilst reshaping Galton's proposals.

Of the three resolutions he put before RGS Council on 24 March 1884, one supported Markham's proposal for lectures for travellers, another supported Galton's proposal for an academic initiative (but with the crucial addition that the co-operation of Oxford and Cambridge Universities should be sought) and the third proposed the appointment (at the expense of not more than £150) of 'an inspector of geographical

Figure 4.5:
Photograph of Douglas
Freshfield (*Source*: RGS)

Figure 4.6:
Photograph of J. Scott Keltie
(*Source*: RGS)

Figure 4.7:
Photograph of H. J.
Mackinder (*Source*: RGS)

appliances for one year 'to collect and arrange in the Society's premises all the best text books, maps, models, diagrams and appliances published in England or on the Continent and to report thereon'.[10] This was the key proposal and Freshfield's own enthusiasm.

Freshfield's scheme was agreed by the RGS Council and the post immediately advertised. The successful applicant was a Scot who had come to London a decade earlier and worked as a journalist, reviewing school text books and writing for *The Times*, the journal *Nature* and the *Encyclopaedia Britannica* on geographical subjects. His name was James Scott Keltie.

KELTIE GETS TO WORK

As Wise reports 'Keltie worked with efficiency and speed. He was a highly skilled investigator and reporter. Clearly too, he had a genuine interest in geography and education.'[11] He visited seven European countries and spoke to teachers and academics in each of them as well as visiting their schools. He corresponded with others in Canada and the

59

USA. He visited a considerable number of both 'public schools' and Board schools in Britain. Wherever he found what he considered to be good practice he collected examples of pupils' work as well as maps, models, atlases and what were then called 'teaching appliances'. His voluminous report of over 150 pages was ready by the middle of May 1985, only ten months after his appointment.[12]

It was broadly supportive of what was going on in elementary schools ('Since the State undertook the charge of elementary education, the position of geography... has greatly improved') but made disturbing reading in relation to secondary schools. Keltie considered geography teaching in Britain to be well behind what was going on in Europe, on which he reported in some detail. In most British secondary schools, he found teachers lacklustre and untrained, textbooks dull and dreary, and pedagogy poor. He favourably compared what was going on in the London Board elementary schools (see Figure 4.8) to 'some of our great public schools':

> In each of the London Board schools for example, there are a special map of the neighbourhood of each school, a map of the division in which the school is situated and a map of London and its environs. (p. 13)

> In one of our oldest and most celebrated public schools I could find only two maps; one a large map of the Dominion of Canada, presented by the High Commissioner, ornamenting one of the passages, and another wretched school map exhumed, after much searching, from a remote recess. (p. 22)

Few of the British schools which he visited were considered strong in geography and he noted that where present, it was only in the lower school, and there taught by the class master who would have had no special training in it. University College School, Hampstead was one of the few schools which were praised, and Keltie included one of its geography examination papers as an appendix to his report, calling it, 'A paper in which even a professional geographer might be plucked, if he had not been coaching himself in the subject immediately before.'

Keltie's report spent almost as much space (22 pages) on his impressions of German education as of British (25 pages). In Germany he had been impressed by the high status of the subject and by the way in which it was taught.

> It is a serious subject of education, taught to a large extent by trained teachers, and with a wealth of apparatus not to be found in this country. (p. 48)

He observed that many German teachers worked on the 'Heimatskunde' principle, first establishing firm understanding of local places and areas, through individual use of large-scale maps, journey-to-

A Board School Leaving Examination

1. Explain the following terms, and give one example of each: *isthmus, promontory, volcano, water-basin, cataract, delta, spring tide.*

2. Explain the cause of Day and Night. Why, in summer, do the days lengthen as we approach the North Pole?

3. Where are the following, and for what are they noted: Aberdeen, Cork, Swansea, Bristol, Munich, Odessa, Aden, Colombo, Port Elizabeth, Mauritius, Zanzibar, Khyber Pass, Peak of Teneriffe, Vancouver's Islands, Falls of Niagara?

4. What articles does this country import to supply materials for clothing? From what countries are they respectively brought, and in what districts are goods manufactured from them?

5. What islands, and island groups, belong to the British Empire? State the position of each, and mention what use it is to this country.

6. Draw an outline map of Australia *or* South America, showing the chief physical features, political divisions, and position of ten large towns.

Figure 4.8:
London School Board Leaving
Examination in Geography,
1893

school exercises and field visits, before going on to consider areas further afield. Keltie was impressed by the results of this approach and also noted that 'this system is finding its way into English Board schools'. But he saw the comparison between enlightened German education and that in British grammar and 'public' schools as very unflattering to his own nation.

He was also complimentary about the position of geography in the Scottish schools he visited:

> Geography has always held such a high place among subjects of school study in Scotland that it is taught in Glasgow Academy neither as compulsory nor optional but as a matter of course. (p. 88)

His overall evidence was selective and impressionistic, but his conclusions were authoritative because of the mass of evidence he had brought back and because of his clear presentation of what he had seen on his widespread travels:

> Except then in our elementary schools, in the high schools for girls and in isolated middle-class schools … geography in this country is almost entirely neglected as a subject of education. (p. 36)

> So far as our schools are concerned, the two great weaknesses seem to me to be want of knowledge in the teachers and want of organisation in the programmes and methods. (p. 77)

The thoroughness of the Report, the forthright nature of Keltie's comments and (at the secondary level, at least) the unfavourable comparisons with Germany and France galvanised the RGS into action when the Report was presented. Lord Aberdare, the president, gave it pride of place in his speech to the AGM of the Society in the following month.

PRINCE KROPOTKIN INTERVENES

One notable supporter of the Report was Prince Peter Kropotkin who used it as a peg to write a substantial article in the influential periodical, *The Nineteenth Century* (December 1885) called 'What geography ought to be'. Kropotkin (1842–1921), was a notable Russian *émigré* whom *Chambers Biographical Dictionary* describes as 'geographer, savant, revolutionary and nihilist'.[13] He escaped from imprisonment in his homeland and first came to England in 1876. He often spoke and wrote on controversial political matters but was also interested in geographical and educational issues, and advanced arguments for a stronger place for geography in the school curriculum (see Chapter 1). However, he did not share Keltie's enthusiasm for 'Heimatskunde' approaches:

> To divide geography into Heimatskunde for the earlier age and into geography proper for an advanced age is neither desirable nor possible. One of the first things a child asks his mother is 'What becomes of the sun when it goes down?' ... we are bound to give them notions of cosmography and physical geography from childhood.

(The echoes of that division of opinion were to rumble on for many years, fuelled by the growing attachment of primary school educators to the Nature School of education principles of Pestalozzi and Froebel; others like Freshfield opposed the Heimatskunde idea strenuously. The support for 'starting local' with younger pupils reached its apogee in the 1950s, though it happened to be coincident with a loss of focus on 'subjects' altogether in the primary school.)

However, Kropotkin did make the point that geography needed to be experienced in a practical way by children, 'with the use of maps, compasses, etc.', if it was to be real to them and he offered support and publicity for the exhibition of appliances which Keltie organised in conjunction with the Report.

THE EXHIBITION OF APPLIANCES

The materials which Keltie had collected in the course of his travels were catalogued and ready for viewing by December 1885. Three large rooms in The Galleries, 53 Marlborough Street in the centre of London were hired. A relief model of the Monte Rosa group of mountains dominated the main room; another major exhibit was a relief model of the sea bed around the British Isles. Around the walls were textbooks, models, pupils' work, atlases, episcopes and epidiascopes, and other 'appliances'. A programme of lectures and discussions was arranged in conjunction with the exhibition.

Almost unnoticed at the time, the visit of one young Oxford graduate (he had first read natural sciences and then history) to the exhibition, had great consequences for school geography:

> As a result of a notice in the paper I came up to London and went to a hall (off) Regent Street where I found a collection of maps, diagrams, books and Dr Keltie. I had never heard of Dr Keltie at that time. I knew very little of the Royal Geographical Society. I got into conversation with Dr Keltie and he was very kind to a young man who put some crude questions to him. It was from that moment that my vague tendencies towards geography began to crystallise.[14]

Thus a chance conversation in an exhibition hall drew Halford Mackinder into geography's orbit and prepared the way for his major contributions to it. Mackinder was later to call Keltie 'my father in geography'.

Over 4,000 people visited the exhibition during its six-month stay in London, many of them schoolteachers. Then it went on to Manchester, Edinburgh, Bradford and Birmingham, coinciding at the latter city with the September annual meeting of the British Association for the Advancement of Science. Freshfield, ever the opportunist, delivered a paper on 'The place of geography in education' at that conference and it was well reported by *The Times* next day. The British Association were also skilfully and successfully lobbied to lend their support to Freshfield's next scheme. The idea which Freshfield conceived was that the most opportune way forward was to attack at the top – to seek to secure a geographical appointment at one or both of the universities of Oxford and Cambridge.

MACKINDER'S 'SCOPE AND METHODS' PAPER

Mackinder meanwhile had gone off to lecture for the Oxford Extension Movement, full of zeal for what he saw as 'The new geography'. He calculated that he travelled over 30,000 miles and gave over 600 extension lectures on 'physiography' and 'the new geography' in seven years. 'He preached the New Geography with all the missionary zeal and

Figure 4.9:
Map of places where H. J. Mackinder gave extension lectures, 1885–93 (*Source*: GA)

fervour of a Wesley' (see Figure 4.9).[15] One of his courses in Manchester was attended by 105 elementary school teachers and, it was estimated, had the potential to affect 6,000 pupils.

Mackinder was a persuasive and charismatic lecturer, though never a great conversationalist. At the age of only 26, he had a command of language and the gift of explaining new ideas which held audiences in thrall. The reported success of Mackinder's lectures led the RGS to invite him to read a paper on 'the new geography' and he did so on 31 January 1887. The paper, 'On the scope and methods of geography', was a landmark comparable to Keltie's Report of 18 months before.[16]

On the occasion of its centenary, Coones[17] conveniently summarised the paper, largely in Mackinder's own words:

> The crucial questions are these: can geography be rendered a discipline instead of a mere body of information? ... is geography

one, or is it several subjects? More precisely are physical and political geography two stages of one investigation or are they separate subjects to be studied by different methods, the one an appendix of geology, the other of history?

If the subject is to be of practical, theoretical, intellectual and pedagogic value, then the reply must be that geography is a unity, embodying the truth that 'knowledge is … one'. One of the greatest of all gaps lies between the natural sciences and the study of humanity. It is the duty of the geographer to build one bridge over an abyss which in the opinion of many is upsetting the equilibrium of our culture. In order to achieve this end we insist on the teaching and the grasping of geography as a whole … lop off either limb … and you maim it in its noblest part … Geography must be a continuous argument.

Consequently no rational political geography can exist which is not built upon and subsequent to physical geography, for geography is the science whose main function is to trace the interaction of man in society and so much of his environment as varies locally… It is the function of physical geography to analyse one of these factors, the varying environment.

Physical geography is not a matter for those already burdened with geology, for the geologist asks different questions and is possessed of a different point of view. Geography is concerned with the distribution of phenomena and with the causal relations which exist between them in the present. Geology, on the other hand, does not deal with the topography of the present but with the riddles of the past.

The distributions on the earth's surface of both physical and human phenomena are geographical only in so far as they act upon each other. These data are grouped regionally, into natural regions and communities; the interaction between them defines the scope of geography and determines its methods. (p. 4)

Mackinder's paper raised the coherence of arguments to justify geography as a distinctive study to a new level and at the same time took on the powerful geological lobby (which wished to keep geography as a sub-set of its own science) head on. His advocacy and demonstration of the unity of physical and political (or, as we would now say, human) studies in the subject (illustrated with examples from south-east England) was a defining moment in the history of the emerging discipline and compelling to those who heard it; its brilliance of exposition was matched only by the perfection of its timing.

The paper caused a stir in a number of ways. One Admiral who sat in the front row was heard to repeatedly mumble 'damn cheek' as the paper was delivered. Others were astonished at the poise and persuasiveness of one so young. Two weeks later, a further meeting was held at the RGS to discuss issues raised by the paper. On that occasion, Francis Galton said 'It is a great thing to have a gentleman like Mackinder, of university distinction, who knows his own mind, ... who is destined to leave his mark on geographical education.' Years later, J. F. Unstead called the paper 'a classic document in the history of the development of British geography'.[18]

Within a few short months Mackinder was lecturing at Oxford University, with the RGS undertaking to contribute half of his annual salary (£300) over a period of five years. Mackinder's early lectures there were attached to no particular degree programme; although distinctive courses were arranged, geography was to remain under the administrative umbrella of geology until 1916. The lectures were delivered to small numbers (he recalled that two ladies, who brought their knitting, were his first lecture audience) but when news of his charisma and knowledgeability got round, he soon attracted a sizeable following, especially for lectures which linked geography to history.

More importantly he had a platform for his views and he was to be a notable figure both in the promotion of geography and in public life in the decades to come. His later working life was spent as a university administrator and as a politician (he was Director of the London School of Economics before becoming a Member of Parliament), but he remained active as a speaker and writer and two of his books advanced interesting and controversial geopolitical theories.[19] Yet perhaps his most lasting and positive memorials are in the general advancement of geographical education which he helped to achieve.

The RGS was less successful in finding a suitable figure for Cambridge, where geography languished in spite of the willingness of the university authorities to co-operate in the same way as Oxford over the matter of a salary. F. H. H. Guillemard was of a delicate disposition and proved to be something of a broken reed, lasting only six months in the post before resigning under the strain. Neither of his successors, J. Y. Buchanan and H. Y. Oldham, had the multiplicity of talents needed to get the subject established and accepted; the genuine advancement of geography beyond the margin in Cambridge was delayed for at least two decades.[20]

THE FOUNDING OF THE GEOGRAPHICAL ASSOCIATION

Mackinder arranged for the new common room at Christ Church, Oxford, to be the venue for a significant meeting which was held in March 1893. B. Bentham Dickinson, then a teacher at Rugby School, conceived the idea of exchanging some of his lantern slides, used to illustrate geography lessons, with other public school masters (see Figure 4.10). He invited some other teachers whom he knew taught some geography (in all honesty they could scarcely be called 'geographers') to

Oxford, 4th of April, 1893.

Dear Sir,

In connection with schemes for the improved illustration of Geographical and other teaching in Schools, which have lately been circulated by Mr. Field of Canterbury and also by Mr. Dickinson of Rugby, it has been arranged to hold a Meeting of School-masters and others interested at Oxford, on Saturday, the 20th of May, at 4.30 p.m. in the New Common Room, Christ Church.

It is hoped that the discussion will lead to the adoption of a practical scheme.

We trust that you may find it possible to be present, and to place your experience at our disposal.

We remain,

Yours faithfully,

DOUGLAS W. FRESHFIELD,
(Hon. Sec. to the Royal Geographical Society.)

T. FIELD,
(Head-Master of King's School, Canterbury.)

H. J. MACKINDER,
(Reader in Geography in the University of Oxford.)

B. B. DICKINSON,
(Assistant-Master in Rugby School.)

C. E. B. HEWITT,
(Assistant-Master in Marlborough College.)

Kindly reply to
B. B. Dickinson, Bloxam House, Rugby.

Figure 4.10:
Facsimile of letter calling a meeting of schoolmasters at Oxford, 1893 (*Source*: GA)

meet to discuss the matter and Mackinder offered support and acted as host.

The fact that geography was an illustrated lesson at this time in some of the public schools is in itself remarkable; one can only presume that those who came to Oxford did not represent the 'great public schools' which Keltie had criticised only eight years earlier. In this minority of schools the use of lantern slides (they would have been of heavy glass and probably at least 4″ × 4″ in size) was distinguishing the subject from its colleagues: it leavened the supposed diet of 'capes and bays' with visual representations of what was being taught.

The lantern slides required large and heavy projectors, and the rooms needed to be totally blacked out for the image to be effectively seen, but a small cadre of enthusiastic teachers nevertheless thought it worthwhile to go to this trouble in order to make their lessons more vivid. In many cases, the photographs had been taken by the teachers themselves whilst on climbing or trekking expeditions in the continent of Europe or in other parts of Britain.

In a similar way printed photographs or wood-block drawings could be viewed if the classroom was equipped with an episcope, though that piece of machinery was even bulkier than the lantern-slide projector.

Dickinson found ten other colleagues interested in coming to the meeting; not a great number, but then geography had only a toehold in the secondary school curriculum and (since geography was only marginally and sporadically taught in universities as yet) even those who came saw geographical education as an interest rather than an area of expertise. They had all been educated in another discipline (though in all probability not trained to teach that subject) and it would be on this which they spent most of their teaching time.

Under the guidance and enthusiasm of Mackinder and Freshfield, however, the meeting gathered momentum. By the time it had concluded, the group had resolved not only to set up an exchange of slides but also association which would devote itself specifically to 'the study and teaching of geography'. A first committee meeting was held at University College School, Hampstead, in June 1893, and a few months later at the first Annual General Meeting, held at the Colonial Institute in Kensington, the Geographical Association was born.[21]

Its membership at the start was exclusively male and exclusively public school, but it took only a few years for both those barriers to be broken down. Indeed, Freshfield, who became the first President, might not have been in a position to have put so much energy into the earliest days of the GA if he had not fallen out with the RGS in 1892 over the question of whether women should be admitted to the Fellowship. The RGS had got itself into a pickle by giving medals to some women explorers, and then admitting some to Fellowship, without seeking the full permission of the Society. Backwoodsmen Fellows came out in droves to oppose this revolutionary step and the Council were forced to back down.

Impatient with the traditionalists, Freshfield penned the memorable quatrain:

Figure 4.11:
A nineteenth-century
geography lesson – note the
model which is on the front
table
(*Source*: London Metropolitan
Archive)

The question, our dissentients bellow
Is can a woman be a Fellow?
That, sirs, will be no question, when
Our Fellows are all Gentlemen!

and transferred his considerable energies from RGS to the newly formed
GA at a vital moment. He was to tell the RGS later:

> The reason why some of us wanted to see ladies in the Society was
> that many ladies are engaged in geographical teaching and often in
> high posts. The Geographical Association was founded to give these
> ladies facilities denied them elsewhere.[22]

Freshfield is not strictly accurate about the reasons for the founding
of the GA, but there is little doubt that his active participation in the new
body brought an early consideration of whether women should be
members. The response was more positive in the GA than in the RGS.
With women beginning to teach in some secondary schools (Maria Grey
College in Bishopsgate, North London, had been founded in 1878 to
train women for secondary school teaching, the first training course of its
kind) it was not long before they found their way on to the committees
and Council of the GA where there was less opposition to and more
appreciation of their contribution.

The GA membership, at first mainly of secondary-level teachers from
the independent (or 'public') schools, grew only very slowly in its early

years. The Association was to begin making its significant contributions from the turn of the century, a time coincident with the greater involvement of A. J. Herbertson, the enthusiastic young assistant whom Mackinder had been able to recruit to Oxford as his own base of influence developed.

In 1880 at Aveton Gifford, in Devon, a mother wrote to the Headmaster of the village elementary school asking him to 'excuse her daughter from learning geography as it puzzled her'.

The headmaster recorded in the school record book that 'I told her that as the child is not afflicted in any way, I could not excuse it – and the puzzling will do her good, if not carried to excess.'

From Aveton Gifford Church School: notes on the early records by R R Sellman, Aveton Gifford Parish Deposit, 328/A add.3/PE3 , in the Devon Record Office.

NOTES

1. Michael Robbins, *The Railway Age* (Routledge & Kegan Paul, London, 1962: reprinted by Penguin Books, London, 1965), p. 151 in the Penguin edition.
2. A. V. Maddrell, 'Empire, emigration and school geography: changing discourses of Imperial citizenship 1880–1925', *Journal of Historical Geography*, 22 (1996), pp. 373–87.
3. 'Editorial', *Daily Graphic*, 2 January 1893.
4. Quoted by Teresa Ploszajska in her PhD thesis (1997), 'Geographical education in London schools 1870–1944', an unpublished manuscript which can be consulted in the University of London Senate House Library (see also Chapter 3, note 5).
5. Author uncredited, *Alternative Geography Readers: Book 3 The British Empire* (Collins, London, undated, but between 1890–1900).
6. For fuller biographical detail on Freshfield see: T. C. Longstaff, 'Douglas Freshfield', *Geographical Journal*, 83 (1934), pp. 257–62; Dorothy Middleton, 'Douglas Freshfield', in G. J. Martin (ed.), *Geographers: Biobibliographical Studies*, Vol. 13 (Mansell, London, 1991), pp. 23–31.
7. For fuller biographical detail on Keltie see: L. J. Jay, 'J. S. Keltie', in T. W. Freeman and P. Pinchemel (eds), *Geographers: Biobibliographical Studies*, 10 (Mansell, London, 1986), pp. 93–8.
8. For fuller biographical detail on Mackinder see: B. Blouet, *Halford Mackinder* (Texas A & M University Press, Collye Station, 1987): W. H. C. Parker, *Mackinder: Geography as an Aid to Statecraft* (Oxford University Press, Oxford, 1982); E. W. Gilbert, 'Seven lamps of geography: an appreciation of the teaching of Sir Halford Mackinder', *Geography*, 36 (1951), pp. 21-43; E. W. Gilbert, *British Pioneers in Geography* (David & Charles, Newton Abbot, 1972), chapters 8 and 9. For a penetrating and critical view of Mackinder's work see, particularly, G. Kearns, 'Halford J. Mackinder', in T. W. Freeman and P. Pinchemel (eds), *Geographers: Biobibliographical Studies*, Vol. 9 (Mansell, London, 1985), pp. 71–86.
9. Royal Geographical Society Additional Papers No. 95, held in RGS archives: memorandum written by Clements Markham, dated 28 February 1884.
10. Royal Geographical Society Additional Papers, held in RGS archives; memorandum written by Douglas Freshfield, undated, 1884.
11. M. J. Wise, 'The Scott Keltie Report, 1885 and the teaching of geography in Great Britain', *Geographical Journal*, 152, 3 (1986), pp. 367–82.

12. J. S. Keltie (1886), *Geographical Education* – 'Report to the Council of the Royal Geographical Society', in RGS Supplementary papers 1, pp. 439–594. The Report was also reprinted as a separate publication by John Murray in 1886 and page references given here are from this version.

13. Entry on Kropotkin in M. Magnusson (ed.), *Chambers Biographical Dictionary* (Chambers, Edinburgh, 1990), p. 843.

14. H. J. Mackinder, *The Geographical Teacher*, Vol. 7 (1914), p. 226.

15. Gilbert, 'Seven lamps of geography'.

16. H. J. Mackinder, 'On the scope and methods of geography', *Proceedings of the Royal Geographical Society*, NS9 (1887), pp. 141–74.

17. Paul Coones, 'Mackinder's "Scope and Methods of Geography" after a hundred years' (research paper, School of Geography, University of Oxford, 1987).

18. J. F. Unstead, 'H. J. Mackinder and the New Geography', *Geographical Journal*, 113 (1949), pp. 47–57.

19. H. J. Mackinder's two seminal books on geopolitics were *Britain and the British Seas* (Heinemann, London, 1902) and *Democratic Ideals and Reality: A Study in the politics of Reconstruction* (Constable, London, 1919; repr. Penguin Books, London, 1944). The latter advanced the theory that whoever controlled the Eurasian heartland would be the dominant world power: written in the aftermath of the First World War, it was said to have been read by Adolf Hitler and to have influenced his thinking about strategy. The idea of the 'heartland' as the key to world power was prominent in the thinking and writing of General Karl Haushofer, a leading academic strategist and student of geopolitics in the inter-war period. Haushofer often referred to Mackinder's theories in his teaching and writing and called Mackinder's 1904 paper ('The geographical pivot of history', *Geographical Journal*, 23 (1904), pp. 421–37) 'the greatest of all geographical world views ... a geopolitical masterpiece'. Rudolf Hess, Deputy-Leader of the Nazi Party, studied under Haushofer and it is known that Hess provided some of the key ideas for Hitler's *Mein Kampf*. However, views now differ concerning the extent of Haushofer's influence in inter-war Germany.

20. The fortunes of geography at Oxford and Cambridge are colourfully and amusingly chronicled in: D. I. Scargill, 'The RGS and the foundations of geography at Oxford', *Geographical Journal*, 142 (1976), pp. 438–61; D. R. Stoddart, 'The RGS and the foundations of geography at Cambridge', *Geographical Journal*, 141 (1975), pp. 216–39 (a revised version is in the same author's collection of essays *On Geography* (Blackwell, Oxford, 1986).

21. For a full history of The Geographical Association, see W. G. V. Balchin, *The Geographical Association: The First Hundred Years 1893–1993* (Geographical Association, Sheffield, 1993).

22. D. Freshfield, 'Presidential Address', *Geographical Journal*, 46 (1) (1915), pp. 1–10. Freshfield resigned as Honorary Secretary of the RGS in 1894. He served as the first President of the Geographical Association from 1897–1911, but restored his links with the RGS in the later part of that period. In 1903 he was awarded the RGS Founder's medal not only for his explorations of the Caucasus and on Kanchenjunga but also 'as a mark of appreciation of his persistent efforts on behalf of the improvement of geographical education'. He was elected as President of the RGS during 1914–17.

5

The Struggle for Recognition, 1900–20

Layton, using science as his example, identifies a three-stage model of the evolution of a school subject:

> 1. the callow intruder stakes a claim – justifying its presence on grounds such as pertinence and utility
> 2. a tradition of scholarly work emerges, along with a core of trained specialists: an internal logic to the discipline develops
> 3. teachers of the subject constitute a strong professional body; students are inducted into a 'tradition'.[1]

The model is helpful as an explanatory tool in some respects, but it ignores some of the essential political and practical landmarks of subject recognition which form key staging points along the journey to acceptance. One of these landmarks (in the British system, at least) is acceptance within the canon of subjects which are able to be studied for external examinations.

At the turn of the century (see Figure 4.3, which represents trends over time in a graphical mode) geography had a strengthening presence in the lower realms of educational endeavour – the elementary schools – but most of the pupils of these schools left at 12 or 13 years of age without any major formal qualifications. In the grammar and independent schools, geography was only a fringe interest for some teachers and heads. Though taught to some for, perhaps, 60 or 90 minutes a week in the lower forms of secondary schools in England and Wales, it was not part of the major corpus of the curriculum which led on towards matriculation and advanced courses for university. And, despite the appointment of academics at Oxford and Cambridge, partly with RGS support, geography had the merest toe-hold in the universities as a discrete subject of study.

Though Mackinder and others were vigorous in their proselytisation of the virtues of geography as they stumped the country speaking to Extension Classes and teachers' meetings[2] the subject, in an educational context, was still an unproven newcomer to the minds of many – and the many included the (mostly classically trained) civil servants of the Board of Education who were apt to look at any proposed innovation with extremely sceptical minds. By Layton's terms, geography had hardly reached the starting point of a first phase of development.

Events national and international, and within and without the world of education, were to change the picture over the next 20 years however.

THE BRYCE COMMISSION

Following the establishment of universal elementary education by the Forster Act of 1870, attention had turned to the secondary sector. Gladstone had appointed a Royal Commission in 1895 to consider the best method of 'establishing a well-organised system of secondary education in England'.

The Bryce Commission, as it was known, proposed a centralised authority to combine major aspects of education under one government minister,[3] but also a counter-balancing scheme of local education authorities over the country (to replace the *ad hoc* Boards of Education set up in 1870) which would be responsible for the actual supply and care of schools in defined geographical areas.

The Commission's preoccupation with structures led it away from any detailed consideration of the curriculum, though it proposed, crucially, to continue a 'hands-off' approach, saying that 'it was not considered desirable to lay down model curricula for schools of various types' and encouraging authorities to experiment within broad guidelines.

The Commisssion identified three aspects as the basis for a well-balanced curriculum: the literary, the scientific and the technical. It also proposed co-education for secondary schools on the grounds of efficiency, and a generous provision of scholarships to bridge the gap between elementary and secondary education. It was far from being locked into the past. There was, however, no particular hope for geography in these formulations, despite the prevailing climate of strong interest in imperial matters.

The reservations about geography in this period were expressed by the Master of Balliol College, Oxford, Dr Benjamin Jowett, in a famous utterance quoted in the first edition of the Geographical Association's magazine *The Geographical Teacher*, which appeared in 1901, 'Yes, but can you teach geography so as to make people think?'. His mind was not closed to the possibility of geography making its way into the curriculum, but from what he saw in elementary schools (whether it was characterised by factual learning or more active pedagogical methods) he remained to be convinced about its coherence, its challenge for higher levels of education and its intellectual depth.

Mackinder's 1887 paper had provided an important insight for those who sought to show that there was a distinctively geographical way of handling the growing amounts of information available about the world, both physical and human, but it was more effective as a rallying point than as a detailed prescription for classrooms. Intellectuals like Jowett accepted that learning about the world was interesting for pupils and could be made real and vivid by good pedagogy; but they saw, as yet, no structured set of key ideas, no worked-through conceptual framework. Preachers of the time often said of Christianity, that 'it had not been tried and found wanting but found difficult and not tried'; with geography almost the reverse was the case – it was not seen to be difficult enough and therefore (at upper levels of education) did not need to be tried.

THE BALFOUR ACT OF 1902

The recommendations of the Bryce Commission were put into practice by the Education Act of 1902. The Act is usually known by the name of the minister who piloted it through Parliament, A. J. Balfour, but it was largely the work of the Acting Permanent Secretary to the Board of Education, Sir Robert Morant (1863–1920). Morant's first educational job had been as tutor to the nephew of the King of Siam following his graduation from Oxford in 1885, and, almost in passing, he set up the foundations of a public education system in that country in his spare time. His flair for administration and his organising abilities soon brought him promotion when he returned to a Civil Service career in England. Though he had elitist views about the curriculum (believing in a mainly utilitarian diet for those who would only attend elementary school), he rescued the Board of Education from potential chaos and set up a system of educational administration in England which was to last for most of the century.

The key to the 1902 Bill was the counter-balance between central government and the newly formed local educational authorities (LEAs); part of the balance involved neither one side nor the other assuming sole responsibility for the shape of the curriculum. Thus, almost by accident, ultimate curriculum control was left in the hands of the schools themselves, a situation which continued until the introduction of a National Curriculum in 1988.

It would be a mistake to take this theoretical position too literally, however. In practice, some external constraints and influences on schools emerged. The Board (later Ministry) of Education (i.e. central government) issued 'Handbooks of Suggestions' for schools which dealt with particular subjects,[4] though the term 'sugggestion' was something of a euphemism: the LEAs developed advisory and inspection systems to monitor the schools for which they had responsibility.

In elementary schools, the system of a specified 'Code of Regulations' continued to operate after 1902, though the force of this was progressively weakened in subsequent years. In 1926, perhaps because of Conservative fears of what a Labour government might do if it came into power, the authority of the centrally devised regulations was diminished and they became rather shadowy advisory documents for teachers from then until 1944 when elementary schools were themselves abolished. The new infant and junior schools which took their place as a 5 to 11 years 'primary sector' were given no such constraint on their curriculum practice.

In the secondary schools, an overall curriculum influence was mediated through the Board of Education. There was a listing of groups of subjects to form courses which were judged suitable for study at advanced levels. The higher education sector had an interest here: universities, themselves growing fast in number after the First World War, began to seek evidence and form requirements for general standards of entry. Examination boards were devised in which they had a strong influence, through the appointment of examiners and the drawing up of syllabuses for the examinations. In 1917 the Secondary Schools Examinations Council was established and the 'School Certificate' came into being, with papers being offered in the same subjects and (theoretically) at the same level by different examination boards.[5]

In origin, these examinations were clearly designed as a testing point for those who wanted to go further in their education and not as a general 'graduation' mark for all. The specification of syllabuses (i.e. the definition of what was proper or appropriate knowledge to have) and the combination of subject passes preferred or allowed was in the hands of university academics; teachers played a somewhat deferential role on most examination board committees. Therein lay much of the heartache for those pupils who struggled to achieve passes in at least five subjects to gain their 'School Certificate' or 'Matric'. To have passed School Certificate was the obvious but somewhat rare badge of 'success' in the days before separate subject examination passes could be given and a wider spectrum of ability tested fairly at a national level.[6]

The 1902 Act offered no particular advantage to geography, though it was to lead to the creation of a swathe of new secondary grammar schools (often marked by their naming in honour of King Edward VII). In these schools, set up by the new local education authorities, original curriculum initiatives might be more freely promulgated than in those schools with strong traditions in the past.

The posse of those in all forms of education who, at this time, would call themselves geographers (as distinct from those who might teach some geography in the course of their school duties) was tiny; the GA was little more than a coterie of independent school masters to whom geography was a spare time interest and its membership was barely in three figures seven years after its foundation. And, if there was to be advancement at secondary level, there was no help from the centre; without convincing intellectual stature or many friends in positions of high influence at this time, geography had little more on its side than some teachers with a gut feeling that the subject had 'pertinence and utility'.

MAKING A CASE

Mackinder was active in promoting a discussion about geographical education at the 1903 meeting of the British Association for the Advancement of Science. Having now moved on from Oxford to a post in London as Director of the London School of Economics, he urged universities to create separate Departments of Geography (as had been done at Oxford in 1899) so that a coherent set of courses might be put together. The ideal of degree studies undertaken exclusively in geography would thus come closer.[7]

Coincident with this Mackinder urged secondary schools to employ at least one teacher who had had some training in geography. But not all teachers at this time had any training in their craft, let alone in the subjects which they taught, since teacher-training was not compulsory; it was still considered acceptable for a graduate with a degree in a particular subject to go straight into school and teach, eschewing any knowledge of education or the arts of pedagogy, and relying on the depth of their subject knowledge to see them through. Not all did this without some qualms; but it must be remembered that only a few secondary teacher-training institutions were as yet in existence.[8]

Goodson criticises Mackinder for omitting the interests of pupils in his campaign to develop the subject in schools but this seems a selective reading of Mackinder's work;[9] in many places Mackinder writes knowledgeably about the interests and the imagination of children.[10] In later years Mackinder maintained his educational interests and his contacts with schoolteachers. He remained more active in the GA, where he was Chairman of Council until 1946, than in the RGS. The Institute of British Geographers was formed in 1933 to represent the growing band of geographers in higher education but Mackinder never became a member nor was ever 'recognised' for his previous services to geography.[11]

THE INFLUENCE OF HERBERTSON

It was one of Mackinder's young lieutenants who made the greater impact in this period, however. A. J. Herbertson (1865–1915), having come to notice elsewhere, was chosen by Mackinder to become the Assistant Lecturer in Geography at Oxford University in 1899, Herbertson had begun an academic career at Manchester University in 1894 and then gone on to Heriot-Watt College in Edinburgh. A small, wiry man, he was not noted as an inspirational lecturer (D. H. Lawrence said that he was 'bored exasperatingly' by him) but many who studied under him later spoke and wrote with appreciation of his intellectual sharpness and great energy.[12] Herbertson, like Mackinder, saw that the future of geography as an academic discipline was bound up with increasing its presence and popularity in schools and he pursued this aim with more practical strategies.

It was typical of Herbertson that he should accept an invitation to take over the honorary secretaryship of the GA in 1900 in addition to his other duties. Under his leadership the Association immediately began to expand its activities and its sphere of influence. The membership was expanded beyond its original 'public school' origins to include teachers from all types of schools and women were welcomed into the membership. A magazine for teachers was begun. Herbertson also lost no time in enlisting the support of the RGS and the British Association for the Advancement of Science (BAAS), asking them to write to the Board of Education and to urge upon it the claims for geography to be taught in secondary schools.

In terms of Layton's model of subject development, this seems to suggest a jump from the first to the third stage of the model; for geography, at least, the second and third stages occurred almost simultaneously with, as we shall see, Herbertson active in both.

The letters, allied to some judicious personal contacts engineered through the RGS, had some effect on Morant who was anxious to avoid secondary schools becoming too narrow or specialised in their curriculum outlook. When the Board of Education produced its *Secondary Regulations* in 1904 (a document with little more than advisory status despite its title) the regulations for the general four-year course stated that:

> The Course should provide for instruction in the English Language and Literature, at least one language other than English, geography, history, mathematics, science and drawing, with due provision for manual work and physical exercises and, in a girls' school, for Housewifery. Not less than 4 and a half hours a week must be allotted to English, Geography and History.

In the following year, a more specific document, *Regulations for the Teaching of Geography in Secondary Schools*, was issued by the Board of Education 'requiring' in each school a course of general instruction in the subject and extending over four years. Then followed the detail of a suggested four-year place-based syllabus which would cover successively; Europe; America and Africa: Asia and Australia: Regional Contrasts (within the British Empire).

Herbertson wrote back on behalf of the GA, quoting a resolution adopted by the Annual General Meeting at the end of 1905:

> One of the most important advances in the position of Geography in our education system has been made this year by the publication of new regulations by the Board in which a four-year course in Geography is recommended for secondary schools. The Board will recognise the teacher's own syllabus if it is submitted and approved. This is a most valuable step on the part of the Board of Education and the Association desires to express its thanks to the authorities who are responsible for it.

Scott Keltie, by now Secretary to the RGS, wrote a letter to the Board on 7 November 1905 saying that there was:

> satisfaction that the Department has taken so important a step as to issue definite regulations for the teaching of a subject that has until recently been so much neglected in secondary schools.[13]

What caused this change of heart? Part of it at least was pure curriculum politicking; a greater realisation by the geographical bodies (the long-established RGS and the newer GA) of the need to build bridges and mend fences. Douglas Freshfield, though now reconciled with the RGS again, remained faithful to the GA and was its energetic President from 1897 until 1911. He had friends in high places and knew how to orchestrate a campaign through a combination of enthusiasm, bonhomie and assiduous use of a network of influential acquaintances.

Part of the change was due to the accident of circumstances; Morant was sympathetic and it suited government interests at this time to 'liberalise' and create a distinctive curriculum for the new grammar schools and not have them follow the entrenched patterns of the older public schools.

A third reason was intrinsic to the subject itelf; geography was gaining a reputation as something more than elementary 'capes and bays'. The view that it was a subject worth studying was constantly fostered and demonstrated by Mackinder in the profusion of his lecturing and writing, by the GA through its newly founded journal, and, not least, through the intellectual impact of Herbertson's own work.

HERBERTSON AND THE NATURAL REGIONS PAPER

Mackinder had published *Britain and the British Seas* in 1902, a book which presented an intriguing theory about how the control of 'heartland continental regions' led to world dominance. It was a provoking book written in some measure to publicise the importance of geography and geographical ideas and it caused considerable discussion in the clubs and smoking rooms of the time, but it was not immediately relevant to geography's position in schools.

Herbertson on the other hand, thinking his way through both academic and educational issues, turned more directly to matters concerned with the development of the subject. After some years of experiment, he formulated a scheme of dividing the world into natural regions, which he propounded in a series of papers between 1903 and 1913.[14]

Herbertson's development of natural regions (see Figure 5.1) was a project to establish that geography should deal not with the distribution of single elements on the earth's surface, but with all. His classification of regions was based primarily on the configuration of the land and on distinctive climates, but in later versions, it was also related to vegetational patterns which, in turn, were influenced by altitude. Herbertson used the figures of seasonal rainfall and the recurring incidence of certain critical temperatures as the key criteria in his work, assuming that these were permanent factors.[15]

His scheme was one which asserted the primacy of physical geography. He acknowledged that a population density map would give an indication of the economic potential of areas and might well be

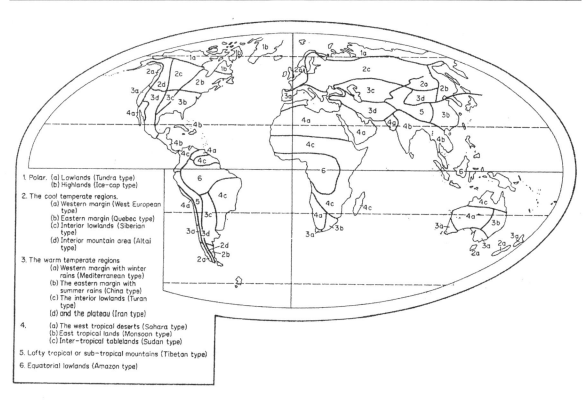

1. Polar. (a) Lowlands (Tundra type)
    (b) Highlands (Ice-cap type)

2. The cool temperate regions.
    (a) Western margin (West European type)
    (b) Eastern margin (Quebec type)
    (c) Interior lowlands (Siberian type)
    (d) Interior mountain area (Altai type)

3. The warm temperate regions
    (a) Western margin with winter rains (Mediterranean type)
    (b) The eastern margin with summer rains (China type)
    (c) The interior lowlands (Turan type)
    (d) and the plateau (Iran type)

4. (a) The west tropical deserts (Sahara type)
    (b) East tropical lands (Monsoon type)
    (c) Inter-tropical tablelands (Sudan type)

5. Lofty tropical or sub-tropical mountains (Tibetan type)

6. Equatorial lowlands (Amazon type)

Figure 5.1: A. J. Herbertson's map of the classification of the world into natural regions

Figure 5.2:
Photograph of A. J. Herbertson

studied in conjunction with a regionalised map, but said that 'political divisions ... must be eliminated from any consideration of regions'. To him, human factors were clearly subservient.

Herbertson's work on natural regions was the development of a significant classificatory device (and major paradigm) in purely geographical terms, but it also provided a key to more systematic teaching in education. Regard the world as one of recognisable regions and it was reduced to manageable and coherent elements of study. Fifty years later, Herbertson's basic work was still being acknowledged by eminent geographers and geography teachers as a formative influence, whilst being re-examined and re-defined.[16]

The idea of teaching a 'regional framework' with clear characteristics for each region was, in its time, an advance on the listing of the characteristics of individual countries, a tedious routine which destroyed motivation in many classrooms, as information about places became more plentiful.

The emergence of the 'natural regions' idea was, for some, the first inkling that geography aspired to be something other than a factually dominated information-gathering subject; it was given further power by Herbertson's willingness to become involved in the writing of school texts which expounded and elaborated the idea at different levels.

It was a salutary example of how an academic idea gains force and momentum if its deviser is willing to both communicate and interpret it at all levels through the education system. The weaknesses of the regional approach would only slowly become apparent (see Chapter 7).

At about the same time, the concept of regions on a much smaller scale ('pays' in the French term) was being espoused by Vidal de la Blache (1845–1918); one of his best-known books[17] deals with the 'small' regions of France one by one, and shows how each has its own distinctive form of agriculture through differing conditions of soil and water supply. The essence of Vidal's small regions are rooted in a pre-industrial rural world, though Vidal also asserted that modern trade had accentuated agricultural specialisations rather than diminished them.

Herbertson admired the work of Vidal and other geographers of the 'French school' but did not link it to his own because of the enormous difference in scale. Vidal's concept was to be an idea more influential in academic than school geography in later years. School teachers found out in the field the practical difficulties concerned with both surveying and defining self-contained small regions in a fast-changing world (see Chapter 6).

In time, books were written by other academics, by teacher-trainers and by classroom teachers, all utilising the essence of Herbertson's great organising idea in various ways. The influence of the French writers led to the idea of natural regions being expanded to embrace the concept of 'human regions', an idea which Herbertson himself began to explore later. The pattern of learning geography in British schools became, largely as a result of Herbertson's work, set in a regional mould for half a century.

THE EMERGENCE OF A JOURNAL

Thus a key organising idea for geography classrooms was set afloat in the years before the Great War, whilst at the same time more teachers were, through Herbertson's influence, encouraged to take part in the Geographical Association by attending conferences, local branch meetings and by reading its journal. With a subscribing membership of only 121 in 1900 (the RGS's membership was 4,026 in the same year – see Figure 12.1) it must have been a bold gesture of faith for the GA to embark on a publication of any kind, yet it was a key step towards the building and strengthening of a 'community of scholars'.

The Geographical Teacher (edited by Herbertson alone after the first few issues) played a vital part in giving its readers a sense of identity and fellowship as well as being a prime transmitter of innovative ideas and good practice. In the very first issue, published in January 1901 there is a mixture of practical and theoretical articles.[18] The first article, by T. G. Rooper, 'formerly one of Her Majesty's Inspectors of Schools' was a trenchant one on 'Methods of teaching geography' and set out seven conceptual approaches for the classroom, drawing on German examples. It was followed by a piece about using Ordnance Survey Maps in the classroom.

Two of the articles were by women and about the education of young women. Ada Bramwell, Lecturer in Geography at Maria Grey College, wrote about the problems of teaching geography in the lower forms of girls' secondary schools with inadequate time and resources; Joan Berenice Reynolds, who, in 1899, had been one of the first students for the Diploma in Geography set up by Mackinder at Oxford, provided a wide-ranging listing and discussion of 'excursions' beyond the classroom which could profitably be taken, particularly using the practical examples provided by her sister who was headmistress of a girls' school in the Lake District.

There were several pages of reviews of textbooks, maps and slides at the end of the journal, and a good number of advertisements. *The Geographical Teacher* clearly served a valuable purpose in providing both a forum and a market-place from the start. These are further key elements in the progress towards disciplinary coherence and maturity which Layton describes in his model.[19]

THE COMING OF THE GREAT WAR

The new pattern of elementary and secondary schooling began to settle down. Much of the nation basked contentedly in an Edwardian summer, its prosperity secure, its Empire expanding. But clouds were darkening the political horizon.

When Britain plunged unexpectedly into war in 1914, many younger male teachers quickly volunteered to go to the Western Front; other teachers found that voluntary war duties on the Home Front took priority. It was not surprising that curriculum development became a minor concern and was put on hold. The nation developed a belated interest in the macro-geography of European alliances and in the micro-geography of the Flanders battlefields.

Times of war increase an interest in things geographical. The poring-over of maps, the assessment of terrain and weather, the consideration of supply and transport lines, form an integral part of what goes on in theatres of action; but also at home interest in the location of events in the zones of combat becomes a daily factor.[20]

It is said that one reason for the introduction of geography as a major subject into into French schools after 1870 was because of the nation's unfortunate experiences in the Franco-Prussian war.[21] Put simply, the German officers and commanders were better at handling the geography of that war. In the same way, the Boer War (1899–1902) increased interest in geographical matters in Britain, as the sieges of Ladysmith and Mafeking (and their relief) were followed with bated breath back at home. But for many people in Britain it was the 1914–18 war, more than any other, which confirmed an appreciation of the importance of geographical knowledge. In strengthening an interest in geography itself it contributed indirectly to the immediate future of the subject in schools.

If part of this sudden appreciation of the importance of geography was confined to the members of the armed forces, equally a widespread folk-knowledge brought back by the returning soldiers, airmen and naval personnel was widespread which reawakened the tradition of telling stories of travel exploits to others and 'following things on a map'. Ypres, Passchendaele and Gallipoli were transformed from strangely spelt anonymity into known and significant places through personal experiences; the characteristics of their terrain formed a sombre litany repeated alongside the casualties and the deeds of heroism with which they were associated.

Post-war there was also another important dimension to add to this; a new found concern for and belief in internationalism, and in the idea that, by banding together, nations could prevent such a cataclysm happening again. Woodrow Wilson's active participation in the Treaty of Versailles and the establishment of the League of Nations were two indications of a greater world awareness. At the same time popular newspapers began to cover more world news. Travel between different parts of the world began to be notably easier to arrange.

All these factors had impact on the world of education and led to a second major campaign to improve the lot of geography in schools – this time in relation to seeking a greater place in the advanced courses of schools and in universities.

THE GROWTH OF UNIVERSITY DEPARTMENTS

In the midst of war, the first university Honours School of Geography was set up. It was inaugurated in 1917 in the University of Liverpool, one of the new 'redbrick' civic universities spawned by the prosperity of the Victorian era. P. M. Roxby was appointed to the Chair.[22]

Prior to this, students could take geographical courses in some universities, but not have geography as the major subject of their degree. The institution of an honours course in geography at Liverpool was swiftly followed by others – at the London School of Economics and at the University College of Aberystwyth in 1918, at University College, London and at Cambridge in 1919, at Manchester in 1923, at Sheffield in 1924.

One of Roxby's first moves was to write to the Board of Education to press for a greater presence of geography courses in secondary schools and for the inclusion of geography in the Advanced Examinations for the Higher School Certificate (a post-matriculation preliminary to university entrance). In the first two decades of the century, geography was conspicuous by its absence from the list of advanced main subjects in the Regulations of Examining Boards for secondary schools. Three groups of options were recognised: Group A – science and mathematics; Group B – classics; Group C – modern studies (language, literature, history).

Roxby clearly had an eye to finding a supply of students who might wish to study in his newly created department, but was firmly rebuffed by the civil servants who responded to his request. An internal Board of Education Minute Paper (2 June 1917), written by 'F.B.S' shows that it was the expansion of 'human geography' which was viewed with most suspicion. It also indicates how far the subject still had to go to achieve some credibility in the secondary sector:

> Mr Roxby's plea, that because Geography is recognised as a subject for study for an Honours course at the University, it should be taken by all boys up to 16 and by those who will later specialise in Geography, from 16 to 18 ... appears to me to be based on a fundamentally false assumption.

> It might equally well be argued that because Economics is a subject of advanced study at the university, it should be included in the school course ... I think we should resist, in general, the efforts of enthusiastic University teachers to impose their own specialisms on the schools.

> As for the particular case of Geography, I am of the opinion that recent developments in Geography teaching – the insistence on the Economic side (cf. Professor Lyde's book on the Continent of Europe) – have made geography less suitable as a subject of school study than it was when the emphasis was laid on map-reading and physical features: and I should have thought that the Geography teachers at the Universities would do well to encourage boys to take advanced courses (16–18) at school not in Geography, but in Science and History.

> I would only add that the school teaching of Geography is suffering

at the present time from the teacher who professes to know Geography and knows nothing else.

There is more than a whiff (especially in the last paragraph) of a defensive attitude here, and the flavour of the internal memorandum was diluted in an anodyne reply to Roxby which referred his comments on to the Chief Inspector of Secondary Schools, who was asked to call on him when next in Lancashire. In turn, the Chief Inspector, Mr Fletcher, no doubt acting on the cherished educational principle that a little temporisation turneth away wrath, suggested that Roxby should come to London at some time in the future to meet with officers of the Board.

Chastened by his first brush with curriculum politics, Roxby sought the help of allies. Herbertson had died tragically early at the age of 50 in 1915, probably by overworking himself to death; his successor as Honorary Secretary of the GA was a cultured, mild-mannered, but wily anthroplogy lecturer at Aberystwyth, H. J. Fleure, who was to serve the Association with distinction in this post for the next 30 years. Fleure joined forces with Roxby to co-ordinate a second approach to the Board of Education in 1919. Fleure urged the more-established and influential Royal Geographical Society to make representations to the President of the Board of Education, and Roxby added the lesser weight of the Liverpool Geographical Society with a pithy resolution:

> The Council of the Society regrets that geography is not included as a main subject (in advanced courses in schools) and urges the Board of Education to reconsider its position.

But other allies outside the subject (or apparently outside the subject) were on the horizon. The British Association for the Advancement of Science weighed in with support, though it is worth noting that their Secretary, O. J. R. Howarth, had studied geography with Mackinder at Oxford. More unusually, the newly formed League of Nations Union was prevailed upon to give its support. Its letter to the Board noted that:

> Geography has a special part to play in providing for a wide outlook and training in world citizenship ... The League suggest that schools should be allowed to offer Geography, if they wish, as a subject in an Advanced Course, in the same way that other subjects are accepted.

A further flurry of letters between the GA and the Board of Education in 1921 brought no result; Mackinder used the occasion of a public lecture at the RGS to seek that body's support for a further campaign.[23] An editorial in *The Geographical Teacher* early in 1922 fumed 'no real change has as yet been made in the official attitude of apathy and indifference, if indeed it may not be called hostility, to geography'.[24]

Yet the co-ordinated campaign, sustained by the growing public interest in international matters in the wake of Versailles and the

Table 5.1: Comparative membership figures for five subject
teaching associations, between 1912 and 1921

	Geographical Association	Modern Languages Association	Classics Association	Association of Teachers of Domestic Science	Association of Science Teachers
1912	1,000	1,060	1,500	1,116	120
1915	1,107	1,140	1,600	1,315	130
1918	1,458	1,100	1,500	1,700	200
1921	4,159	1,300	1,800	1,870	360

Comment: Note the spectacular increase in the membership of the Geographical Association's membership in the years immediately following the First World War, compared with the marginal increases recorded by the other associations.

evidence of obvious success in the teaching of geography in some schools, was ruffling feathers at the Board. One internal memo noted 'Now that Geography is recognised as an Honours subject at Cambridge, London and elsewhere it is more difficult than it was to resist the plea that it should be given full recognition in the post-matriculation work of schools' – it seemed that the classicists who dominated the civil service of the Board were beginning to bow to the inevitable.

Under increasing pressure the dam of obstruction eventually cracked. The 1922 Board of Education Regulations for Secondary Schools recognised the possibility of Advanced Courses in Geography for the first time. Three years later the tide had moved so swiftly, that the new set of regulations noted that 'the curriculum must provide for instruction in certain subjects of which Geography is one'. As Proctor notes in chronicling this episode, 'the subject's subsequent growth in schools and universities was dramatic'.[25]

GEOGRAPHY TEXTBOOKS OF THE PERIOD

A glance at any collection of geography texts of the 1900–20 period will reveal that, in size at least, most of them remain small scale. Books were almost invariably produced in crown octavo size (seven and a half inches by five inches) hard back and cloth bound.

They remained, for the most part, of two broad types – the informational geography (such as Ellis Heaton's secondary series of six *Scientific Geographies* published by Holland) and the reader (such as Longman's *Pictorial Geographical Readers*, known as the 'Ship' series).[26]

Heaton's books are written in lucid, utilitarian prose, enlivened with bold case and italic interventions, and divided into short sections. Their clear aim is to be an aid to the learning of information and as revision for an examination. Their 'excitement' or 'wonder' quotient is practically zero (see Figure 5.3).

Fig. 20.—Comparison between Japan and the United Kingdom.

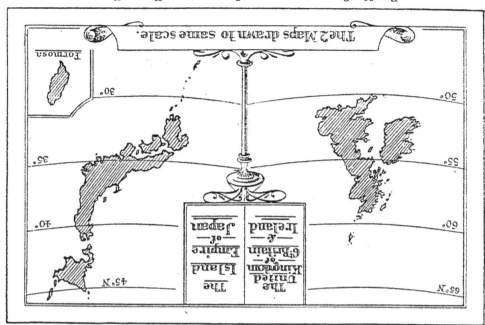

East Indian Archipelago to the *Andaman* and *Nicobar* chains in the Bay of Bengal. This long line of islands is the most remarkable seismic line in the **Old World**. It is studded with *volcanoes* throughout its length. Many of these are still active, and *earthquake shocks* are common. Several of the volcanoes attain a height of 15,000 feet. *Fusi-yama*, one of these, in *Hondo*, is the sacred mountain of the Japanese.

In *Kamschatka* the volcanoes are on the outward flank of the mountain axis; in the Japanese group, they are mostly on the inner flank. The strips of *coastal plain*, which are very narrow both in Korea and the Japanese islands, are covered with *Tertiary* deposits (*cf.* Thames Basin). The mountain axes are built up of ancient rocks. Just outside the Japanese island-chain the *Pacific* drops to a depth of 27,000 feet (in the **Tuscarora Deep**). Within the island-chain the seas are comparatively *shallow*. The "*seismic line*" therefore corresponds with the true border of the continent.

Hondo is the main island. Its latitudes are those of the *Mediterranean Sea* and *California*. Separated from Hondo by narrow channels (sea-filled rift-lines) are the islands of *Kiushiu* and *Shikoku* in the warmer south and *Yezo* in the colder north. The long chain of the *Kurile Islands* links Yezo with the Kamschatkan peninsula. The islands belong to Japan, the peninsula is Russian territory. A similar chain of volcanic islands links Kiushiu with Formosa. The islands of the Empire thus enclose three seas: the *Yellow Sea*, the *Sea of Japan*, and the *Sea of Okhotsk*. The Yellow Sea is always open, the Sea of Japan is liable to ice in the depth of winter, and the Sea of Okhotsk is sub-Arctic in character, although its latitude is only that of the British Seas.

Climatic Conditions.—Formosa, Korea, and Hondo (and the smaller islands to the south) belong to the **Monsoon Region.** They receive their heavy rains from the *South Monsoon*, which corresponds in time (summer) to the South-west Monsoon of

Figure 5.3: Double-page from *A Scientific Geography* by E. W. Heaton (1909) (reduced size)

20 WHITE CLIFFS AND ROCKY CRAGS.

the middle of the Strait, and resting on a tower which is built on the rock.

7. This bridge was the first of its kind, and when it was opened in 1850, the people cheered loudly as the train came through.

8. The town of Holyhead on the north side of Holy Island is joined by a causeway with Anglesey. A railway crosses the causeway, and many people travel by it, because Holyhead is the chief starting-place for those who wish to go by steamer to Dublin, the capital city of Ireland.

MENAI BRIDGE.

7. WHITE CLIFFS AND ROCKY CRAGS.

1. The coast of England and Wales owes its many good harbours to the dashing of the seas on every side and the gradual wearing of the land. The hardest rocks, which are not so easily worn away, are left jutting out into the sea, and they often enclose quiet waters which form good harbours where ships can take refuge in stormy weather.

Figure 5.4: Double-page from *Our Own Country*, anonymous (1918) (reduced size)

The Pictorial Geographies, on the other hand, as their name implies, are illustrated with pictures and prints, though these occur at a frequency of only one every six or seven pages, and even then of such size (half or quarter-page) as to make only a moderate impact. At the end there is a factual appendix, together with half a dozen full-colour, full-page maps of the area studied.

Another reader series of the time, *Our Own and Other Lands*, published by McDougall's Educational Company with no attributed author,[27] was a little more arresting to the reader as it included large hand-tinted colour photographs and delicate sketches of notable landmarks in the countries being described (see Figure 5.4). The book about 'our own country' begins with the forthright assertion that 'Many countries are larger than England, but none is more important.' It goes on to encourage a good look at the map of England and Wales (with hints about where to look and what to look for) and sections on the climate and the seas, before settling into conventional regional descriptions. The section on Cambridge in the McDougall reader is typical of others. It offers random information with no explanantion or analysis:

> Cambridge has not so many students as Oxford. King's College Chapel, of which King Henry VI was the founder, is the finest of its buildings and Trinity College is the largest. Cambridge is in a very low-lying part of England, and the town itself, without the University, is not very interesting. The finest part is behind the colleges, where the grounds and gardens are called 'the Backs'. The river Cam, which is there crossed by several bridges, flows through 'the Backs'. (p. 165)

The 'Other Lands' represented in the series have a strong emphasis on the British Empire. It was noted by Marion Newbigin[28] amongst others that teaching based around the organising framework of Herbertson's natural regions could aid imperial knowledge, since there was some part of the British Empire in each major region. What could be more 'natural' than to exercise an imperial preference in the educational sphere?

AN AMBITIOUS EFFORT

Ernest Young, the first Headmaster of the Harrow County School for Boys (one of the now-encouraged unendowed local grammar schools opened by the newly formed Harrow Education Committee in January 1911), was one of a new breed of educationalists. Young believed in 'progressive' approaches to teaching, a liberal and innovative curriculum and plenty of extra-curricular clubs and activities.[29] He involved himself thoroughly in all aspects of school life and was a strong proponent (and exponent) of Scouting and of school journeys, two key elements in the development of environmental education at the time.[30]

Young (1869–1944) had gone to Borough Road Training College, served in the Siamese Education Department under Robert Morant, and had begun his teaching career as a science teacher. But his interest in the physical environment, both in study and activity led him towards geography and both at the Lower School of John Lyon (where he became Head in 1902) and at Harrow County he took on responsibility for geography teaching in the school and promoted it vigorously as a subject. May, whose school history of Harrow County is unusually readable and informed by the standards of most dutiful volumes of that ilk, regards Young as a 'great' Headmaster, and counts it fortunate for the school that he taught geography 'since in method this was one of the most advanced subjects of the time'.

Young was the writer of an ambitious three-part series, aimed at the lower forms of secondary schools, and published by George Philip and Sons[31] between 1908 and 1912, price 1s 6d per copy. *A Rational Geography* tried to cover both the 'cosmographical approach' to geography and the descriptive regional approach in each of the three volumes. Thus Part 3, the first part published, linked together, somewhat curiously, scale and direction, surveying, projections, geology, flora and fauna, Asia, Australasia.

The books are almost certainly based on Young's own classroom teaching; they cover the ground thoroughly, but they read in a staccato style, with ceaseless questions and injunctions peppering the text. Here is a sample paragraph:

> In what direction does the coast run beyond Aden? What islands lie off the coast? To whom do they belong? The southern coast of Arabia is very regular, and possesses few good harbours. On what gulf does Maskat stand? What is the gulf called when it narrows? Into what gulf does the strait lead? The Persian Gulf is of great political importance and contains a portion of the submarine cable which connects Europe and India. The Strait of Ormuz is only about 50 miles wide and is nowhere more than 50 fathoms deep, so that in time of war, an enemy in possession of the Gulf could easily destroy the cable. To whom do the Bahrein islands belong? They are the centre of a flourishing pearl industry. The eastern waters of the Persian Gulf are too deep for pearl fishing. What river runs into the northern end of the gulf? Is there a delta? Does this point to the probability of the gulf ever being filled up? (Book 3, p. 88)

The number of questions is double the number of statements; one can almost hear the replication of a hectoring classroom style in the text here. The extract reveals the strong intention to develop an interactive pedagogy, but one cannot help harbouring the suspicion that such a plethora of questions might mean in the end that the students could not see the wood for the trees.

The Development of Public Examinations in England and Wales

The School Certificate (requiring five subject passes) and Higher School Certificate (requiring three subject passes) remained as the major certifications for secondary school pupils from 1917 until 1952. They were then replaced by the General Certificate of Education (GCE).

The GCE allowed students to gain certificates for passes in individual subjects at 'O'- or 'A'-Level, and thus increased the number of those who achieved some success, but the target audience remained the 'top' 25 per cent in ability of the school population. Other bodies, such as the Royal Society of Arts and the College of Preceptors provided examinations of lower academic intensity and in a greater range of subjects (some vocational) but qualifications gained by these routes tended to have variable credibility with employers.

The Certificate of Secondary Education (CSE) was then introduced as a nationally recognised qualification for a wider spectrum of academic ability (notionally, the percentage between 25–75 per cent of the school population of that age). CSE boards pioneered a much more local control of examinations, and encouraged experiment in examination forms, including a greater emphasis on coursework as against a terminal examination. 'Mode 3' CSEs could be devised by individual schools, and were sometimes highly innovative in form, but they often lacked strong external moderation and were thus variable in standard. This soon caused a loss of confidence in their notional comparability to GCE qualifications.

The phenomenon of two parallel examinations run by different bodies and confusion and ambiguity about the relationship between them led to a limited experiment with a pilot single '16-plus' examination. This was followed by the combining of GCE and CSE with well-intentioned idealism but uncomfortable practical consequences, as the General Certificate of Secondary Education (GCSE) in 1988. The GCSE now operates (monitored by the Qualifications and Curriculum Authority) with 'tiered' examination papers in order to cater adequately for pupils of widely differing academic ability. GNVQs have now entered the scene as alternative vocationally-oriented examinations.

A SUCCESSFUL ELEMENTARY TEXTBOOK

Rather less wearing in style were the *Oxford Geographies*, a series of books for elementary schools edited by A. J. Herbertson. Herbertson's wife Frances[32] wrote several texts in the series with admirable clarity, and a feeling for appropriate shortness of sentence and vocabulary. Though they appear disarmingly simple, the books probe fundamental geographical issues; here is an example from *A First Physiography* published in 1911:

> *26. The influence of the Sea.* Take off your shoes and stockings, some hot day, and walk on the pavement on the sunny side of the street. You will find it painfully hot. You will be glad to dip your feet into the nearest running water. This will feel deliciously cool. Why does the pavement or the road feel hot, when the water feels cool? It is because land heats much more quickly than water. You have often bathed in the sea in summer. You know quite well that the sea is cooler than the land in summer. The land cools more quickly than the sea in winter. In winter the sea is warmer than the land. It was never so hot as the land, but it has kept its heat longer. (Vol. I, *Physiography*, p. 22)

Frances Herbertson pointed out in her preface that 'it is hoped that teachers will never forget that the exercises [at the end of each chapter] are an essential part of the book. They should be worked through by every pupil using it.' The combined text and work book was clearly emerging, even though the overwhelming predominance of space was given to exposition.

ON THE PRACTICAL SIDE

Another popular book of the period which exhibited similar characteristics was *A Class Book of Practical Geography* published by George Philip in 1911.[33] In this there were a great number of exercises concerned with taking weather observations, measuring heights and distances and carrying out simple survey tasks, as well as using maps and compasses. The book was divided almost equally between instruction and 'Exercises' (187 of them).

The authors commented that they had 'endeavoured to keep in mind the limited time available for this kind of work in most schools' but it was an encouraging sign that an increasing number of teachers of geography in the lower forms of secondary schools saw the subject as more than just 'book learning'. The full flowering of field work as a formative element of school geography was just around the corner.

One of the authors of 'Practical geography' we have already met – the notable Ernest Young, Headmaster of The County School, Harrow. The other, of whom much more needs to be said in a following chapter, was the Geography Master of The William Ellis School, Gospel Oak, in North London, James Fairgrieve.

NOTES

1. D. Layton, *Science as General Education*. A pamphlet in the *Trends in Education Series* (HMSO, London, 1972).
2. Even after his appointment to Oxford University, Mackinder continued to speak at many 'extension class' and teachers' meetings. Besides expounding 'the new geography' he was constantly urging the cause of geography as a subject and campaigning to have it instituted in secondary schools and in higher education.
3. Report of the Royal Commission on Secondary Education (Bryce Commission) 1895. Aspects of education at this time were handled by the Charity Commissioners, and the Department of Science and Art as well as the Board of Education itself.
4. See, for instance, *Suggestions for the Consideration of Teachers and Others Concerned in the Work of Public Elementary Schools* (HMSO, London, first edn 1905; repr. with revisions, 1912).
5. The situation was appreciably different in Scotland, where a Leaving Certificate had been instituted in 1888. Geography could be taken as a subject of study in both higher and lower grades.
6. It is appropriate to note here that the system which required success in a combination of subjects for a 'School Certificate' (at 16 years) or a 'Higher School Certificate' (at 18 years) persisted until 1952, when a revised national examination structure (the General Certificate of Education) was introduced (see box on p. 90).
7. It is ironic that, despite the early formation of a Department at Oxford, that university did not allow students to take an Honours degree in Geography until 1933, 46 years after Mackinder's appointment and 34 years after the formation of a Department of Geography.
8. There were however a significant number of institutions training (mainly female) teachers for elementary schools in this period. For more detail on this, see Chapter 19, 'The training of teachers', in Josephine Kamm, *Hope Deferred* (Methuen, London, 1965).
9. I. Goodson, 'Becoming an academic subject; patterns of explanation and evolution', *British Journal of Sociology of Education*, 2(2) (1981), pp. 163–80.
10. See, for instance, H. J. Mackinder, 'The development of geographical teaching out of nature study', a pamphlet published by George Philip, London, 1908; H. J. Mackinder, 'The teaching of geography and history as a combined subject', *The Geographical Teacher*, 7 (1913), pp. 4–9.
11. R. W. Steel, *The Institute of British Geographers: The First Fifty Years* (IBG, London, 1984). The IBG merged with the Royal Geographical Society in 1995.
12. See, in particular, the A. J. Herbertson, Centenary Special Issue of *Geography*, No. 229 (November 1965), including major articles by E. W. Gilbert, 'Andrew John Herbertson: an appreciation of his life and work', pp. 313–31 and by L. J. Jay, 'A. J. Herbertson: his services to school geography', pp. 350–62. There are also personal reminiscences of Herbertson contributed by J. F. Unstead and H. J. Fleure, pp. 343–9.
13. This episode is chronicled in N. Proctor, 'The pioneers of geography: a new and currently relevant perspective', *Transactions of the Institute of British Geographers*, 11 (1986), pp. 75–85.
14. The most often quoted of Herbertson's papers on this topic are 'The major natural regions: an essay in systematic geography', *Geographical Journal*, 2 (1905), pp. 300–12, and 'The natural regions of the world', *The Geographical Teacher*, 3 (1905), pp. 104–13 (a reprint of portions of the GJ paper), but they were prefigured by 'What is geography?', *Journal of Geography*, 2 (1903), pp. 532–3.
15. We are now, through concern about 'global warming', much more aware of the unreliability of this assumption.
16. L. D. Stamp, 'Major natural regions: Herbertson afer fifty years', *Geography*, 42 (1957) pp. 201–16. Stamp comments, 'It is difficult to cite any other single communication which has had such far-reaching effects on the development of our subject.'

17. Vidal de La Blache, *Tableau de la Geographie de la France* (Hachette, Paris, 1903).
18. *The Geographical Teacher*, 1 (1). The publication began as a termly one, and then converted to four times a year in 1907. It was renamed *Geography* in 1928 (not without some internal opposition in the GA) and has retained that name ever since. In 1974 the GA began to produce a second journal, *Teaching Geography*, which took on the role of publishing more practically-oriented material, leaving *Geography* to publish longer and more 'scholarly' articles.
19. Layton, *Science as General Education.*
20. A brilliant contemporary example of the wide sweep, cogency and interest of this kind of geography is provided in Harold A. Winters *et al.*, *Battling the Elements: Weather and Terrain in the Conduct of War* (Johns Hopkins University Press, Baltimore, MD, 1998).
21. For a fuller justification of this belief and a description of the episode see N. J. Graves, *Geography in Education* (Heinemann, London, 1975), pp. 48–50.
22. There is an admiring vignette of Roxby in Chapter 11 of E. W. Gilbert, *British Pioneers in Geography* (David & Charles, Newton Abbot, 1972); see also T. W. Freeman, 'P. M. Roxby', in T. W. Freeman and P. Pinchemel (eds), *Geographers: Biobibliographical Studies*, Vol. 5 (Mansell, London, 1981), pp. 109–16.
23. H. J. Mackinder, 'Geography as a pivotal subject in education', *Geographical Journal*, 57 (1921), pp. 376–84. The paper also offers Mackinder's reminiscences of events related to geography and schools from the 1880s onwards.
24. Editorial in Spring 1922, *The Geographical Teacher*, 11, pp. 268–70. The correspondence between O. J. R. Howarth, secretary of the BAAS, and the Board of Education, is reported in the same issue. The resolution of the matter is reported in the Editorial of the autumn 1922 issue of the journal, p. 330.
25. N. J. Proctor, 'Fight for Geography', *The Geographical Magazine*, February (1986), pp. 92–4.
26. E. W. Heaton, *A Scientific Geography*, a series of six books (Holland, London, 1910): author uncredited, *The Pictorial Geographical Readers* (Longman, London, 1904). Another series of readers of the time (author uncredited *Highroads of Geography* (Nelson, London, 1914)) used 'masterpieces' by great artists to illustrate the text and included a section of poetry with geographical interest 'for recitation'.
27. Author uncredited, *Our Own and Other Lands*, a series of four books (Holmes McDougall, London and Edinburgh, probably *c.* 1918).
28. Marion Newbigin, *The British Empire Beyond the Sea: An Introduction to World Geography* (Bell, London, 1914).
29. Trevor May, *The History of the Harrow County School for Boys*, published by the Harrow County School for Boys (now Harrow High School), Gayton Road, Harrow, Middlesex, 1975.
30. The remit of providing general environmental education for school pupils is often seen by geography teachers as part of their task, especially through field-work, though environmental education has not figured notably as a separate subject of study in English or Welsh schools in this century. The educational role of voluntary youth organisations, such as the Scouts, Guides and Woodcraft Folk (in some cases promoted in school, and in other cases out of school) has been significant in this context (see Chapter 6). Note also the abortive campaign to introduce an Environmental Science A-level to schools, described in Chapter 7. Environmental education was one of the 'cross-curricular themes' espoused in the original version of the 1988 National Curriculum, but these were not followed through strongly. In the late 1990s concern for general environmental education seemed to be re-emerging.
    The origins of concern for environmental education can be traced with certainty to the work of Patrick Geddes and his Outlook Tower in Edinburgh in the 1880s and probably before that; W. E. Marsden has recorded some of these early initiatives in 'Environmental education: historical roots, comparative perspectives and current issues in Britain and the United States', *Journal of Curriculum and Supervision*, 13 (1997), pp. 6–29.
31. E. W. Young, *A Rational Geography*, a series of three books (George Philip, London, 1908–12). George Philip & Sons were destined to have greater fame and impact in geography as publishers of maps and atlases. George Philip himself worked closely with

teachers and geographical bodies to produce appropriate material for schools. The long-running series, 'Philip's Visual Contour Atlases' included four-page county map supplements for different parts of Britain to encourage local study.

32. F. D. Herbertson, *The Elementary Geographies: Vol. I, A First Physiography* (Clarendon Press, Oxford, 1911). Frances Herbertson (*née* Richardson) was a god-daughter of the redoubtable Headmistress of Cheltenham Ladies College, Dorothea Beale, and a graduate of London University. She wrote a life of Frederic Le Play (see Chapter 6), and, together with Joan B. Reynolds, was one of the earliest women to achieve national prominence as a distinctively geographical educator. At the Oxford Summer Courses, she was described as 'busy, energetic – even more so than Herbertson, a driving force at the summer schools, always everywhere, keeping everyone up to scratch' (R. N. Rudmose Brown, *Geography*, 23 (1948), p. 106).

33. E. W. Young and J. Fairgrieve, *A Class Book of Practical Geography* (George Philip, London, 1911).

6

Field-Days, 1920–40

Britain emerged from the First World War in optimistic mood – the warring of nations would be solved by the Treaty of Versailles, the creation of a League of Nations and a new-found concern for international understanding; those who had fought (and survived) would be cherished, valued and given new homes in 'A land fit for heroes to live in': the darker shades of the workhouse, the nineteenth-century industrial slum and Dotheboys Hall had been banished.

The creation of new secondary grammar schools, encouraged by the 1902 Education Act, was creating a new pathway to success for bright children from poor homes; and though elementary schools (by Morant's deliberate policy) offered a more utilitarian curriculum than their independent preparatory school neighbours, the quality of their teachers was rising and the school leaving age had now been raised to 14.[1] Investment in good education for all was slowly coming to be seen as a passport to prosperity rather than a danger to the state's stability. At the higher levels, the rapid expansion of existing universities, the proliferation of new ones and the growth of scholarships for bright pupils indicated the potential emergence of a meritocracy based not on power and privilege of birth but on ability.

Those who were involved with geographical education shared the general optimism of this period. There was a growing 'international' consciousness amongst the population to add to (and sometimes to challenge) more traditional imperial perspectives. Geography was widely taught and enjoyed in elementary schools. Two successful campaigns had been undertaken to persuade the Board of Education that geography should be included, first, as a subject for study in 'School Certificate' courses (i.e. included in examinations taken at the age of 16) and then in 'Higher School Certificate' courses (those taken as a preliminary to university entrance between 16 and 18).

Yet the campaigns opened up only a possibility not a compulsion to take the subject at Certificate level; much work still remained to be done to convince many secondary head teachers and parents that geography could hold its own academically with more established subjects, and that the brightest should even consider it for study.

And at less-exalted levels geography was cast in a minor role: when the government-initiated Hadow Report on The Education of the Adolescent (1926)[2] made its recommendations about a desired curriculum for less academic pupils 'work in music and art: work in wood and metals; work in literature and the record of human history' were specifically mentioned in the major summary of hoped-for new courses. Geography was not, though its educational virtues were strongly commended elsewhere in the Report.

Even so the opportunity for advance was at hand. A circle of opportunity was now linking together: children who were introduced to geography in the elementary schools could continue to take it to School Certificate and beyond; the subject could be studied in the higher forms of secondary schools in readiness for university entrance; there were now newly established degree courses in geography; the number of geography graduates would proliferate, and an attractive option to them at this time was to teach their subject; geographers could thus be trained as geographical educators and return to schools to invigorate and refresh geography lessons with their specialist geographical knowledge; this in turn could improve the quality of lessons and motivate more pupils to an interest in the subject. Here, at least, there was potential for development if the purposes and practice of geography teaching could catch the interest of parents and the motivation of pupils. This was notably different from the situation only 40 years before when there were no geography courses of any significance taught in the higher forms of schools or in higher education.

One key link needed to maintain this circle was a programme of specialist subject training for teachers. The main route of training for most of the nineteenth century had been through pupil–teacher schemes where a craft apprenticeship model was followed. In the later years of the century, training institutions for elementary teachers, most of them founded by the Church of England, had grown in number (from nine in 1846 to 26 in 1891). Their courses varied considerably in length, between a few months and two or three years, and there was also variability in standards. In some colleges the desire to develop academic learning (indeed, to provide the trainees with enough knowledge to teach a range of subjects) drove teaching about 'method' into a minor role.

In secondary schools, for many years the prevailing view was that the possession of a university degree was enough to command the classroom – knowledge was all and pedagogical and psychological issues were pushed firmly to the background. But the work of educationalists such as Dorothea Beale (1831–1906), Frances Mary Buss (1827–94) and Maria Grey (1816–1906) had been responsible for changing the climate about the necessity of training at this level.[3] Besides establishing the first college to train women teachers for secondary schools, Maria Grey founded, in 1877, the Teachers' Training and Registration Society (TTRS). The TTRS aimed to ensure that all teachers were properly qualified and to monitor the adequacy of their qualifications and their professional conduct (i.e. a forerunner of a General Teaching Council).[4] In 1885, Frances Mary Buss helped to found the Cambridge Training College (now Hughes Hall), which was intended to provide training for students from Girton and Newnham Colleges who wished to teach. Between 1885 and 1897 Dorothea Beale founded three training institutions for women teachers, associated with Cheltenham Ladies College. By 1897 Cambridge University had established a Teachers' Training Syndicate to develop examinations for teachers at both elementary and secondary level. The scheme was soon patronised by suitably qualified women who came to predominate in the numbers passing the examinations.

One significant event in the teacher-education sector was the establishment in 1912 of the London Day Training College. Initially it trained teachers for schools in London and it has grown into the University of London Institute of Education of the present day. When appointments to the new College were made, it was natural that an eye should be cast over those who were already teaching in London schools. One candidate who attracted attention was a dynamic geography teacher at the William Ellis Secondary School in Gospel Oak, Hampstead.

FAIRGRIEVE'S INFLUENCE

James Fairgrieve (1870–1953) was destined to be an influential educator in the period between the wars, and is, without doubt, one of the major figures in the history of geographical education (see Figure 6.9). Yet he had no academic or professional qualifications in geography, save a certificate acquired by part-time study from the London School of Economics. He was, like so many other early figures of influence in British geographical education, a Scot, but went to the University of Wales at Aberystwyth to take a degree in maths and physics in 1889. He stayed as a university demonstrator for a couple of years before taking a further maths degree at Jesus College, Oxford, from where he graduated in 1895.

He then returned to Scotland to teach at Campbelltown Grammar School but was attracted to London in 1898 by a clergyman with whom he had been friends as a student in Oxford. The clergyman knew Fairgrieve's educational views were broadly liberal and wanted him to head a private school which would offer a more progressive curriculum than that currently in operation in the elementary Board of Education schools of the time.

Fairgrieve's own personal interests inclined him to gardening, walks in the countryside and to understanding the politics and economics of an expanding Empire. He became interested in geography as a school subject, joined the Geographical Association in 1906, and attended Mackinder's classes at the LSE in the evenings. As a result of a recommendation from Mackinder he was appointed geography master at the William Ellis School in 1907, a specialist teacher for the first time at the age of 37.

One of his biographers records that he was 'bubbling with fresh ideas and astonishing energy'[5] at this time. His teaching at William Ellis School (where he had set up a geographical laboratory in 1911), and his energetic writing of textbooks (some with Ernest Young, mentioned earlier) brought him to the attention of the newly appointed Principal of the Day Training College, James Adams, who had once been his Headmaster at Campbelltown. The Vice-Principal, Percy Nunn, had come from being Senior Maths Master at William Ellis, so Fairgrieve's abilities were well-known to him. When appointed, he became one of the first specialist full-time trainers of secondary school geography teachers in the country.

Fairgrieve's commitment was equally to pedagogy as to geography. Though he saw the importance of a knowledge base for geography, he was far from being a didactic teacher or a 'capes and bays' practitioner. He believed in the development of active teaching methods and promoted the use of maps and models, artefacts and pictures, as essential adjuncts to geography lessons. He advocated that children should explore their own local surroundings and that geography should form strong links with other subjects. Reg Honeybone, one of his successors in leading the geography department at the London Institute, remembers him from the days when he was a postgraduate student in Fairgrieve's teacher-training course at the London Day Training College in 1934–35. 'He was a remarkable man ... I remember him saying, "We must work from the known from to the unknown; not like some teachers – who work from the unknown to the unknowable!"'

Fairgrieve's magnum opus was *Geography in Schools*, published in 1926.[6] Though it was not the first manual written about the teaching of geography,[7] it was certainly the one which captured the potential audience of its period most comprehensively. It contains within it, Fairgrieve's own famous definition of the objectives of geography teaching.

> The function of geography is to train future citizens to imagine accurately the conditions of the great world stage and so help them think sanely about political and social problems in the world around.

His further explanation of this included

> History deals essentially with the drama, geography deals with the stage on which the drama, and specially the present act of the drama, is played ...

> No one man, even during a long and busy life, ever set eyes on the whole of the world, and in geography we are concerned with much more than we can see. We cannot understand a fraction of the world unless we make an effort to imagine things as they are. (pp. 18–20)

Subsequent chapters on 'Reality in geography', 'The grammar of geography' and, most notably, 'Geographic control' revealed, in philosophic terms, a mild determinism characteristic of the period, but what shone through was the author's grasp of practical classroom situations and the skilful and persuasive way in which his ideas were presented. He mixed both geographic and educational wisdom in equal parts.

To give a flavour of his work here are two extracts. The first passage concerns the understanding of structure as one of the elements of physical geography:

> Structure – The skull feels hard to the touch. In the middle of the face there is something projecting, the nose: it is softer than the skull but does not 'give' easily; it has some definite shape. On the cheeks there is something softer still. Now, as a result of the different proportions of the hard and the soft and the softest in the structure, one's head has a certain shape, it has a certain relief. The relief is the shape, and it is there as result of the structure. In the same way the surface of the globe has acquired a certain shape, as a result of certain events in the past during which forces have acted on the structure. (p. 40)

and, linking to it, this extract from another chapter:

> The important thing in teaching geography, as in teaching everything else, is to remember that we are concerned not with logical order, but with psychological order. The logical order may be quite in place in the university; in the school it has no place. Begin where you can begin, as you catch fish. If you can hook them by the mouth, do that; if you can hook them by the tail, do that; if you can catch them by the middle, do that …

> Classes, circumstance, individual boys and girls vary so much that what might be the right way in one class may be the wrong one in another. A way that may be right with a class in one year may be less good with a class at the same stage next year.

> Some general principles of course there are. It is quite obvious, for example, that one must not start with structure in Standard I, or Standard III, or the corresponding classes in a secondary school. Structure comes in logically at the beginning, but psychologically, it comes, if anywhere, at the end … this is in accord with what we know of the development of the child. (pp. 89–90)

Fairgrieve's influence on a generation of geography graduates who passed through the Day Training College (later the London Institute) was considerable; he enthused many of them to take up teaching with commitment and his beliefs about teaching and learning were lively and motivating for pupils.

Fairgrieve was also responsible for setting up the Colonial Education Centre (now known as the Centre for the Study of Education in Tropical Areas) at the Institute in 1927. He was elected President of the Geographical Association in 1935, one of the first teachers to achieve this high office, and he remained active in the Association's work until his death in 1953, though increasingly crippled by infirmity and able to attend meetings only with the help, successively, of sticks, wheelchair, and basket-bed. One of his last acts was to order the seed for the coming year for the Friern Barnet Allotment Holders Association, whose President he was, and whose activities he had supported since his arrival in London over 50 years before. Though, from a contemporary perspective, some of his imperial views jar, his name and his work is revered by those who were his students, many of whom went on to key positions in education, and his place in the history of geography teaching in schools is assured.

Yet his influence was not all-pervasive. Michael Wise, later Professor of Geography at LSE, recalls that 'we didn't hear of Fairgrieve or his work' in his PGCE training course at the University of Birmingham in 1939–40 and notes that Fairgrieve did not lecture to the Birmingham Branch of the GA in the period 1934–39; it seems probable that in his own time Fairgrieve's influence was much stronger in London and its schools than in the rest of the country.

GEOGRAPHY AND FILM

Fairgrieve championed the use of film in schools, realising the potential of this infant art-form to bring other parts of the world alive for pupils in classrooms. He was responsible for setting up film-monitoring committees of London teachers, for writing numerous reviews of film material in *The Geographical Teacher* and for many demonstrations of the usefulness of film in geography teaching.

Film was an art-form of rapidly growing importance in the inter-war years. The addition of sound to silent pictures in the late 1920s increased its attractiveness and its versatility. A generation of children and young adults across the class-divides, found themselves newly addicted to 'two pennorth o'dark' and the glamorous stories acted out within the cinemas, the newly built cathedrals of the suburbs which were springing up everywhere.[8]

Though most feature films were romances, historical dramas, music and dance spectaculars or light comedies, there was also a strong documentary film movement growing-up in Britain at this time led by John Grierson, Basil Wright, Harry Watt and others.[9] Grierson, a thoughtful and dedicated Scot, had a firm conviction that the motion picture could play a vital educational role in a democracy and had extraordinary gifts of adminstration and organisation as well as artisitic creativity. He almost single-handedly put the documentary film movement on its feet in Britain and was devoted to producing examples of what he called 'the creative treatment of actuality'.[10]

Grierson's work at the Empire Marketing Board Film Unit and later the GPO Film Unit and the Crown Film Unit produced notable short pieces of major geographical interest, most famously 'Drifters' (1929),

'ANNUAL CONFERENCE NOTES AND DISCUSSIONS'

INSTRUCTION BY CINEMA

'On the Friday afternoon members of the Council were invited to attend a class lesson at which Mr Fairgrieve illustrated the use of the cinema in the teaching of geography. The lesson was a glorious triumph over a long sequence of obstacles and was, incidentally, a model of adaptation.

One did not suspect that things were going wrong when just before the demonstration was due to begin, an unperturbed Mr Fairgrieve left the building, as we later discovered, to look for his boys. He returned without them.

It was next discovered that the plugs in the room allotted were out of order and a select group followed Mr Fairgrieve, determined though very cheerful, from room to room, until one was discovered which would meet our needs in respect of electrical power. The room was otherwise most unsuitable, as the film had to be projected against a strong light on to the space between two windows, a severe handicap for a small instrument. In the absence of the class, Mr Fairgrieve, with the aid of two films, outlined a lesson on the production, collection and preparation of rubber. He also gave a practical demonstration on the use (and possible misuse) of the instrument.

A disturbance outside announced the arrival of the class, a high-spirited group of Standard IV boys, who had sacrificed an afternoon's holiday to this end. To witness the response of the boys to what is ordinarily, one would imagine, a very difficult lesson was an experience which will not readily be forgotten ...

It was explained that, as yet, there are available only a few films of a type so well suited to geography teaching as the one exhibited ... it would be ungrateful not to put on record our appreciation of the noble sacrifice made by the boys on behalf of the Association.

H.K.'

(From GEOGRAPHY Vol 14 (4) Spring 1928, pp 345-46).

The GA's 1928 Annual Conference was held at the London School of Economics. Fairgrieve was demonstrating 'Gill's School Cinema Projector price £6.10.0'

Figure 6.1:
'Instruction by cinema' –
extract from *Geography* (1928)
(*Source*: GA)

and 'Night Mail' (1936).[11] These films were often less than 30 minutes in length and therefore eminently usable in classrooms; new mobility to travel in the inter-war period was matched by the advance of new media technology and the short documentary film revealed graphically ways of life and sights of wonder which previously had only been related by word. Geography benefited from the additional power that the moving visual image could provide and its motivating effect in classrooms was seized on by lively teachers. Grierson expressed enthusiasm in eloquent, even prophetic tones:

> We can, by propaganda, widen the horizons of the schoolroom and give to every individual, each in his place and work, a living conception of the community which he has the privilege to serve.[12]

Arthur Knight, a notable historian of the film, provides an important gloss on this in pointing out that:

> What [Grierson] meant [by propaganda] was not the calculated cynical distortion of truth as practised by the totalitarians, but its function of spreading information.[13]

This concern for the visual followed in the tradition of Dickinson's desire to exchange with other teachers lantern slides for use in classroom lessons (which led to the founding of the GA)[14] and the still frequent use made of the epidiascope[15] in geography lessons at this time.

Fairgrieve was to be frequently found at GA conferences demonstrating the use of film with classes brought in from London schools, mixing his pedagogical and rhetorical talents with a rare flourish (see Figure 6.1).

GEOGRAPHY AND RADIO

A second major development of mass communication in the 1920s and 1930s was the advent of radio. This, like film, brought a new external dimension to classroom learning. Geography again, by its nature, stood to benefit. Early experiments by the Marconi Company in the 1920s led to the founding of the British Broadcasting Corporation in 1927.[16] Lord Reith, the first Director-General appointed was, like Grierson, a Presbyterian Scot with an educational vision, and he determined that the new medium should shoulder the responsibility of uplifting the nation as well as entertaining it.[17]

It was not long before experiments were being made with broadcasts specifically for schools, though timetables often had to be re-arranged, because the broadcasts had to be received 'live' off the airwaves in the absence of any widespread tape-recording technology available at this time.

The first programmes were designed for secondary schools and schools 'signed up' as listeners and received supplementary notes and

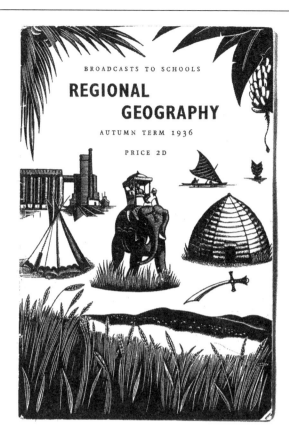

REGIONAL GEOGRAPHY

The New World

TERM I—North America

planned by C. D. FORDE, Ph.D.
Professor of Geography and Anthropology in the University of Wales
broadcast by GEORGE B. BARBOUR, Ph.D.,
P. R. CROWE, Eric ASHBY, D.Sc., *and* ALAN SULLIVAN

FROM THE NATIONAL TRANSMITTER AND FROM SCOTTISH
TRANSMITTERS

Thursdays 11.30–11.50 a.m.
24 September–10 December 1936

TO THE SCHOOLS

The whole of North America in four hours! That is the actual amount of time we shall be 'on the air' for the geography of a country eighty times the size of Great Britain. It can't be done. And yet, after all, we know a good deal about Canada and the United States already; for many of the people in the New World are our own folk and left the 'old country' only a few years ago. I know a village over there where all the old people speak Gaelic and where every other man is a MacSomething. And yet there are American villages where you hear more German spoken than English; half the city of Quebec is French. Much of what we know about the people of our own country and the rest of Europe will be true also of their relatives in North America, even though they've been settled there for generations. What we want to see is how they have changed their New World surroundings, and how those surroundings have changed them.

Obviously there won't be time to talk about everything. Instead, we shall have to divide the country into large regions within which the conditions are more or less uniform—the Wheat Lands, the Corn Belt, the Far North, and so forth—and emphasize the typical things in each.

GEORGE B. BARBOUR

3

Figure 6.2: Cover and introductory page from BBC's 'Regional Geography' pamphlet (*Source*: BBC) (reduced size)

scripts to help teachers explain and interpret the material in the broadcasts. In geography there were series developed called *Travel Talks* and *Regional Geography* (see Figure 6.2). The former included contributions from travellers and explorers as well as from teachers; both Ernest Young and James Fairgrieve were amongst the broadcasters, though the latter had less success in this venture than in many others, judging by the comment of at least one radio critic.[18]

Programmes for elementary schools began in 1934 (Ann Driver's famous, 'music and movement' was the first of this kind) and *Travel Talks* became a junior-oriented geography programme. The GA encouraged teachers to use the programmes and the geography series drew a steadily increasing audience until the advent of television in the 1950s. Specialist subject producers were appointed by the BBC as were field-based Education Officers by the Schools Broadcasting Council who commissioned and monitored the output.

Schools television educational programmes supplanted radio from the 1960s onwards, despite the belated development of tape-recording techniques and of tape-slide presentations marketed separately. Television made its way in education, just as it largely supplanted radio in the home. The independent television companies who came into existence post-war also made provision for schools programmes and geography was well-served in television's early days. Financial cutbacks at the BBC and a shift in priorities, as channels chased ratings, eventually led to the loss of the glossy and well-produced supporting pamphlets for schools which had been a feature of the 1950s and 1960s as well as a loss of the specialist producers.

The widespread advent of video-recorders made it possible for the broadcasting companies to shift transmission times to the middle of the night, and these days programmes are rarely heard or watched 'live' off-air. It has also to be said that the attraction of specially made programmes has also lost some of its appeal as school pupils have become satiated by television output and blasé about material with specific educational connotations. Teachers, these days, are more likely to make use of programmes (or extracts of programmes) from the regular schedules of radio, television and film, especially news and documentary pieces.

The advent of film, radio and television, allied to much increased personal mobility has changed the whole milieu of teaching since the 1920s, and of geography teaching in particular. The idea, once held, that knowledge of the world was a precious gift to be revealed bit by bit by the geography teacher to pupils now has no validity; educators know well that pupils gather a multiplicity of world images from other sources through watching TV from their earliest days. The task now is to challenge the veracity and the adequacy of such images, which mostly emanate from the entertainment-oriented context of soap operas, feature films and cartoons. The view of Australia once mediated by geographical reader texts as a vast out-back (see Figure 4.3) is now more likely to be replaced by a vision of it as a nation of suburban Ramsay Streets, the context of the much-watched daily television serial *Neighbours*.

INTO THE FIELD

Fairgrieve had been a proponent of field walks for pupils, in his schoolteaching career, though he was by no means the first person to do this. The origin of the strong tradition of fieldwork as a part of the education of pupils goes back to days before the subject of geography itself was recognised distinctively on the curriculum.

Scott Keltie's Report to the RGS noted that the boys of Robert Gordon's Hospital Aberdeen, were, as early as 1876, taken 'out to the country and in a simple, rough, but effective, and to them interesting and instructive way… taught to draw maps of a small area for themselves'.[19] Brunsden provides a comprehensive and entertaining introduction to the origins of fieldwork for schools, locating it in general concerns for environmental education and tracing the story back to Rousseau, Pestalozzi and Froebel in the eighteenth and nineteenth centuries.[20]

It was, however, only the exceptional Board elementary school which did other than take occasional lessons in the playground; in most cases, neither location, nor the implications of cost, nor inclination persuaded teachers beyond the confines of their classroom. The wealthier public schools might organise a 'tour' for some of their older pupils from time to time, but it was not until the 1920s that we can see the development of a significant field-work component in British geographical education.

On a wider front, The School Journey Association was instituted in 1901 and the School Nature Study Union in 1903. Adventurous teachers, like G. G. Lewis (who led his pupils on to Hampstead Heath to recreate the sense of being explorers and colonisers by making decisions about the landscape in miniature) were active in these organisations but they were pioneers, rather than representatives of the norm.[21]

The first half of the twentieth century was, however, to see a great flowering of field-activity, both in schools and beyond. In the first issue of *The Geographical Teacher* in 1901 Joan Reynolds had urged the application of field-teaching approaches already common in Switzerland and Germany.

> while these excursions are still innovations we must remember how important it is that such as are carried out should be successful from all points of view. They must prove themselves to have a direct as well as an indirect educational value ; or British parents who will have to bear the extra expense and are slow perhaps to perceive the value of this new form of training, will taboo them as a needless extravagance.
>
> ... we may realise in time the ideal held up by Ruskin when 'the country will become an outer and uncovered classroom, a Divine Museum utilised by our teachers'.[22]

Well before the First World War some teachers and teacher-educators (J. H. Cowham, who ran formal school trips from Croydon to Godstone, notable amongst them)[23] regularly took their students out of the classroom for lessons in the physiography of the landscape and nature study. But it was after the Great War, as the new secondary schools flourished, that fieldwork came into prominence both as a general activity (in school journeys and expeditions) and as an academic exercise. In Britain, when part of the geography curriculum, it assumed a flavour which was different from that found in American and Australian schools where the emphasis was (and still is) often on the 'experience' itself – the raw encounter with 'wilderness' or 'outback'. British teachers tended to provide an academic edge to the work, encouraging accurate mapping and recording to be done as a preliminary to the analysis and synthesis of material. The influence of the fashionable French school of academic regional geography could be seen in the way in which small-scale surveys were carefully compiled, but there was also a link back to the work associated with the Outlook Towers advocated and built by Patrick Geddes and to the spatial-cum-sociological explorations of Frederic Le Play.

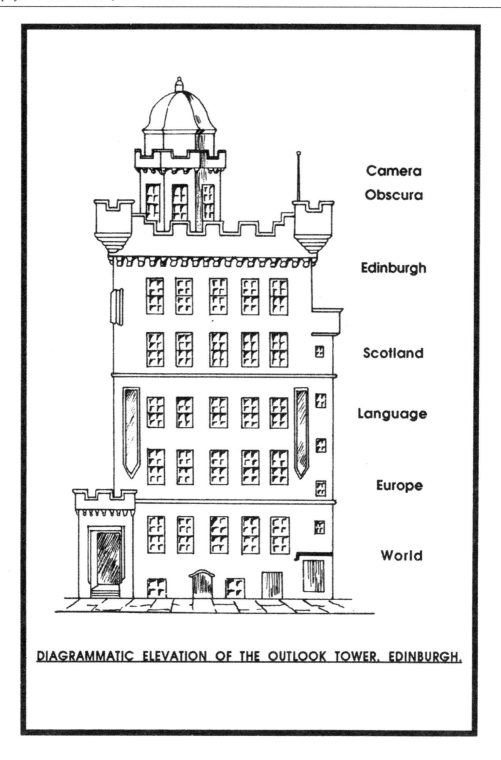

Camera
Obscura

Edinburgh

Scotland

Language

Europe

World

DIAGRAMMATIC ELEVATION OF THE OUTLOOK TOWER, EDINBURGH.

Figure 6.3: Geddes' Outlook Tower in diagrammatic elevation, with indications of the uses of its storeys. (*Source: Cities in Evolution*, Williams & Norgate, London, 1915)

TWO PIONEERS OF FIELD WORK

Geddes and Le Play, in their different ways inspired geography teachers to become field workers, though neither would have called themselves 'geographers' as such. They were largely responsible for the regional survey movement which grew strongly in the 1920s.

Geddes (1854–1932) was a remarkable polymath whose ceaseless fecundity of ideas and schemes was astonishing.[24] He established an 'Outlook Tower' on Castle Hill, Edinburgh in 1892 and the young A. J. Herbertson was one of those who helped him to establish it. The tower was designed to be both a museum and a centre for study and survey, though those mundane terms hardly do justice to the vision and breadth of Geddes's plans for it. In it were represented three of the central themes of his vision – sight – synopsis – synthesis (see Figure 6.3). The camera obscura installed at the top of the Tower in a darkened room was particularly important in that it provided an unusual clarity of vision; it gave a distinctiveness of 'sight'. Stoddart says that 'it came to symbolise a form of observation and a definition of subject matter which has governed field studies since that time'.[25] An outside panoramic gallery which went all the way around the camera tower provided the synopsis. The tower itself, with galleries below representing successively Edinburgh, Scotland, the English-speaking world, Europe and the oriental civilisations, was designed to be the gathering-place for the information and a meeting place for scholars from many disciplines – the synthesis.

> Given the panorama, Geddes considered that 'the first contribution of this Tower towards life is purely visual, for from here everyone can make a start towards seeing completely that portion of the world he can survey'…Standing on his tower, Geddes was developing the most basic technique of the geographer teaching in the field, that of pointing and talking from a highpoint.[26]

Geddes would later go on to say 'the only complete science – the synthesis as the mother of them all – is Geography'.[27]

Le Play, in origin trained as an engineer, travelled widely in Europe in the first half of the nineteenth century and developed the idea that local field survey could form the basis both for insights into the plight of the working classes as well as for social reform.[28] His view was that the three main determinants of society were the impact of the environment, the jobs which people did, and the strength of their kinship. He linked the three in a persuasive triptych: *Lieu – Travail – Famille*. (When translated by Geddes, who was an admirer of Le Play's ideas, the third part was crucially widened in scope, so that the English-language version became known as *Place – Work – Folk*.)

Le Play also developed a clear methodology for his investigations (observation – the collection of facts – the classification of facts – the determination of linkages and causations between facts – a prescription for action) which formed an attractive pedagogical recipe for early field-workers. There was a flourishing Le Play Society in Britain from 1930–60 and it ran almost 100 survey expeditions/excursions during its life. Schoolteachers formed a large part of the Society's membership and joined enthusiastically in many of these projects.

> A battery of cameras was always an essential part of the equipment of a Le Play party and a vast collection of lantern slides is in existence and dozens of files and folders containing reports and photographs.[29]

Le Play's approach was linked to a prevailing belief in the 1920s that regional survey field-work was the thing to do. The GA set up a Regional Survey Committee to encourage schools in this, but the evidence gathered began to suggest that, for schools at least, the method worked best in very small rural communities (just as Vidal de la Blache had shown) and became a quite overwhelming (and somewhat nebulous and superficial) task in areas where the complexities of urban and industrial living had taken hold. At best, even when carried out by adults, it promoted the education and enjoyment of the participants, rather than made great contributions to original knowledge.

LAND-USE SURVEY

One young lecturer who observed this thoughtfully was Laurence Dudley Stamp (1899–1968). He had graduated with first-class honours from London University before taking off for Burma, where he became Professor of Geography and Geology in the University of Rangoon at the ripe old age of 26. Returning to Britain in the late 1920s Stamp joined the GA's Regional Survey Committee and was interested to observe the results of a survey done by Northamptonshire schoolchildren under the direction of an enthusiastic teacher, E. E. Field, at the county town's grammar school. Field, supported by the Northamptonshire director of education, J. L. Holland (an early member of the Geographical Association), had enlisted the support of elementary and secondary schoolchildren in parishes all over the county in making a land-use survey, based on a simple three-fold categorisation of land – grassland, arable and woodland.[30]

Stamp was struck as much by the logistics of the successful completion of the work as by the nature of the task and the simple but elegant maps which were displayed (and later published) at the end of the project. He mused that here was a practical task for school groups, efficiently completed and with important informational conseqences. National knowledge about land-use was almost non-existent and yet the British countryside was undergoing huge changes, both in farming practice and through urban development at this time.

Within a few weeks Stamp had hatched an idea with far-reaching

EDUCATION WITH A PURPOSE

'Hi! Come here!' I shouted, and the two boys, who had not observed my approach along the far side of the hedge, started and looked up. The natural alarm of the young trespassers upon the advent of a farmer was apparent on their faces, and for a moment they seemed to contemplate flight; however, after a moment's hesitation the older of the two came timidly towards me, followed at a strategic distance by his companion.

'What are you doing here?' I enquired.

'Surveying.'

'Surveying what?'

'Surveying your crops.'

'Let's have a look' and I held out my hand for the paper one of them carried. It was surrendered without demur, and sure enough, there was a section of a six-inch to the mile survey map, which covered the district in which my farm is situated. The boundaries of the fields were marked on it and pencilled on each square was letter A or M.

'Hmm,' I said, 'what's it all about?'

The older boy explained.

'All right,' I remarked, 'carry on, but don't damage any fences.'

'Thank you sir, we won't,' answered the younger boy, who up to now had been silent.

Returning home, I ran into their schoolmaster, and asked him for further particulars, which he readily gave. 'Thank you, sir,' I said, 'but don't you find it rather hard to get the children to give up their time to this work? Wouldn't they rather play games and so forth?' 'Twenty per cent would,' was the reply, 'but the remaining eighty per cent are quite sufficient to do the work. Of course, they don't need to give up many nights and it's quite a voluntary task. I find no difficulty in obtaining their willing co-operation, and they are learning valuable lessons in self-help and initiative; besides, look what a feeling of pride will be theirs when the final printed map is published and they are able to point to a section of it and say "I did the work of surveying that".'

It seems to me that this is education with a purpose; to so interest children that they work in their spare time, find pleasure in that work and give to the community a valuable record as a result of their labours.

Figure 6.4:
Reproduction of text of 1930s newspaper article about an episode from the 1st Land Utilisation Survey (*Source*: GA)

This article, written by a farmer and published in an English local newspaper, was quoted by L. Dudley Stamp, Director of The (First) Land Utilisation Survey of Britain when speaking to the Annual Meeting of the National Council of Geography Teachers at Evanston, Illinois, USA in December 1933.

consequences.[31] He suggested to the GA that there should be a national land-use survey undertaken by schools to ascertain the true facts about the nation's land uses. The GA applauded the idea but rather timidly left Stamp to create his own organisation and finance for the survey, which he did by dint of talking enthusiastically to charitable trusts and his own college, the London School of Economics, and persuading them to give him some money to set up a survey office.

With the aid of a young graduate, E. C. (Christie) Willatts, who had passed through Fairgrieve's postgraduate course at the London Institute, but who had yet to land a teaching post, Stamp had, by 1931, spoken to hundreds of schoolteachers at conferences and got the survey underway.[32]

It was a momentous task. Stamp devised a simple eight-fold category (more complex than the Northamptonshire one, but still practically usable by children of all ages) and a survey handbook and recruited his followers, who flocked to the colours with alacrity. The task had the appeal of relative simplicity, allied to the feeling of making a contribution to a topic of national importance.[33]

Stamp's charm and good cheer persuaded the directors of education in many counties to let their schools take part, and even to support the scheme financially. Scores of teachers enlisted their pupils into well-organised teams to scour the countryside for information. They were aided by Scout troops and Guide Companies, university students, women's institutes, even groups of nuns. Sometimes the novelty of the activity raised eyebrows or aroused the suspicions of those whose day-by-day business was on the land (see Figure 6.4) but fears were generally assuaged by the combined earnestness, zeal and *joie de vivre* of those who were taking part. There was a feeling that it was all being done for the sake of a better Britain – the results would help to make sure that the land was used responsibly and in the best possible way. As Rycroft and Cosgrove have observed,[34] it was a classic modernist enterprise.

Once the individual surveys were undertaken, and the observations entered on to the field maps, the maps were returned to the survey office. There they were painstakingly transcribed by hand from six-inch to one-inch scale and then (as the money became available) printed and published. Stamp himself took on the task of making transects across the maps to check for accuracy; the story goes that he taught his wife to drive so that he could be released for survey duty. He would stand on a platform placed on the front passenger seat of a Morris Eight and, with his considerable bulk wedged half-way through the sun-roof, would look over the tops of the hedges, as they toured through the byways of England and Wales. An appealing image, which conjures accurately Stamp's willingness to be thoroughly and practically involved in any enterprise which he started.

Stamp was also a textbook writer of considerable success. His command of factual material and his memory was remarkable and his simple, polished prose flowed effortlessly on to the page. His secretary for many years, Audrey Clark, remembers that he would dictate a text to her non-stop for an hour and then rarely have to make any emendations

Figure 6.5:
A primary-school class on survey during Land Use-UK 1996. The *Independent* called the project 'the biggest geography lesson in the world'. (*Source*: author)

to the work that she had typed out. His books would not win prizes for originality, but they synthesised valuably and they hit a far more rewarding target – sales. Stamp is the only geography textbook writer to have sold a million copies of a single book; his compendium *The World* was in print for 50 years and was the staple, reliable diet in many geography classes of the 1930s and 1940s.[35]

Stamp used the royalties from his textbooks unselfishly to plough more funds into the *Land Utilisation Survey*. As the maps were produced, he commissioned (or wrote himself) valuable memoirs for each county; incomparable records, analyses and assessments of the state of agriculture and urban development at a particular time, based on the mass of detail accumulated by the youthful surveyors.[36]

Stamp estimated that a quarter of a million schoolchildren were involved in the survey; as an educational enterprise alone (quite apart from its later and greater significance as a record of Britain's misuse of land and a warning about the effect of unplanned urban growth) it was a monumental achievement.[37] Participation in the Stamp survey is still remembered 70 years on with pride by those school pupils who took part in it; and for many it was a vivid and important way of showing the 'pertinence and utility' of geographical study, as well as providing a memorable experience.

Improbably, one of Stamp's colleagues in the Joint School of Geography at the LSE and King's London, Alice Coleman, set out almost single-handed to organise a replica of the survey 30 years later, this time using a much more extensive set of categories.[38] The state of Britain revealed by Stamp's survey had led eventually to the post-war Town and Country Planning Acts; Coleman's underlying purpose was to see if planning had actually 'worked' in the 1960s.[39] Though the complexity of the survey deterred the production of county memoirs of the kind that Stamp had created, printed maps on a 1:25,000 scale were produced for some areas. Field mapping for the whole of England and Wales was completed, with school pupils from geography classes once again the main voluntary surveyors in the vast enterprise.

A third national survey (though this time using sample areas, rather than an overall survey of every square yard of land) was undertaken by 1,500 schools in the Land Use-UK project of 1996, organised by the Geographical Association, in association with the Institute of Terrestrial Ecology and the Ordnance Survey.[40] It owed much to the Stamp and Coleman methodologies, though it also added a further dimension – a reflective section for surveyors who commented on their 'Views and Visions' of the land which they were surveying (see Figure 6.5).[41]

THE CLIMATE OF THE TIMES

The work of schools in the *First Land Utilisation Survey* was the high-profile end of field-work in the 1920s and 1930s. But there were many other individual examples of teachers enlivening their geography by taking classes out of the classroom. Many of these occasions were day or half-day visits and they were usually conducted by coach or bus, to rural rather than urban locations, with the teacher acting as expositor as the landscape unfolded. The role of the pupils was to listen, learn and take notes; thus would they come to appreciate the way the landscape had been formed, the influence of locality on the built form (pointing out the use made of 'local building materials' was a favourite teacher observation) and the linkages between landscape and human activity. A mild determinism prevailed in many of the observations made, with a preference for taking pupils to relatively 'unspoilt' rural spots so that a sense of regionality could be divined – these were areas where the 'geography' was more obvious than in the expanding, sprawling suburbs or the towns.[42]

How had teachers acquired the expertise, knowledge and confidence to run such trips? Very often by going on such a trip themselves. The trips would have been organised by local branches of the GA or Le Play Society, by the local Workers Educational Association, or by some other voluntary organisation. The new lecturers and professors of geography in the universities were well aware of the need to canvass a public for prospective students and many of them genuinely wanted to share their own knowledge with wider audiences.

The spirit of Mackinder's peregrinations around the British Isles at the end of the nineteenth century was revived by keen field-workers like Sidney Wooldridge, Charlotte Simpson, C. C. Fagg and Geoffrey Hutchings,[43] who gave up many weekends to lead field excursions.

> I submit that the object of field teaching, at least in the elementary stage, is to 'develop an eye for country', i.e. to build up the power

to read a piece of country... an easier but grossly incompetent method for the ignorant or unpractised is to deliver a roadside lecture of guide-book or textbook information borrowing freely but irrelevantly from history, geology or agriculture. The question is, rather, what can you see from here, and more particularly, what can you see that the map fails to portray.[44]

As a young and enthusiastic lecturer at King's College, London, Wooldridge (1900–63) seemed addicted as much to Gilbert and Sullivan operettas, in which he performed with brio, as to the nuances of denudation chronology, but his field classes drew large audiences of keen teachers, some of whom had graduated from the same department only a few years before. His own influential book on 'The Weald' was a masterly survey of the geological, geomorphological, vegetational and agricultural aspects of the region.[45] It was significant, though, that London was only mentioned in the very occasional passing reference. The social realities of the commuting fringe were, one suspects, consciously held at bay.

The sketch which adorns the cover of Wooldridge and Hutchings' subsequent book 'London's Countryside' is of a lecturer with his field class sitting attentively as he points out some distant feature.[46] It is a telling image as David Matless has pointed out.[47] It is representative of a whole spectrum of recreational and leisure pursuits which grew up after 1918, as the British people had time and inclination to discover their own landscape.

Rambling and cycling clubs flourished, and the urban and suburban nation took to the countryside on Bank Holidays and summer weekends. The Ordnance Survey discovered that there was a new market for their maps – walkers, ramblers, campers, who were using their newly acquired mobility to escape from the town and the suburbs at every opportunity. The development of mass-produced and moderately reliable motor-cycles and small cars at affordable prices moved them from being the enthusiasts' play-things of Edwardian times to accepted everyday modes of transport for many. Those who could not afford them could nevertheless join a charabanc trip or a railway excursion at the weekend. A resident of the inner London suburb of Kilburn between 1915 and 1936 remembers:

> We had no car, nor even a bicycle ... but at the weekends we would walk up to the railway station on Kilburn High Road and go out for a ride into Hertfordshire. 'Metroland' they called it. They would give you maps to show you where you could go for a good day's ramble. And sometimes there was the excitement of a fair on Hampstead Heath or at the Welsh Harp at Hendon.[48]

The increased interest in the environment benefited geography in schools, not least in promoting mapwork. Teachers themselves might well be part of the weekend exodus to the country, gathering a greater range of travel experiences with which to infuse their work.

All this field-work was linked consciously or otherwise to an ideal of making school pupils better citizens. By experiencing the environment (and particularly the countryside) children would learn to appreciate it and thus work to conserve it, went the thinking of many teachers. The activities of 'townies', (as against country-dwellers and country-lovers), holiday-campers, (as against ramblers and hikers) and motor-boaters (as against sailors) were regarded with clear disfavour. The latter group were memorably represented by the 'Hullabaloos' who unthinkingly moor near a bird's nest on the Broads, play noisy music on their gramophone, and nearly come to a muddy end in Arthur Ransome's popular children's story of the period, *Coot Club*.[49]

J. A. Steers, later to be Professor of Geography at Cambridge, lecturing to the Royal Geographical Society in 1944 about the need to 'save the coast', encapsulated the thinking more consciously:

> Education must begin at school and might well be associated with the teaching of geography. This is the subject above all directly concerned with the study of landscape – and intelligent knowledge and appreciation of the local region by school pupils should do much to guarantee the proper use of the countryside in the future.[50]

There was also in some quarters a conscious move to develop and encourage an 'aesthetic geography' so that (hopefully) an objective beauty would be recognised and acknowledged by all; Vaughan Cornish[51] led this movement and expounded its philosophy, amongst other places, to the GA in his Presidential address in 1928.[52] 'The laws of scenery may be compared with those of music. They are the laws of harmony.'[53] The education of the visual sense was seen as a vital part of an orderly design for modern living and it was suggested that geographers should take their place alongside artists in promoting this.

THE TOURING BRANCH AND ITS DOWNFALL

The idea of going on field excursions had enthused teachers of geography some time before most had been able to introduce them into the curriculum of their schools. Early photographs in the GA archives show intrepid bands of members mounting Shap Fell on motor-cycles and embarking on tours through the Grampians in three-wheelers.[54] The GA formed the idea of organising a 'Touring Branch' in 1922 and the initial programmes of continental tours and domestic excursions in school holidays were immediately booked out by members and their friends. The transport arranged was rather more luxurious than that of the pioneer excursions: travel by 'coaches specially commissioned for long-distance travel ... replete with every appliance which will contribute to the passengers' comfort and enjoyment' was advertised. The Touring Branch programme became an immediate success.

An unfortunate occurrence brought it to grief and also, incidentally, had severe consequences for the GA's relationship with the RGS for several decades. A brochure for the programme of the 'Touring Branch' in 1926 ascribed, probably by poor editorial scrutiny, the authorship and organisation to 'The Geographical Society' rather than to the Geographical Association.

Arthur Hinks, Secretary to the Royal Geographical Society at the time, saw the brochure and was furious, believing that readers would assume that the RGS was involved and in the business of 'sordid commercialism' by running tours. Hinks was a peppery individual, whose dominance of RGS affairs in the period was absolute and whose interests were almost exclusively on the physical side of geography. He kept close links with explorers, but had little interest in teachers. The best the official historian of the RGS can do is to describe his 30 years at the helm in the following terms

> He brought to the affairs of the Society academic distinction as both an astronomer and cartographer and a painstaking if idiosyncratic attention to detail.[55]

His opposite number (though in an honorary capacity) at the GA, H. J. Fleure, was Hinks' antithesis in almost every respect (see Figure 6.7). Fleure was a kind and gentle spirit, a professor at Aberystwyth and later at Manchester, whose interests were in human geography and anthropology. He was the ceaselessly working guiding hand in the GA's affairs over almost the same period as Hinks at the RGS.[56]

Chalk rubbed up against cheese. Hinks resented the success of the 'upstart GA' as he saw it and created a storm in a tea-cup over the error in the brochure. The GA were forced to make a public apology in *The Times* and the RGS turned its back on educational matters until the end of Hinks's tenure as Secretary. The irony was that the 'Touring Branch' ceased activity soon afterwards; fears had emerged that its commercial success as a business activity might lose the GA its status as a charity.[57]

GIRLS AND GEOGRAPHY

Fairgrieve included in his *Geography in School* a chapter on 'Geography for boys and girls'. Considering the evidence of examination results (the year is not given, but it must be around 1925) which showed boys performing better than girls, he commented that

> the syllabuses of the new geography have been drawn up almost entirely by men; the women who have been most successful at examinations are those who have best done this man's geography, for there has been no other … it is at least conceivable that the women who teach geography in girls' schools, while adjusting their methods somewhat to their pupils, still retain so much of what has been found successful in teaching boys, that it militates against complete success.

Figure 6.6:
Photograph of James Fairgrieve
(*Source*: GA)

Figure 6.7:
Photograph of H. J. Fleure
(*Source*: GA)

He is tantalisingly vague here about what 'methods' he means, though in a later passage he quotes a sample of boys as expressing a marked liking for having 'the reasons of things' explained whereas the girls in the sample expressed a preference for 'the humane side of geography'. Fairgrieve goes on to advocate single-sex geography classes and teachers of the same sex for such classes, whilst concluding 'there is no evidence that girls cannot do geography'.

External examination entries in geography from that time to this have never shown a great preponderance of entries from one sex or the other; and neither has there been (at least in secondary education) an undue bias in the number of men and women who taught the subject, compared with some other subjects (e.g. the physical sciences, home economics, craft subjects).

Some recent writers[58] have followed Fairgrieve in postulating that in this period geographical knowledge was 'masculinised', using popular adventure stories of the late nineteenth and early twentieth centuries as evidence. The point made is that there were few female role models. Writing in the mid-1920s, Enid Blyton, education editor as well as well-known children's story teller, implicitly accepted a dimension of the 'masculinising' charge, whilst asserting the equality of girls with boys (my italics in the quotation):

> Girls, some people tell us, do not take so well to geography. I am inclined to think, however, that this is much less true today than it may have been ten or twenty years ago. There is so little difference nowadays in the tastes of young boys and girls that the wise teacher of mixed classes treats them *all as boys* as far as geography is concerned. The modern girl reads the same adventure books and is just as eager to go a-voyaging in strange lands as the modern boy.[59]

The 'masculinising' effect in geography may have been apparent in the 1920s but the charge seems more difficult to sustain in the 1930s. There were, by then, as many women as men teaching geography and the many women teachers who led girls' classes into the field could provide alternative role models.

There was a liberation of what was considered a proper sphere of activity for women from the late 1920s onwards,[60] epitomised by the much-publicised and dare-devil exploits of figures such as Amy Johnson and Fay Taylour.[61] Marjorie Hessell Tiltman's 'Women in modern adventure', a popular illustrated reading text of the period,[62] has literally a score of examples ranging from Freya Stark's explorations to Isobel Hutchinson's adventurous botanical field excursions. *The Girls' Own Paper* (a sister publication to the *Boys' Own Paper* with almost as large a circulation) consciously went out of its way in non-fiction articles to show readers that there were plenty of women doing non-traditional things. The Girl Guides were as numerous and as adventurous as their brother Boy Scouts. Girls' fiction of the period (taking Dorothy Hann, Ethel Talbot and Elinor Brent-Dyer as representative authors) is full of daring 'modern' girls, most of whom would not blink an eye at adventure in the great outdoors.[63]

David Matless in discussing an illustration of J. W. Tucker's 1936 painting 'Hiking', which shows three young women poring over a map at a hilltop resting place, comments

> The open-air could be presented as a space of equality and freedom for women and men, offering a direct democratic combat with landscape which did not respect conservative conventions of gender.[64]

The increasing desire to venture beyond the classroom was enjoyed as much by girls as by boys. As 'field-work', developed in geography classes it does not seem, in its British style, at least, to have been lastingly characterised or monopolised by masculine tendencies. This apparent gender-neutrality has frequently been demonstrated since. The almost universal introduction of field-work activities in schools has produced no significant change in the ratio of boys and girls who choose to study geography. If anything, the movement has been the other way. In contemporary outdoor activities with a geographical and environmental ambience, such as the Duke of Edinburgh's Award, the number of girls achieving awards is now greater than the number of boys.

It is appropriate to note here that a commitment to geography field-work continued to grow in the post-war period. The Field Studies Council was founded in 1943 and created a network of specialist study centres in England and Wales which school classes could visit.[65] Local authorities and even individual schools purchased their own study centres. The idea of progression in field-work skills and undertaking field-work in each year of a pupil's education was developed. One notable post-war field-worker was Henry Wilks, Secretary to the GA's Fieldwork Committee for many years and an inveterate organiser of excursions at the annual conference. His articles outlining a field-work policy and programme in a school were significant contributions.[66]

Field-work was eventually officially 'written in' to geography through the arrival of a National Curriculum in 1988. The current syllabus for National Curriculum geography (5–14 years) includes a requirement for field-work in all Key Stages, though it is not specified that this should be extended or far flung. An attempt by the National Curriculum Working Group (1989) to have 'residential field-work in an unfamiliar environment' made an entitlement for secondary school pupils was rejected by government advisers because of its cost and resource implications.

TEACHING TIMES AND EXAMINATIONS ENTRIES

How much time was given to geography in schools in the 1920s and 1930s? An American educator, Rose Clark, who had travelled in Europe, reported in 1935:

In England and Wales, there is little uniformity in courses of study or in requirements. However common practice allots 2 or 3 hours per week to geography in elementary schools and in intermediate and secondary schools up to the 'first examination' at age 16.[67]

The Incorporated Association of Assistant Masters in Secondary Schools (IAAM) published a compendium written by practising geography teachers for their colleagues in 1935.[68] It records that the average time given to the subject in the secondary school varied between 60 and 150 minutes per week in the first and second years and between 120 and 150 minutes per week in the third, fourth and fifth years of the course. The IAAM advised that three 45-minute lessons (135 minutes) per week, approximately one-twelfth (i.e. 8.5 per cent) of the total time of the secondary school curriculum, should be given to the subject and that this 'must be regarded as just rather than generous' (p. 29). It is interesting to compare this with present-day figures allowed by head teachers anxious to fulfil all the demands of the National Curriculum – in the 1990s the amount of time allowed has rarely been over 120 minutes.

As far as examination entries went, there was a gradual growth for geography to be discerned through the inter-war years, 1918–39. Over the period about two-thirds of school pupils who were entered for the School Certificate examinations included geography as one of their five choices. In the Northern Joint Board School Certificate Examination geography was taken by 83.5 per cent of all candidates in 1922. But this was a high point, and the figure declined to 70.1 per cent in 1928, and thereafter kept steady at around the 70 per cent mark. A similar percentage was reported from the London General School Examinations in the 1930s. Here geography settled into the pattern of being the sixth most popular choice of subject, after English, French, arithmetic, elementary mathematics and history.

At Higher School Certificate levels, where geography was given no presence until the early 1920s, the proportions were much lower, though they steadily increased from a starting point in 1925 when 5.0 per cent of all candidates for the London Higher School Certificate took geography as a main subject. The figure rose to 17.3 per cent in 1929 and to 19.2 per cent by 1931.

This latter figure is almost comparable with the percentage of candidates taking A-level geography in the present-day (see Figure 11.4), but it should be remembered that in present times there are many more subjects fighting for a share of the A-level cake (as well as an overall increase in candidates). The current figure of 40,000-plus students taking A-level geography each year (20 per cent of all candidates) represents a significant strengthening of the subject compared with the pre-1940 years.[69]

FIG. 2. – North Corner of the Geography Room at the William Ellis School.

FIG. 4. – East Corner, showing map cupboard, geological cupboard, screen, and map-hanging devices.

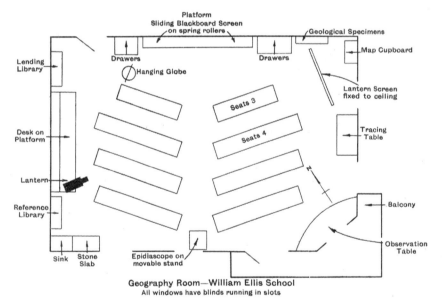

Geography Room—William Ellis School
All windows have blinds running in slots

Figure 6.8:
Illustrations and diagram from *The Modern Geography Room*, 1932 (reduced in size)

GEOGRAPHY ACCOMMODATION

The inter-war years also saw the first concerns to provide specialist geography accommodation. In most elementary schools in the twentieth century as in the nineteenth, classes were taught different subjects in the same classroom; a globe would be a standard feature in most rooms (a geographic illumination of benefit to the whole of the curriculum) and there might be hanging maps at the front.

In secondary schools, it was the exceptional school which had anything other than a normal classroom with tables (or desks) and chairs for geography teaching – partly because, until examination recognition was gained (see Chapter 5), the equipping of geography teaching was considered to be low in the hierarchy of school priorities. (It must also be admitted that some teachers of geography had little knowledge of what they needed to ask for.) The secondary schools developed by the 1902 Act were the places where good practice began.

Pictures of the geography room at William Ellis School, where Fairgrieve taught (in an appendix to his 1926 book)[70] demonstrate his belief that the room should be both classroom and laboratory (see Figure 6.8). They reveal how he had been a pioneer in equipping it as a specialist base.

There are long tables with three chairs at each, map chests and glass-fronted cabinets and cupboards (to contain visual-aids, models, instruments and specimens) surrounding three of the walls. A south-facing window (deemed important for 'outlook') in the other wall leads on to a balcony at the other (an echo of Geddes' Outlook Tower). The names of famous explorers (starting from Ptolemy and reaching up to the present day) are to be seen in large letters as a decorating frieze, adding 'the human touch, without which even the very material facts of the geography room would be incomplete'. A large blackboard globe hangs down from the front. Fairgrieve considered that 'indoors' work for which special provision should be made', should involve the following:

1. the drawing and constructing of maps, plans and diagrams...
2. modelling
3. consulting large-scale maps, plans and charts
4. observing the heavenly bodies, especially the sun
5. observing specimens, geological, botanical and economic...

He also specified as desirable requirements, bookcases, a 'lantern screen', dark blinds, a blackboard, supports for displaying wall-maps, a sink and a slate slab and a tracing table. There are detailed formulations and measurements for how the desks should be arranged (he favoured everyone facing the teacher, whose desk was to be sited on a raised platform), where the globe should be sited in relation to the lantern (to allow the demonstration of day and night), and even where the electric light switches should be and how the teacher should carry out his surveillance of tasks.

A later Head of Geography at William Ellis School, V. C. Spary, wrote a pamphlet in 1932, which capitalised on Fairgrieve's pioneering installations.[71] He continued to urge specialist provision in no uncertain terms.

> In recent years, it has become an accepted fact that a Geography Room is a necessity in every well-equipped school...there is no doubt that in the near future all architects designing school

buildings will be instructed to make special accommodation for geography... even in the leanest of post-war years some authorities embarked upon expenditure for this purpose.

Spary's ideal specification was even more detailed than that of Fairgrieve, down to the requirement of a meridian line marked in the floor, a gas point and a special 'postcard rack'.

Rooms with such equipment were almost always aspiration rather than the norm, but the campaign to provide specialist accommodation was an incidental help in giving geography a profile as a serious contender for curriculum time and money, and for continuing to link it to its scientific and mathematical origins, as well as to the 'humanities' curriculum.

At the end of the twentieth century, however, many geography rooms provided in new schools do not reach such a level of specification or provision as Fairgrieve and Spary optimistically envisaged.

BEYOND THE GEOGRAPHY ROOM

Not all geography learnt in the inter-war years was learnt in the formal surroundings of the classroom, however. The popularity of the organisations founded by Baden-Powell (Cubs and Brownies, Scouts and Guides, Rovers and Rangers) and other 'outdoor' organisations such as the Boys Brigade, the Girls Life Brigade and the Woodcraft Folk meant that many teenagers were exposed to some supplementary environmental education in their leisure pursuits.[72] In the days before other leisure opportunities and more commercial influences jostled for attention, over half the nation's youth belonged to such organisations. The zeal with which 'woodcraft' pursuits and community-linked activities were pursued by these organisations had many incidental benefits and linkages with more formal education.

Attendance at Scout, Guide and Brigade camps was the major event of the year for many who might have no other holiday and little experience of the 'countryside'. The Scouts and Guides operated in a less 'militaristic' way than the Brigade organisations, but, in both spheres, life at such camps was invariably linked to some definite exploration of the environment, the development of mapping skills and some teaching about the kind of behaviour which was and was not appropriate when in the 'great outdoors' – a kind of 'moral geography'[73] taught through woodcraft and camp-fire tales. Given that many geography teachers were 'outdoor types', and enjoyed working for voluntary youth organisations, such as Scouts and Guides, in their spare time, it was perhaps no coincidence that an increase in map work, in local studies and in field-work can be discerned in the formal school curriculum of this period.

There were other informal influences of benefit to geography even closer to the classroom. In the school playground of the 1920s and 1930s, one of the enduring favourite pastimes was the swapping and comparing of cigarette cards – tiny artefacts which had huge popularity with both young and old in the days before the dangers of smoking had been comprehended. The cigarette cards (usually devised in sets of 50 individually different cards around a common theme) were inserted into each packet sold. Each card contained a capsule of written information on one side and attractive sketches or photographs, often of considerable artistic merit, on the other. Two thousand sets were devised by over 100 different manufacturers in the 1920s and 1930s; one set (Wills' 'Railway Engines' of 1936) had a print run of 600 million. The makers were well aware that the attraction of a good topic might create a change of brand-use in the smoker. Children pestered adults for unwanted cards, on a regular and good-natured basis.

Amidst the film-stars, sports celebrities, wildlife, modern inventions and motor-cars, aspects of geographical information were well-represented in the sets. Lambert and Butler's 'Empire Air Routes' was one of many transport-oriented sets and combined maps of flying-boat journeys to Australia and South Africa with pictures of the places at which they stopped; Churchmans' 'Holidays in Britain' were a beautifully coloured scenic portfolio; another Churchman's set, 'Wonderful railway travel' showed trains crossing bridges and embankments in exotic locations full of physical geographic interest. Perhaps most geographic of all were the distinctive large-size photographic cards produced by J. A. Pattriouex for Senior Service smokers; their subjects included 'Coastwise', 'Britain from the Air', 'Beautiful Scotland', 'Our countryside' and others in the same vein. One former headmaster, later to be Minister of Education, Dr Rhodes Boyson, professed that he learnt more from the cigarette cards that he collected than from all his formal schooling in the 1930s.[74]

Stamp collecting was another popular pastime of the period with geographic potential, though like cigarette-card collecting it inevitably emphasised the fascination of fact and of particularity in geography, rather than broad themes or general issues. The minature scenes shown on stamps and the flags and logos which often decorated them were attractive and informative as well as of commercial value. A good number of stamps included maps as their key feature. Many youngsters of the 1930s and 1940s gained both interest in and knowledge about the world through collecting and swapping stamps and poring over their albums. Shrewd teachers often encouraged this by running lunchtime stamp clubs. The hobby was given the accolade of approval through articles in *The Geographical Magazine* and by at least one major lecture based around the stamp by a famous Professor whose name was eponymous.[75]

H. C. Barnard, then the Professor of Education at Reading University, writing in a major text about geographical education in 1948 was positive about the hobby.[76] He felt that 'stamps afford a really valuable stimulus to the pupil in cultivating geographical imagination and amplifying geographical knowledge'. Matless interprets this as:

THE STAFFORDSHIRE GEOGRAPHICAL EXHIBITION OF 1933

The Staffordshire Geographical Exhibition was held between 13th – 19th July 1933 at the County Technical College, Stafford. It was arranged by the Staffordshire local education authority, in conjunction with members of Her Majesty's Inspectorate and teachers in the county.

'The exhibition was probably the largest, the widest in scope, and the most comprehensive that has ever been devoted to the presentation of a single educational subject in this country. It was intended to close after three days, but owing to requests received from all parts of the country, it was decided to keep open for three additional days'

The exhibits were titled as follows:
1. The influence of the physical relief, geology, and climate on plant and animal life and human occupations
2. The effect of geology on plant life
3. A study of a forest area. (Needwood Forest)
4. Traffic on the Shropshire Union Canal
5. A regional survey
6. Industries and occupations of Staffordshire
7. World products section
8. The development of world transport
9. The development of local transport,
10. The household geography section.
11. Japan; a junior school project.
12. The value of broadcast lessons in geography teaching.
13. A method of teaching geography to backward children (using a 40' x 24' map stencilled out on the floor of a school hall)
14. School journeys and camps.
15. Sources of supply of films and slides.'

From: J H Stembridge & H Milford (eds), A demonstration in the teaching of geography; published by Oxford University Press, 1934

'For the child , the study of geography has been made, in a way, as exciting an adventure as befell...those conquistadores who, coming upon new lands, gazed at each other with wild surmise. There is no royal road to learning, it is true, but this exhibition indicates a pleasurable road and one that has evidently been traversed by teachers and pupils in no perfunctory or otiose spirit'.
**Editorial about the exhibition in the Birmingham Post,
July 14th 1933**

'Geography, taught as a humanistic science, as a complete study of 'the home of mankind'...is of such fundamental importance to this great mercantile nation, as well of such primary importance in the general cultural education of its people, that this demonstration of progress in its teaching deserves the widest publicity and recognition'.
**Sir Francis Goodenough, in a letter about the exhibition to
THE TIMES , July 1933**

Figure 6.9:
Extracts about Staffordshire Geographical Exhibition of 1933

A PORTRAIT OF A GEOGRAPHY TEACHER IN THE INTER-WAR YEARS

'Colonel Jameson, as he was known to hundreds of Carthusians, came to Charterhouse in 1919, and, because no doubt he was partly appointed for that purpose, assumed almost at once the command of the Corps, taking over at the same time, the headship of the Geography department. He made his mark in both capacities.

His originality as a teacher of Geography, his exquisite craftsmanship in the construction of solid contour models and his delicate skill in the drawing of plans and maps, made his classroom a wonder and a delight to schoolboys, and indeed to School Inspectors.

Never was there a man with so many fascinating hobbies, most of them requiring meticulously neat work with his hands. His lantern slides (and being somewhat of an expert of military and naval history he had a large collection illustrating most of the battles and campaigns in our history), his sand-table models in Armoury, his water-colour sketches and his model ships were miracles of accurate and loving workmanship...he achieved his success not because he was a martinet, but because he managed to infect others with his own enthusiasm and because his invariably kind and gentle manner, in some strange way, gave him perfect control...'

From *The Carthusian*, June 1956
(the magazine of Charterhouse)
'H P Jameson: Obituary'

---

the stamp-album serving 'as a minature geographical world-exhibition for the child' ... the stamp album becomes a kind of orientation chart pictured with essences, each place characterised and categorised, great distances spanned in the imagination yet always sustained by their layout on an accompanying map, the exotic brought home with its difference essentially preserved.[77]

Sometimes the geographical work achieved in schools itself spilled out into the public domain. There were 'geographical exhibitions' mounted by schools or by local educational authorities, in several parts of Britain in the 1930s.[78] One of the most notable was the Staffordshire Geographical Exhibition (see Figure 6.9) which attracted national interest, and which arose from the projects done by children and from innovative teaching initiatives which were thought deserving of a wider audience.

Figure 6.10:
Illustrations of geographical matter in cartophily,
and geography in philately

CLOUDS DESCENDING

The many who passed time in school and leisure in vigorous enjoyment of the sunny outdoors could not hide the fact that dark political clouds were looming in the later part of the 1930s. Following the rude shock of the Depression and the collapse in world trade that had brought in a National Coalition Government to rescue the country's ailing economic fortunes in 1931, there were now ominous international developments.

As Mosley's Blackshirts gained prominence in the East End of London, Hitler was assuming power and developing the panoply and the territorial ambitions of the Third Reich. The optimism of 1919 and Versailles seemed a world away. Britain (and other nations also) seemed to want to avert its gaze from what was happening; the relief over Chamberlain's return from Munich waving a piece of paper in his hand was a straw-clutching exercise; Europe tumbled unhappily and reluctantly into war.

The effect on geography teaching was curious. Several GA Annual Reports of the period echo that of 1936. A drop in membership over the year is ascribed to the fact that 'the increased difficulties of international co-operation in public life have reacted upon the teaching of geography in schools', presumably making the presumption that geography had no appeal when what could be studied was in the grip of malevolent forces. At any rate, there seemed little desire for general educational or curriculum reform in the years immediately before the war.

Rather, it was a time when teachers consolidated what they had. Geography, was by now reasonably well-established in the grammar schools at secondary level to supplement its strong presence in elementary education. It was, by reputation, a pleasant and motivating subject, enlivened by the enjoyment of film, radio and periodic field-study trips – but still a little lacking in intellectual fibre at the highest level. 'Bright children' liked geography in their younger days, but, as they got older, they were still wont to give it up for the more exacting pastimes of experiments in the chemistry lab or literary analysis of Shakespeare.

NOTES

1. Though today we think of primary/preparatory and secondary schools as successive chronological stages of schooling, it should be noted that in the 1920s the term 'elementary' was still being used in a qualitative rather than a stage-oriented way. The Hadow Report on The Education of the Adolescent (1926) recommended the establishment of separate primary and secondary education for all pupils (with secondary 'central' schools catering for those who might leave at 14) but the implementation of this did not fully take place until 1944 and both the name and the fact of 'elementary schools' survived in some areas until then.

2. Report of the Consultative Committee on the Education of the Adolescent (Hadow Report) (HMSO, London, 1926).

3. See J. Kamm, *Hope Deferred* (Methuen, London, 1965); J. Kamm, *Indicative Past* (Girls Public Day School Trust, 1982); I. M. Lilley, *Maria Grey College, 1878–1976* (published by

Maria Grey College, Twickenham, 1981). Maria Grey College is now part of the School of Education, Brunel University.

4. In spite of long-term support for this idea from government, as the twenty-first century dawns, the idea of a General Teaching Council is only just being implemented for the teaching profession.

5. R. C. Honeybone, 'James Fairgrieve', in T. W. Freeman and P. Pinchemel (eds), *Geographers: Biobibliographical Studies*, vol. 8 (Mansell, London, 1984), pp. 27–34. See also N. V. Scarfe 'James Fairgrieve 1870–1953; pioneer geographical educationalist', in W. E. Marsden (ed.), *Historical Perspectives on Geographical Education* (University of London Institute of Education, London, 1980).

6. J. H. Fairgrieve, *Geography in School* (University of London Press, London, 1926).

7. As representative of earlier books written in this sphere see, Archibald Geikie, *The Teaching of Geography in Elementary Schools* (Macmillan, London, 1887); R. L. Archer, W. J. Lewis and A. E. Chapman, *The Teaching of Geography in Elementary Schools* (Black, London, 1910); W. P. Welpton, *The Teaching of Geography* (University Tutorial Press, London, 1923). Fairgrieve lists ten previous books on geography teaching in his bibliography, p. 349.

8. Jeffrey Richards, *The Age of the Dream Palace* (Routledge & Kegan Paul, London, 1984).

9. F. Hardy, *John Grierson: A Documentary Biography* (Faber & Faber, London, 1979).

10. Some critics of the genre think that the films, chasing memorable images, were prone to romanticise working life at the expense of the exploration of social and industrial problems.

11. Among the better-known of the other films which linked to work done in geography classrooms were *Weather Forecast* (1934), *Song of Ceylon* (1934), *Coal Face* (1935) and *North Sea* (1938). Later Shell Oil took on the role of sponsor to many similar documentary films, with geographical links.

12. Quoted in A. Knight, *The Liveliest Art* (Mentor Books, New York, 1957), p. 211. See also 'Propaganda and education', in J. Grierson, *Grierson on Documentary* (Faber & Faber, London, 1946).

13. Knight, *The Liveliest Art*.

14. The GA maintained both book and lantern slide libraries for use by teachers until after the Second World War. In December 1930, the GA library had 3,900 books and 2,744 lantern slides available for use.

15. The epidiascope, now rarely seen except as a museum piece, was a popular piece of apparatus for over eighty years. Books or illustrations could be placed under its lens and the pages or pictures projected on to a screen. Its drawback was that it was too large and bulky to be moved easily and therefore had to be kept in situ, and that rooms needed total blackout to see the image clearly. These days the advent of photocopying and the provision of multiple copies of books and sheets of source material for individual study has largely obviated its use.

16. A. Briggs, *The History of Broadcasting in the United Kingdom* (five volumes) (Oxford University Press, Oxford, 1961; 2nd edn, 1965).

17. K. V. Bailey, *The Listening Schools* (British Broadcasting Corporation, London, 1957).

18. Professor Bill Marsden has drawn my attention to an article in the 18 June 1936 edition of *The Schoolmaster and Women Teacher's Chronicle* by 'Kritikos' titled 'Two geography talks contrasted'. Talks by Ernest Young and James Fairgrieve are considered and Fairgrieve's pace of delivery and use of unnecessarily specialist vocabulary in a talk about Norweigan fiords is roundly criticised.

19. Quoted in T. W. Freeman, *A Hundred Years of Geography* (Methuen, London, 1965), p. 19.

20. D. Brunsden, 'The science of the unknown', *Geography*, 316, 72 (3) (1987), pp. 193–208.

21. W. E. Marsden, 'The School Journey Movement to 1940', *Journal of Educational Administration and History*, 30 (2) (1998) pp. 79–95.

22. Joan B. Reynolds, 'Class excursions in Wales and England', *The Geographical Teacher*, 1 (1) (1901), pp. 32–6.

23. J. H. Cowham, *The School Journey: A Means of Teaching Geography, Physiography and Elementary Science* (Westminster School Book Depot, London, 1900).

24. H. Meller, *Patrick Geddes: Social Evolutionist and City Planner* (Routledge, London, 1990). See also W. Iain Stevenson, 'Patrick Geddes', in T. W. Freeman and P. Pinchemel (eds), *Geographers: Biobibliographical Studies*, vol. 2 (Mansell, London, 1978), pp. 53–65.

25. D. R. Stoddart, *On Geography and its History* (Blackwell, Oxford, 1986), p. 144.

26. D. Matless, 'Regional surveys and local knowledges: the geographical imagination in Britain 1918–39', *Transactions of the Institute of British Geographers*, 17 (4) (1992), pp. 464–80.

27. A. Defries, *The Interpreter Geddes: The Man and His Gospel* (Routledge, London, 1927).

28. F. Le Play's original thoughts are to be found in *Les Ouvriers Europeans* (1855), but this book has never been translated into English. His ideas are most easily accessed in *Frederic Le Play on Family, Work and Social Change*, ed., trans. and with a substantial Introduction C. B. Silver (University of Chicago Press, Chicago, IL, 1982).

29. S. H. Beaver, 'The Le Play Society and fieldwork', *Geography*, 47 (1962), pp. 226–39. Though the Society was not founded until 1930, tours were organised by Le Play House from 1920 onwards. The Geographical Field Group was an offshoot of the Le Play Society and still survives. Other aspects of The Le Play Society's work were taken on by the Sociological Association. One member of the society, Professor Frederick Soddy, a somewhat solitary Nobel laureate in Chemistry, gained much solace and enjoyment from Le Play tours and at his death founded a charitable trust to further the study of regional survey. As the twenty-first century begins, the Frederick Soddy Trust is still active in providing grants to schools whose field-work is in the spirit of Le Play approaches.

30. E. E. Field, 'The Land Utilisation Map of Northampton', *Geography*, 15 (5) (1930), pp. 408–12.

31. See L. D. Stamp, *The Land of Britain: Its Use and Misuse* (Longman, London, 1948). For a definitive account and assessment of Stamp's contribution to many areas of geography see: Michael J. Wise, 'Laurence Dudley Stamp', in T. W. Freeman (ed.), *Geographers: Biobibliographical Studies*, vol. 12 (Mansell, London, 1988), pp. 175–87.

32. E. C. Willatts contributed his reminiscences of the survey in Chapter 17 of R. Walford, *Land Use–UK: A Survey for the Twenty-First Century* (Geographical Association, Sheffield, 1996).

33. When preparing material in 1995 and 1996 for a survey similar to Stamp's, I met a great number of people who could recall their land-use survey experiences of the 1930s as pupils in photographic detail, and who recounted them with evident satisfaction and nostalgia.

34. S. Rycroft and D. Cosgrove, 'Mapping the modern nation: Dudley Stamp and the Land Utilisation Survey', *History Workshop Journal*, 40 (1995).

35. L. D. Stamp, *The World* (Longman, London, 1929). The book continued in print through to the nineteenth edition (revised by Audrey Clark), published in 1977. It has become the fashion to dismiss Stamp's textbooks as 'curriculum fodder' but David Stoddart, one of the most eminent twentieth-century geographers, recalls, 'I can still recall the pleasure and stirrings of imagination provoked by reading of Nigeria and New Zealand in Stamp's, *Intermediate Geography* when I was a boy' (*On Geography*, p. 50).

    Besides being the first geographical author to write a million-seller single text Stamp also has the distinction of being (so far) the only professional geographer to appear on the long-running weekly BBC radio programme, *Desert Island Discs*. However, his choice of records in 1963 was not geographically distinguished, apart from The Blue Danube Waltz and Bali Ha'i from 'South Pacific'; his chosen book luxury was *Everyman's Encyclopaedia*.

36. The memoirs for each county of Britain were published by Geographical Publications, the publishing company Stamp himself set up and financed.

37. For two contemporary articles on the survey see those written by E. C. Willatts, *Teachers' World*, in the issues of 8 May 1935, pp. 193 and 225 and 22 May 1935, pp. 287 and 297. The 8 May article forms the front page of the magazine and is given multiple headlines: 'Schoolchildren's great gift to the nation: every acre of Britain surveyed and mapped in four years. School cartographers' triumph vindicates modern education.' The 22 May article is headlined 'The Children's Survey of Britain – how the Land Utilisation Survey maps will help schools. E. C. Willatts, B.Sc., continues his story of the children's triumph'. The story of the survey and a summary of the work is found in L. D. Stamp, *The Land of Britain*. A contemporary evaluation of the work is made in D. Cosgrove and S. Rycroft, 'Mapping the Modern Nation', and, by the same authors, 'The Stamp of an idealist', *Geographical Magazine*, October (1994), pp. 36–9.

38. A. Coleman 'Land use planning; success or failure?', *The Architects Journal*, special issue on 'The use and misuse of our national land resources', 19 January 1977, pp. 94–134.

39. A. Coleman, 'Is planning really necessary?', *Geographical Journal*, 142 (3) (1976),

pp. 411–30 and subsequent 'Discussion', pp. 430–7.

40. For a full account of the genesis, process and results of the 1996 survey see R. Walford, *Land Use–UK*. The book also contains retrospects of the first and second Land Utilisation Surveys.

41. See M. Robertson and R. Walford, 'Views and visions of Land Use in the United Kingdom', *Geographical Journal*, September (2000), pp. 239–54. R. Walford and D. Cooper, 'Views and visions', *Primary Geographer*, July (1999). M. Robertson, 'Young people speak about the landscape', *Geography*, 85 (1) (2000), pp. 24–36.

42. Teresa Ploszajska, 'Down to earth? Geography fieldwork in English schools 1870–1944', *Environment and Planning D: Society and Space*, 16 (1998), pp. 757–74, argues, however, that 'fieldwork was more highly valued for its social, moral and civic benefits, rather than for its contribution to geographical education, narrowly defined'.

43. C. Simpson, *The Study of Local Geography* (Methuen, London, 1930); C. C. Fagg and G. E. Hutchings, *An Introduction to Regional Surveying* (Cambridge University Press, Cambridge, 1930). The heart of Hutchings' work is encapsulated in a later article: G. E. Hutchings, 'Geographical field teaching', *Geography*, 47 (1) (1962), pp. 1–14. For biographical detail see W. G. V. Balchin, 'S. W. Wooldridge', in T. W. Freeman and P. Pinchemel (eds), *Geographers: Biobibliographical Studies*, vol. 8 (Mansell, London, 1984), pp. 141–9; Keith Wheeler, 'G. E. Hutchings', in T. W. Freeman and P. Pinchemel (eds), *Geographers: Biobibliographical Studies*, vol. 2 (Mansell, London, 1978), pp. 67–71.

44. S. W. Wooldridge, 'The status of geography and the role of fieldwork', *Geography*, 40 (2) (1955), pp. 73–83.

45. S. W. Wooldridge and E. Goldring, *The Weald* (Collins, London, 1953). Goldring's contribution was largely photographic.

46. S. W. Wooldridge and G. E. Hutchings, *London's Countryside* (Batsford, London, 1957).

47. D. Matless, 'Visual culture and geographical citizenship in England in the 1940s', *Journal of Historical Geography*, 22 (1996) pp. 434–9.

48. Quoted in R. Walford, *A Contemporary Geography of Britain* (Longman, London, 1993), p. 84.

49. A. Ransome, *Coot Club* (Jonathan Cape, London, 1934). Most of Ransome's other children's stories, including *Swallows and Amazons*, contain episodes with similar implications.

50. J. A. Steers, 'The coastline of England and Wales', *Geographical Journal*, 1944, pp. 7–27.

51. A. Goudie, 'Vaughan Cornish', *Transactions of Institute of British Geographers*, 1972, pp. 1–16. See also, Brian Waites, 'Vaughan Cornish', in T. W. Freeman and P. Pinchemel (eds), *Geographers: Biobibliographical Studies*, vol. 9 (Mansell, London, 1985), pp. 29–35.

52. V. Cornish, 'Harmonies of society', *Geography*, 14 (1928), pp. 275–83.

53. V. Cornish, 'The science of scenery', *Nature*, 121 (1928), pp. 309–31.

54. I. Cameron, *To the Farthest Ends of the Earth* (Macdonald, London, 1980), pp. 204–5.

55. When Fleure was elected a Fellow of the Royal Society in 1936, there was an irony in that Hinks was the only other geographer FRS at the time.

56. Fleure included reminiscences about his time as Honorary Secretary of the GA in 'Sixty years of geography and education; a retrospect of the Geographical Association', *Geography* 182(4) (1953), pp. 231–64. For biographical detail see T. W. Freeman, 'H. J. Fleure', in T. W. Freeman (ed.), *Geographers: Biobibliographical Studies*, Vol. 11 (Mansell, London, 1987), pp. 35–51.

57. This episode is chronicled in W. G. V. Balchin, *The Geographical Association: The First Hundred Years, 1893–1993* (Geographical Association, Sheffield, 1993), a history of the GA which provides much other detail about the affairs of the Association.

58. Avril Maddrell, 'Discourses of race and gender and the comparative methods in geography school texts 1830–1918', *Environment and Planning D: Society and Space*, 16 (1998), pp. 81–103; R. Phillips, *Mapping Men and Empire: A Geography of Adventure* (Routledge, London, 1997).

59. E. Blyton, General Editor's Foreword to volume II of the *Modern Teaching* series; *Geography* by R. J. Finch, 1924.

60. See, for instance, 'The flappers come of age', pp. 49–50. D. Porter *et al.*, *Yesterday's Britain* (Reader's Digest, London, 1998), pp. 49–50. In the accompanying picture two young

women, dashingly dressed, have stopped their motor-cycles at the roadside for a cigarette.

61. Amy Johnson, a 26-year-old typist, flew solo from England to Australia in a tiny D. H. Tiger Moth in 1930 – see C. Babington-Smith, *Amy Johnson* (Patrick Stephens, Cambridge, 1988); Fay Taylour competed as an equal against men in the early days of 'dirt-track racing' at High Beech and Belle Vue, Manchester – see M. Rogers, *The Illustrated History of Speedway Racing* (Studio Publications, London, 1978), pp. 13–14, and p. 117.

62. Marjorie Hessell Tiltman, *Women in Modern Adventure* (Heinemann, London, 1935).

63. See Kirsten Drotner, *English Children and Their Magazines, 1751–1945* (Yale University Press, New Haven, CT, 1988), especially chapter 13; Mary Cadogan and Patricia Craig, *You're a Brick, Angela!: The Girls Story, 1839–1985* (Gollancz, London, 1986).

64. David Matless, *Landscape and Englishness* (Reaktion Press, London, 1998).

65. The Field Studies Council currently administers a score of field centres in England and Wales; its headquarters is at Preston Montford, Shropshire.

66. H. C. Wilks, 'A scheme of fieldwork throughout a school', *Geography*, 41 (1) (1956), pp. 15–24 and in *Geography*, 41 (2) (1956), pp. 108–13.

67. Rose B. Clark, 'Geography in the schools of Europe', *Journal of Geography*, 35 (1935), pp. 67–77.

68. IAAM *Memorandum on the Teaching of Geography* (Incorporated Association of Assistant Masters, 1935).

69. The public collation of overall national examination statistics is comparatively recent; currently the task is undertaken by the Qualifications and Curriculum Authority (QCA). Past statistics have to be disinterred from the record of individual examination boards, most of whom have been submerged in larger groupings in the last decade.

70. Fairgrieve, *Geography in Schools*, pp. 342–8.

71. V. C. Spary, *The Modern Geography Room* (George Philip, London, 1932).

72. In relation to scouting see, essentially, R. Baden-Powell, *Scouting for Boys* (Scout Association, first published 1908, with many editions since) but also E. E. Reynolds, *The Scout Movement* (Oxford University Press, Oxford, 1950). Tim Jeal's lengthy biography of the Chief Scout, *Baden-Powell* (Hutchinson, London, 1989) contains a balanced account of some scouting issues in Chapters 9–16. The Scouts reached a peak membership of 472,000 in 1933.

The Guide Movement is chronicled in Alix Liddell, *The Girl Guides 1910–75* (Girl Guides' Association, London, 1976); O. Baden-Powell, *Window on my Heart* (Hodder & Stoughton, London, 1972). The Guides also reached a membership of nearly half a million at some stages in the 1930s.

J. Springhall's, *Youth, Empire and Society: British Youth Movements 1883–1940* (Croom Helm, London, 1977) provides some basic data and framework on the many youth organisations which flourished in this period, but self-confessedly does not explore the environmental perspective in any detail.

Other youth movements with strong environmental emphases founded in this period included the shortlived Order of Woodcraft Chivalry and the Kibbo Kift Kindred (see Springhall, *Youth, Empire and Society*). The Woodcraft Folk, also founded in the 1920s, have proved more durable. See especially, Leslie Paul, *Angry Young Man* (Faber & Faber, London, 1951), Chapter 3.

Less environmentally linked at this time, but nevertheless enthusiastic organisers of summer camps and outdoor activities and with substantial memberships in the inter-war period were: The Boys' Brigade, the Girls' Life Brigade, The Girls' Guildry, The Church Lads' Brigade, The Church Girls' Brigade, the Jewish Lads' and Girls' Brigade.

For the history of the Boys' Brigade (BB) see J. Springhall, *Sure and Steadfast* (Collins, 1983, 1991). The BB reached a peak of almost 100,000 members in 1934.

For the history of the Girls' Life Brigade (GLB), see E. M. Want, *The Rays Outspringing*, vols 1 and 2 (Girls' Life Brigade, London, 1951, 1961). The Girls' Life Brigade, the Girls' Guildry (mainly strong in Scotland) and the Girls' Life Brigade (Ireland) merged to form the Girls' Brigade in 1965. Their current membership is over 30,000. The GLB alone reached a peak membership of over 60,000 in the mid-1930s; the Girls' Guildry had a membership of about 25,000 in 1939.

For the history of the Jewish Lads' and Girls' Brigade see S. Kadish, *A Good Jew and a*

Good Englishman (Vallentine Mitchell, London, 1995).

73. See F. Driver, 'Moral geographies; social science, and the urban environment in nineteenth-century England', *Transactions on the Institute of British Geographrs* (1988), pp. 275–87; D. Matless, 'Moral geography in Broadland', *Ecumene*, 1(2) (1994), pp. 127–55.

74. For insights into the history of cigarette-card collecting (cartophily) see London Cigarette Card Company. *The Complete Catalogue of British Cigarette Cards* (Webb and Bower, London, 1981); issues of *Cartophilic Notes and News*; annual catalogues of card values produced by Murray Cards (International) Ltd.

75. For insights into the history of stamp-collecting (philately) see Bill Gunston, *The Philatelist's Companion* (David and Charles, London, 1975); Hunter Davies, *The Joy of Stamps* (Robson, London, 1984); J. Holman, *The Stanley Gibbons Guide to Stamp Collecting* (Stanley Gibbons, London, 1989). See also L. D. Stamp, 'Philatelic cartography', *Geography*, 51(3) (1966), pp. 179–97.

76. H. C. Barnard, *Principles and Practice of Geography Teaching* (University Tutorial Press, London, 1948).

77. Matless, 'Regional surveys and local knowledges'.

78. See also Ploszajska's account of an exhibition of results from the field-work of Dulwich Central School at the South London Art Gallery in 1938 in 'Down to earth?'

7

Regions and the Road to Ennui, 1940–60

WARTIME

'War depends on three things – good administration, good morale and geography – but the most important of these, I think, is geography', said Field Marshal Montgomery of Alamein, Britain's most famous commander of the 1940s.

In the Second World War (1939–45), as in the First World War (1914–18), geography became a prime topic of interest and concern as the ebb and flow of battle preoccupied the nation. Popular newspapers and magazines printed prominent maps in their columns day by day – on Monday, it might be a representation of the breaching of the Maginot Line, on Tuesday a map to show the sinking of a U-boat in the Atlantic, on Wednesday a contextual illustration of some far-off battle field on which little publicity had so far been expended. Lines and arrows showed directions of flow; myriads of symbols represented supposed troop concentrations or air bases; different gradations of shading showed if territory had been lost or won in the recent past. The question of terrain became significant; a generation pored and puzzled over the maps with interest, and sometimes with agony or delight.

Max Beloff, at the time one of the nation's leading historians, writing later of the Battle of Britain, echoed Montgomery's judgement about geography:

> I find it natural to think of the problem of war in Europe as one of transition between different territorial settlements and of the respective strengths and weaknesses of the expansionist and status quo powers at any given juncture. Physical and human geography are the keys.[1]

So in schools, the importance of learning geography (or at least certain parts of geography) again became self-evident. Geography teachers sometimes gained an enhanced reputation as they explained to their colleagues or to their pupils the geographical ramifications of the stand at El Alamein, the siege of Tobruk or the storming of Monte Cassino.

These teachers were the older generation; the younger ones had been called up long ago and were doing their bit at the front or (in the case of some academic geographers) in various vital intelligence roles, where the practical use of their knowledge was being vindicated.[2]

THE GEOGRAPHICAL ASSOCIATION IN WARTIME

Membership of the Geographical Association dropped as teachers enrolled in the forces, but the Association valiantly kept its publications and annual conference going, even though the latter was forced out of London by the bombing. In 1942 it found itself at Exeter, narrowly missing Hitler's 'Baedaker' raids on the city.[3]

There, the conference had, as its opening contribution, a provocative address from the principal of the University College of the South-West, Professor John Murray. Murray, a noted classicist, took the opportunity to poke a little fun at geography, whilst innocently disclaiming much knowledge of the subject:

> I have sought to discover, from likely persons, what geography – up-to-date geography – is and what it aims at. These persons became instantly embarrassed! I was told of Human Geography and Physical Geography and Historical Geography and, rather more vaguely of Economic Geography, and still more vaguely of Social Geography. I was even told that geography was Regional Psychology.
>
> Many geographies, but no Geography? The magisterial element of geography has had to yield, apparently, under the democratic egalitarian pressure of 'the geographies' ... this is a gathering of orphans.[4]

Mackinder, still active in GA affairs at the age of 82, was scheduled to give the following address and was immediately at pains to respond to Murray's barbs, off-the-cuff:

> Is not Dr Murray's address a challenge to geographers to make more evident to the educational public what it is that geography aims at doing? ... Would it not be well to come to some understanding among ourselves as to the relationship of our specialisms to the technique and philosophy of the subject as a whole?

Mackinder defended specialist geographies by pointing out that tasks of analysis had to be achieved before the synthesis of patterns could be developed. But he claimed that geography itself, in its unified form, was an 'art of expression' of the highest kind:

> It culls its data from the geographical aspect of a number of sciences ... it integrates its conclusions from the human standpoint, and so

departs from the objectivity of science, for it ranges values alongside of measured facts. Hence 'outlook' is its characteristic – it is a philosophy of Man's environment.[5]

This rather tendentious justification for the subject reveals a recurring problem for geography in the first 50 years of the twentieth century; the need to find a coherent way of expressing the synthesising objectives of geography as a field of study without being seen to be essentially hybrid or else grotesquely overbearing in the claims made. This afflicted university geographers more than schools, but the backwash of the argument seeped down into secondary education, where, in its less attractive manifestations, geography was often accused of being little more than a large rag-bag of content. The desire to link physical and human science together in explaining landscapes and societies created methodological puzzlements; the inclusion of 'values' as an aim, as Mackinder attempts here, created even more suspicion amongst traditionalists.

The attempt to state the synthesising qualities of geographical analysis was losing some credibility at this time, because the argument had historically depended on deterministic premises (about the way in which the physical characteristics of the land 'controlled' or 'influenced' agricultural practice, industrial activity, the location of towns, etc.) and these premises were being visibly eroded. It would need the discovery of a new potential binding force of overall spatial geometries to revive it.

In spite of this (or perhaps because of it?) there have been increasing fissiparous tendencies in higher education from the 1950s onwards, as academic geographers have multiplied, sought their own distinctive niches and developed their specialisms. One trenchant critic of this tendency has been David Stoddart, who offered a warning of the perils of disunity whilst giving the Carl Sauer Memorial Lecture in 1986, asserting that geography should take the 'high ground'

> too many of our colleagues have either abandoned or failed to recognise what I take to be our subject's central intent and indeed self-evident role in the community of knowledge.[6]

The editor of *Transactions* (Britain's most prestigious academic geography journal) was similarly concerned in his valedictory editorial a year later, re-casting the famous Yeatsian epigram to 'Can the centre hold?' as a title for it:

> the subject will flourish if it can demonstrate that it has a commonly agreed core or centre (and that core must include both physical and human geography), that it does straddle the sciences and the humanities, and that it is (can be?) about the interplay between those two great facts of existence.[7]

Another published 'Comment' in *Transactions* around that time noted that there was an invisible thread between the intellectual preoccupations of academe and school life:

> Can we now usefully ask of ourselves and of our somewhat fragmented discipline 'Whither the geography of today and tomorrow?'. For surely on the answer to this question will depend decision-making regarding the educational value and popularity of our subject in schools and its role as a university discipline and in other institutions of higher education. As geographers today probe and strive to expand our frontiers further and further, would our answers now be too disparate to command attention?[8]

The reference to the contemporary disparate nature of geography has some poignancy. These were the last published words of Professor Alice Garnett who had spent most of her life, beyond her duties in the University of Sheffield, in working tirelessly for the Geographical Association. She succeeded H. J. Fleure as its Honorary Secretary in 1947 and was the GA's gentle and genial guiding light for 20 years. She, more than most, understood the mid-century struggle to make geography a coherent, acceptable and widely available subject in schools and the impact that university-led preoccupations might have.

THE 1944 EDUCATION ACT

Even before the end of the Second World War, government thinking had turned towards 'the broad sunlit uplands' of reconstruction. Fresh thinking about the education system formed part of the plans. The 1944 Education Act, initiated by R. A. Butler, was a far-reaching attempt to put in place a new education system fit for post-war Britain. Working from the recommendations of the pre-war Spens Report (1938)[9] and what was then the apparent certainty of psychological data, Butler was persuaded that children could be examined at 11 and allocated to different kinds of schools as best fitted their needs.

The key decision was that there should be separate secondary education for all, with children moving on from elementary (now to be called primary) schools. A tripartite system of grammar, technical and secondary-modern schools would be set-up with an '11-plus' examination identifying which kind of school a child should be sent to. A government propaganda film of the time[10] which was made to expound the idea to the public has a cheery optimism and a wonderful naievety about the ability of the tests to make the right decision; only belatedly was it realised that an 'off-day' at examination time might blight a child's life chances and that separation in schooling would also breed resentment and division in an increasingly egalitarian-minded society.

The three kinds of schools were (notionally) to have 'parity of esteem' though they would follow different kinds of curricula. Once again, however, the government stopped short of making any pronounce-ments about the curriculum; only a form of worship was made a statutory requirement.[11]

The Changing Place of Geography in the School Curriculum of England and Wales 1950–1992

Post 1945 – Fewer specialist teachers in 5–11 schools

1964 onwards – 'Madingley' conferences
1967 – Plowden Report encourages more 'topic work' in primary schools

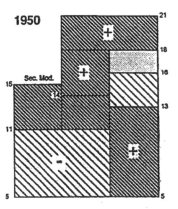

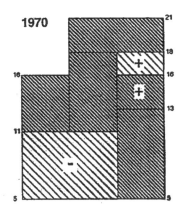

1970/80s – Greater emphasis on topic work, 'humanities' and process-dominated learning.

1991 – Geography National Curriculum introduced into schools, following Reform Act (1988)

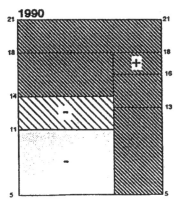

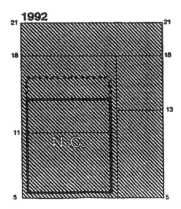

Figure 7.1:
The changing place of geography in British schools
(*Source*: author)

137

George Tomlinson, gritty Yorkshire Minister of Education in the post-war Labour government which replaced Churchill's wartime administration, once notably said in the House of Commons 'Minister knows nowt about curriculum' in response to a Parliamentary question. He meant, of course, not that he was ignorant of it, but that it was none of his business. It would remain not so for only a few years longer.

THE STATE OF THE SCHOOLS – PRIMARY

What was the general health and nature of geographical education in British schools in the war years and after? Viewed merely from the perspective of 'presence' it was not doing at all badly (see Figure 7.1).

In most primary schools there was a weekly period of geography on the timetable. In the junior section (7–11 years) it was likely that a book such as Archer and Thomas's First Series Geography would be used.[12] This was a popular series, first published in 1936, in which stories of the lives of particular children were used to characterise the life of a region. The teacher would read the story (or have pupils read it aloud around the class) and then the pupils would be encouraged to draw a picture related to the story and perhaps make some notes. The famous opening chapter of book 1 of Archer and Thomas was of 'Bombo of the Congo', a Pygmy boy who lived a simple life in an African village. Subsequent chapters dealt with 'Tooktoo the Eskimo', 'Hirfa the Bedouin girl', 'Pedro the South American Indian', 'Ahmad the Egyptian boy' and 'Roshil the Bengali'.

There are 11 pages about Hirfa, and 19 photographs and sketches of Bedouin life, as well as six 'activity' sections which include questions and imaginative exercises (see the sample section in Figure 7.2).

By now the judgemental approach to Bedouin life and morality which characterised eighteenth- and nineteenth-century geography books has been replaced by an altogether more empathetic approach. However, Hirfa's family's economic circumstances are not alluded to; she is presented as a girl content with her lot, who likes to go occasionally into the town to see the shops but who is 'so happy living in the desert that she would not like to live anywhere else'.

'Bombo of the Congo' was later to be regularly ridiculed for a time as a token image of a primary geography rooted in the rural, the picturesque and the essentially antique, but in fact the series went on to deal with more complex environmental relationships and more developed societies. By book 4 there were chapters about Tokyo, Pittsburgh and Calcutta, albeit the cities were dealt with in a fairly sanitised way. In post-war editions (the books were still reprinting 20 years after they were first published) there are also oblique allusions to the effects of the Second World War on Europe, though no indication given of why the war was fought or at what cost in human life. Lifestyles were explained as linked to different physical environments in a moderately deterministic way (entirely in tune with the academic

HIRFA

Each tent in the Bedouin camp is the home of one family

Hirfa's father builds a little fire of dry twigs on the ground outside the tent. Then he makes coffee in a copper coffee-pot. Hirfa runs into the tent, and brings out a jug of camel's milk and a bowl of dried dates. Her mother brings out two kinds of cheese. One kind is made of camels' milk and the other kind of goats' milk.

If we stay with Hirfa's people for a while we shall find that all their meals are much alike. They live mostly on the milk of

their animals, and on the cheese that they make from the milk. Now and then they buy a few dates and a little coffee and flour at the towns in the desert.

Some things to do

1. Make a little paper model of a Bedouin camp in the desert.

2. Pretend that you are Hirfa talking to Tooktoo. Tell him why he could not travel on a dog sledge or in an umiak in the desert.

35

Figure 7.2:
Page from *Little People of Many Lands* by A. B. Archer and H. Thomas (*Source*: Ginn & Co.) (reduced size)

thinking of the times). Of imperialism there is scarcely a whiff through the four books. The attitude to other people had become more compassionate and the studies were now in greater depth, but the geographic textbook still only told half of the story.

Some teachers of under-11s also took their pupils out for local field-work projects and/or for a school journey at some stage during the year. These activities were encouraged through the training which many young primary school teachers received from teacher-training colleges, many of which had now embraced Froebelian ideas with enthusiasm.

One key institution of influence in this sphere was the Froebel Educational Institute at Roehampton and the senior geography teacher-trainer there, Olive Garnett, (sister of Alice), produced the most significant and widely read book of the 1930s, 1940s and 1950s about teaching geography to young children. It challenged the dominant practice of 'telling stories' to younger children and advocated a vigorous, 'open-air' approach to geography with a stress on 'discovery learning'.

Garnett's *Foundations of School Geography*[13] was still in print and being used as a Bible of primary school practice in the 1960s and it was a world away from the factual and classroom-bound learning of some Victorian schools. Based on Froebel's philosophy that young children learn best by discovering things for themselves Garnett proposed schemes of work which took young children outside the classroom into their own school grounds and the lanes and streets beyond. The environment would provide the best learning-ground for an understanding of the world and the important thing was to stimulate the curiosity and wonder of young children, not stuff their heads full of factual material at too young an age.

> Children come to school full of a desire to know and learn about all manner of things. There is no necessity for the teacher to hunt round for topics to interest the children, for they bring quite enough with them. Yet, in the past, instead of satisfying a young child's hunger for knowledge concerning, for instance 'what the men are doing in the hole in the road' etc., a new subject is presented to him about which the teacher knows something (admittedly a very little) – 'Children in Other Lands'!

> The child may be interested in this up to a point – he is interested in almost everything that comes his way (if it is to some extent within his grasp) and especially in stories. But his curiosity concerning the real things about which he wanted to know remains to be satisfied, if at all, outside school, which is a pity.

Texts like these were influential in radically changing the nature of learning for the under-11s, but they also incidentally loosened the grip of subjects in the elementary school timetable. In the minds of the disciples of Froebel and Pestalozzi, learning was a seamless robe, and the codification of material into separate disciplines an unnecessary, or at least an unimportant task. What grew up in primary schools, to reach its zenith in the Plowden Report of the 1960s was a view of the curriculum in which all things merged into each other – the 'integrated day' was to become the Holy Grail of primary education for a time and the emphasis shifted from product to process. As in Tom Lehrer's wondering comment about 'new math', 'The important thing was to understand what you were doing rather than to get the right answer.'

The system flowered creatively and wonderfully as an idea –– the theory was that topics were to blend with one another, the rhythm of the school day would be flexibly tuned to the motivational span of particular tasks, the cross-curricular links of all things would be exploited – and the ultimate justification was that the 'real world' did not take account of subject boundaries. This worked successfully when handled by experienced and expert teachers. The problem, as it later turned out, was that in the hands of less skilled practitioners the system also allowed curriculum mayhem, with some essential components of knowledge and skills rarely visited, and with some children quite at sea in an apparent jumble of projects.

THE SECONDARY SCHOOL

At the secondary level, geography was making its way forward in the grammar and the central schools, aided by the development of the circle of opportunity which now took some students on to university to study the subject in depth and then, frequently, back into schools to teach. Whereas in 1921 there had only been six professors of geography in universities, by 1937 there were 21, including those who headed flourishing schools of geography at both Oxford and Cambridge.

The subject did not yet, however, quite have the cachet of being a suitable subject of study for first-class brains. Many of those who went to university to read geography were seen by their colleagues to do so either because they were attracted by the 'outdoor life' of the subject (and likely to go on to jobs overseas or to be 'rolling stones') or because they had assessed the intellectual demands as not quite as great as those in older-established disciplines. Significantly, though geography flourished in the grammar school sixth forms of the land, it was not so strong in the independent schools and neither Eton nor Winchester had yet admitted geography to its examination curriculum in the upper school. (At Harrow, aided by the earlier interest of Viscountess Strangford, the subject had a stronger footing and the first group of upper school geography specialists took their exams in 1930.[14])

The reason for this was not that geography had no methodology (indeed, with its frequent reliance on visual aids, it was probably taught with a good deal more variety and liveliness than many of the more traditional subjects) but that its intellectual structure was seen as limited and lacking in development.

Herbertson's seminal paper on 'The natural regions of the world'[15] had opened up a classificatory framework for the subject as early as 1905, and provided a way of dealing with increasing amounts of information. Its principles had spread to the development of 'human regions' as teaching vehicles in schools, influenced by the academic writings of the French school of geography led by Vidal de la Blache, and later Brunhes and Febvre.[16] Both in physical and in human geography the regional approach reigned.

THE ROAD TO ENNUI

The road to regions was also the eventual road to ennui. Geography textbooks packaged and repackaged the world's information in a variety of regional ways and some authors became adept at working the material into examination-friendly forms; the acquisitive mind could gather information through assiduous study and careful memorisation; the addition of illustrative maps and diagrams provided refreshment to the wordy diet. But however elegantly shaped the regional description was, it could not disguise the fact that there seemed relatively little to excite the mind at higher levels, no in-depth study of issues or controversies, few tools of analysis or organising principles to supplement the eye of faith and the palimpsest of description. Or, if there were, they were predicated on such precarious evidence that only those internal to the subject took the debate seriously.

The study of the world was reduced to a repeated formula, which carried no progression, and which, in its conceptual scale, was not linked to the experience of pupils. And there grew to be serious geographical reservations as well as pedagogical ones. Why had Herbertson's criteria to regionalise the world by become such a 'gospel' of supposed geographical truth? (Perhaps, because it was such an outstanding event in its time – but now time had moved on.) The division of the world into natural regions took no account of the political realities and boundaries of the world – a key matter for the 1930s and 1940s – let alone the obliteration of the friction of distance through greater mobility. Perhaps most important of all, the later development of the regional approach to encompass human and economic activity suggested (at least implicitly) that physical environment controlled (or at least strongly influenced) human response; if geographers pursued this argument as a central tenet of study, its determinist cast would become increasingly difficult to sustain.

Of even more significance was the fact that regional study came to be seen as essentially a portrayal of a static view of the world – a way of presenting it in 'snapshot' terms. What was becoming increasingly apparent was that the world was a highly dynamic place and that to study the processes behind what was happening was as important as systematically laying out the pattern of things.

The promise of Stamp's land-use survey work as an example of the use of geography as an aid to citizenship was never quite realised in the 1940s and 1950s; what happened, through the distractions of war, was that the subject lapsed back into a refined version of 'Capes and bays' – a 'Cook's Tour' of the continents over five years of the secondary school curriculum. The Southern Continents (Africa, South America, Australia) were studied in the first year (on the premise that they were emptier and thus each able to be 'covered' in a term); in subsequent years there would be study of Asia, North America, Europe and the British Isles in a variety of combinations – but premised on the fact that the more developed a country was the more difficult it would be to understand. The complex, more developed parts of the world would come later in the progression of study, though the same regional approach was applied in each case.

Honeybone warned about the difficulties in a significant paper in 1954:

At one time there existed the much derided 'capes and bays'; at another what we might call 'economic capes and bays', lists of products related in the flimsiest ways to their environments; at another the pseudo-scientific 'capes and bays', the era of the isobars and the plantary wind system; and, at the present time, we seem to be over-emphasising the 'regional account capes and bays' ... do not let us delude ourselves that a regional account under the headings of Position, Relief, Climate, Natural Vegetation, Occupations, etc, necessarily represents a true geographical synthesis.[17]

The attraction of the regional curriculum frame was that pupils could be said to 'cover the world' if they stayed with geography over five years of study; the knowledge base was complete, if superficial. The drawback, however, was that no matter how carefully and elegantly the textbook writers packaged the material, by the time it reached the notebooks and the minds of 3C or 4X, it was scarcely more than a disjointed collection of phrases, some of which were idiosyncratically memorable for life ('jam-making in the Carse of Gowrie', 'short, sharp summers, and warm, wet winters' ..., etc.), others which were speedily confined to oblivion after the relevant examination had been taken. And the quick regional summaries of areas sped by, lesson by lesson, so that they often remained only as a blur in the mind.

THE TEXTBOOKS THAT EMPHASISED COVERAGE

The neat and efficient octavo-size series of texts of Thomas Pickles[18] and Preece and Wood[19] were best-sellers in the years which spanned the Second World War and its aftermath.[20] Designed for the 'School Certificate' forms of secondary schools, both of them were well-produced and illustrated with neat maps and diagrams (see Figure 7.3). They sought to offer concrete examples to supplement the factual knowledge which they represented but did so, not at length, but only with glancing sentence-long references, since they aimed to be comprehensive in their areal coverage. But, looking back on it, there seeems to have been little joy, wonder, imagination or stimulation in the geography. The shadow of what was examinable, as well as the economic gloom of the age had come to colour the aspirations and the nature of what was taught

Pickles explained his pragmatic aims in his preface for the series:

Within the limits imposed by such practical considerations as the number of school periods available, the age of the pupils, and the demands of the examinations, the attempt has been made to provide a survey of the geography of [...] which will not only be a workmanlike aid to preparation for the examinations in questions, but will also form the basis for intelligent appreciation of our social and economic problems.

143

The *Southern Railway* runs from Waterloo, Victoria, and London Bridge Stations, to Plymouth, Southampton, and all the chief ports and holiday resorts of the south coast, utilizing the dry gaps and river gaps in the North and South Downs (see Fig. 60).

Other towns of the London basin may be considered in

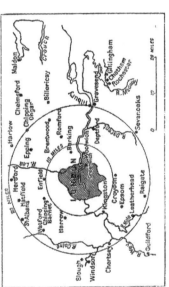

FIG. 69. LONDON AND ITS ENVIRONS
(Note the 10-mile and 20-mile circles)

relation to their manufacturing industries, which may be grouped as follows:

(1) Old-established industries which owe their origin to local supplies of raw material. *Luton*, for example, developed the straw-plaiting industry because in the locality a specially fine white straw was grown. The industry still survives though all the raw material is now imported, chiefly from China and Japan. *High Wycombe* has for long been famous as the centre of the chair-making industry. Originally the chairs were made by hand from the local beech wood, but

nowadays the industry is carried on chiefly in factories, and a large part of the timber is imported. It will be seen that the industries of these towns form excellent examples of the principle of industrial inertia (see p. 62). *Reading* has an old-established biscuit industry, which originally drew its supplies of flour from the locally grown wheat.

(2) Industries which still depend on local supplies of raw material. The chief of such industries is the manufacture of cement at Rochester and Gillingham, the materials used being chalk and mud dredged from the bed of the Medway.

(3) Modern industries which owe their origin to the supply of electrical power from the 'grid' system, the facilities for assembling raw materials, the proximity of the London market, the abundance of labour supply, and the comparatively low cost of land for factory sites. Most of these recently established industries specialize in products which are valuable in proportion to their bulk and to the amount of raw material which they contain, e.g. wireless sets, electrical apparatus, household utensils, prepared foods, etc. One of the most important of the new industrial centres in Greater London is *Slough*, two miles north-east of Windsor.

EXAMINATION QUESTIONS

1. Describe and account for the distribution of population *either* in the Humber basin (excluding the Trent) *or* in the Thames basin. A sketch-map should accompany your answer. (L. M., 1922.)

2. Where are the chief chalk belts of England, and how do you account for their existence? (L. M., 1920.)

3. Examine the land approaches to London *either* on the north side *or* on the south side. Indicate the natural features which have rendered these approaches suitable for railway building, and point out the importance of the various railways. (L. M., 1921.)

Figure 7.3:
Page from *The British Isles* by Thomas Pickles (1935) (*Source:* J.M. Dent & Co.) (reduced size)

In Pickles' 240-page book on *The British Isles*, East Anglia is covered in under three pages. There are five lines on rock type, 12 on coastal erosion and the Broads, 13 on farming. Mention of Cambridge has now shrunk to it being one in a list of towns which are said to be 'at the inland limit of the Fens, and at the former head of boat navigation on the rivers'.

A typical Pickles paragraph is as follows:

> *Norwich* grew up round a castle built on high ground near the confluence of the Wensum and the Yare. It is an agricultural market town and manufactures mustard, starch, boots and shoes, agricultural implements and traction engines.

Little sense either of being a historic 'fine city' or a large and influential regional centre is revealed in such a pedestrian description, let alone an indication of what life is like for the inhabitants or why they make what they do. It also appears that Pickles, perhaps through the overwhelming need to compress the text, has listed the prime manufactures of Norfolk rather than Norwich.

Preece and Wood (Book II: *The British Isles*), a book of 274 pages, does better, with five pages allocated to East Anglia. The description of Norwich is more extended:

> NORWICH. A city of Saxon origin, Norwich is situated on the River Wensum, near its confluence with the River Yare ... It was of early importance as a fortress and an ecclesiastical centre (it has a castle and a cathedral) and in the Middle Ages was an important river port, trading largely in wool. The convergence of river valleys gave Norwich a high degree of nodality, so that it became an important road, and later a railway, centre. This nodality gave it pre-eminence as a market town for the whole of the Norfolk region. It has a variety of industries, including the manufacture of agricultural implements, leather goods, and especially, footwear, fertilisers, mustard, starch, vinegar, beer, etc, all of which are connected with the agricultural activities of the region.

Both books show the same fact-filled, comprehensive, and inevitably superficial approach. This is what the study of geography, based on the regional coverage of the world in a school lifetime, had spawned.

This might have been acceptable when pupils were more easily motivated and at the acquisitive stage of development[21] but was less so as they matured and began to search for deeper meanings and principles in what they studied. It explained the comment of one public school headmaster of the time (which echoed Jowett's famous turn-of-the-century question, see Chapter 4), 'Geography – ah yes, an excellent subject, but best studied, I think by the younger boys ...'.

THE BEGINNINGS OF SAMPLE STUDIES

Some teachers and teacher-trainers were aware of the diminishing returns of the undiluted regional approach and cast around for ways to enrich and enliven it. One of the most active in this respect was Neville Scarfe, who had succeeded Fairgrieve at the London Institute in 1935. Scarfe was a dynamic and ebullient character, a real enthusiast for geography and particularly its supposed potential to develop international understanding. His personal charisma made him a powerful communicator at seminars and conferences and carried over into his ideas about what could be attempted in the classroom. In the 1940s and 1950s he propounded the value of the development of teaching 'sample studies' within regions so that pupils could be relieved of the burden of exhaustive regional information and, at the same time, interact more vividly with the lives of real people. G. M. Hickman and Scarfe's colleagues Roberson and Long wrote key articles to publicise and codify these ideas,[22] though the historical origins of them were much earlier.[23]

A 'sample study' would concentrate on providing the detail of a particular farm or factory or village and would usually be chosen for its ability to help the teacher to draw out the regional and national implications by working from the particular instance to the general situation.

In some ways this was to borrow from the primary schools, where Archer and Thomas' stories already offered a 'sample study' flavour and to develop more thoroughly the individual illustrative material which decorated some of the better textbooks of the inter-war period. Fairgrieve and Ernest Young had verged on the idea in their *Human Geography* series for secondary schools,[24] but their specific examples of the life of Siberian peasants or Ceylonese tea-pluckers were never personalised, although they were sometimes illustrated by photograph.

Another E. Young (not to be confused with the earlier Ernest Young, though by coincidence, he attended as a pupil the Harrow grammar school at which Ernest had been head) also rose to fame as a textbook writer in this period, getting his start, as he later explained, largely by accident:

> A term or two after I got back from the war I was in the book room at City of Norwich School one day, wondering what the hell I could do with Form 3, who had textbooks that I didn't like at all. The Head of Department walked in and showed me a letter inviting him to submit a synopsis for a series of books for the new Secondary Modern Schools. He didn't want to take it on, but offered to put my name forward instead. ... My synopsis was accepted and I wrote *Our World* during the next three or four years. It bore very little relation to the synopsis, but it was published and it paid off, fortunately.[25]

E. W. ('Bill') Young's Head of Department, J. E. G. Mosby, also prudently claimed a share of the authorship however. *Our World* (later

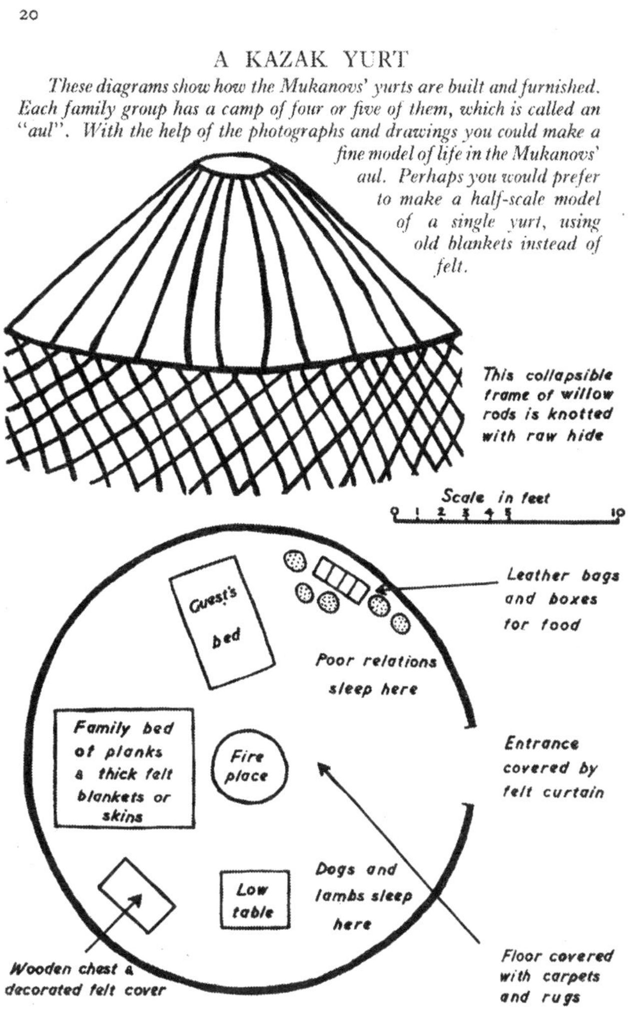

20

A KAZAK YURT

These diagrams show how the Mukanovs' yurts are built and furnished.
Each family group has a camp of four or five of them, which is called an
"aul". With the help of the photographs and drawings you could make a
fine model of life in the Mukanovs'
aul. Perhaps you would prefer
to make a half-scale model
of a single yurt, using
old blankets instead of
felt.

This collapsible
frame of willow
rods is knotted
with raw hide

Scale in feet

Guest's bed

Leather bags
and boxes
for food

Poor relations
sleep here

Family bed
of planks
a thick felt
blankets or
skins

Fire
place

Entrance
covered by
felt curtain

Low
table

Dogs and
lambs sleep
here

Wooden chest &
decorated felt cover

Floor covered
with carpets
and rugs

Figure 7.4:
Page from *Our World* by E. W.
Young and J. E. G. Mosby
(*Source*: Edward Arnold, 1951)
(reduced size)
This page is preceded by a
double page headed 'A Way of
Life that did not Change for
Centuries', and followed by
one headed 'The Kazak
Nomads are Settling Down',
which relates that many Yurt
dwellers have now become
farmers or factory workers.

Our Changing World) by Young and Mosby became one of the first
successful post-war series, not only for its practical concentric approach
(starting from the geography of the local community and working
outwards) and its strong sample-study element (see Figure 7.4) but also
for the fact that it broke new ground in having its text portioned and
designed page-by-page and in double-spread layouts.[26] This was in
contrast to the setting out of text as a continuous narrative as had almost
invariably been the case in the past.

Young (1915–97) was later to co-author, with J. H. Lowry, *A Course
in World Geography* which was a staple and popular classroom series in
the 1960s, mostly based on an areal framework.[27] Edward Arnold,
Young's publishers, reported that, of all their authors, only the books of
E. M. Forster sold more.

Young, a man of wide interests, firm beliefs and generous spirit, went on to a headship of a secondary modern (later, comprehensive) school in Royston, Hertfordshire (a school which, remarkably, has had eminent school geographers as three of its four head teachers) before retiring in the 1960s. He went to Norfolk to become a full-time writer, living on the UK's finest terminal moraine.

He told David Wright in an interview published in *Teaching Geography*,[28] 'I feel that geography teachers have a great social responsibility and that geography teaching should have a moral – even a spiritual – motivation.' Like many ex-geography teachers, he devoted much of his retirement to the application of geographical insights in community life by serving (as an Independent member) on parish and district councils and by working with voluntary conservation bodies

THE GROWTH OF SAMPLE STUDIES

The idea of sample studies enlivened the, by now traditional, regional diet of secondary school geography and the GA issued a booklet about the use of them; several other specialist bodies (notably the Association of Agriculture) then began to produce detailed material about farms and factories which could be utilised in a classroom context. They were often in packs rather than books, so that photographs, maps and diagrams could be handled separately. This became a well-used approach in post-war geography classrooms, as the material filtered through and teachers gained confidence in presenting the detail of the material. Eventually, one set of textbooks[29] for schools went to the extreme of presenting exclusively sample studies from different parts of the world, accompanied by study questions but no other linking text.

The London Institute team of geography educators, were the main authors of an influential, high-selling (and almost definitive) set of textbooks which incorporated this idea in the 1950s[30] under the guiding editorship of R. C. Honeybone and Mary Goss. Regional description was balanced, on the one hand, by sample studies, and, on the other, by practical map exercises. A generation of children learnt about south-eastern Australia through being taken on a vicarious tour of Mr Walker's fruit-orchards at Ardmona, and of California by reading of Mr Wileman's ranch at Fresno. Though the books retained the prevailing popular octavo size and hard-backed covers of the time, they included map extracts, plentiful numbers of half-page photographs, extracts from literature and a much wider range of class activities than previous series had done. Pedagogical factors were dominant.

Importantly, the books gave up the struggle to maintain comprehensive coverage of all regions. Thus, in *Britain and Overseas* (Book 1) six British areas were exemplified (south-west England, south-east England, Lancashire and Yorkshire industrial areas, East Anglia, the Highlands of Scotland, London), but Ireland was represented by a study of a single farm and Wales not at all. The withdrawal from comprehensive coverage had begun …

This meant that 15 pages could be spent on East Anglia, with sketches, pictures, diagrams and maps embedded in the text. There was a map of the main features of the geography of Norwich and an aerial view of the centre. The reader was told 'Before we leave East Anglia, we will take a short visit to Norwich, the county town of Norfolk' but instead of descriptive text, the reader was invited to interact with the map and pictures:

29. Locate in the picture the Cathedral and the old castle.
30. In your atlas find Norwich and the places named on Figure 78.
31. What features in the map suggest that Norwich is an important town in East Anglia?
32. Can you suggest what is the use of the circular road?

BUT WHAT'S THE USE OF IT ALL?

As utilitarian strains re-emerged in educational philosophies, the question also increasingly arose, at least for bright pupils, as to what was the use of studying geography? In the hands of lively teachers, the lessons were tolerable and the world was made interesting, but what could you do with it in future life – except lounge with an atlas, provide answers for crosswords, and stray enquiries, and, if pressed for a job, teach geography to others? Pupils pondering and perspiring over the products of Peru and Paraguay could empathise with Josie Pye in Anne of Green Gables – 'Last year I concentrated on geography and where did it get me? Nowhere. This year I'm going to concentrate on boys.'

Two other members of the strong London Institute geography department, B. S. Roberson and I. L. M. Long, produced a secondary schoolteachers' manual in the 1960s.[31] It was the fruits of their own long experience and encapsulated the received wisdom about geography teaching in the immediate post-war period. 'Bertie' Roberson and Molly Long were a personable and influential pair and they had both made a success of London secondary school geography departments through creative pedagogy before being recruited to train teachers.

Their experience was evident in the practical approaches which they explained and espoused in the book. Their preface was bullish, but also mindful of criticisms levelled at the subject:

> The whole trend of our argument is that children should be led to think about the subject matter offered. It is less than a century since geography emerged from its academic disrepute of Victorian times and it was the absence of any intellectual content that led to its low standard in schools. The idea of geography as a 'soft option' for the unintelligent remains.

Their second chapter was titled 'The regional approach' and makes a strong case for teaching regional geography. It includes a realistic appraisal of pedagogical difficulties in geography teaching and prefigures some of the issues later considered by Egan in a more general context:[32]

> We suggest that the early years should be on a regional basis, to give children factual knowledge of countries and to ensure that they study places that are real to them. It is from this basis, in later years, that generalisations can be made. It is only from known facts that children can make generalisations for themselves.

In the end, however, it concludes:

> Meanwhile, we have nailed our flag to the regional mast. and those who would not place the main emphasis on regional geography in school must justify themselves with some other viable philosophy.

It was a challenge that would be vigorously taken up in the decades that followed.

THE SOCIAL STUDIES EPISODE

In the wake of the 1944 Education Act, efforts to devise a 'new curriculum' for the secondary modern schools took a non-academic and utilitarian turn. It was proposed that vocational subjects (woodwork, metalwork, technical drawing, domestic science, shorthand and typing) should take up a major part of curriculum time alongside Maths and English. Bearing in mind the reduced time available for other subjects, the idea of evolving and teaching a general mix of understandings about life in Britain began to form. In this, it was suggested, geography and history might be combined with aspects of other areas such as civics, economics and an understanding of the way Britain is governed. The combination, it was reasoned, would form a concise and more immediately practical preparation for life for those who were not going on to higher study.

Within a few years a band-waggon was rolling for something which came to be called 'social studies' and which drew on the experience of American education, where it had been introduced in the 1930s. The November 1950 issue of the Journal of Education was given over to a series of articles on the topic, a 'Handbook' of Social Studies was published and a small 'bible' about the teaching of social studies in secondary schools emerged.[33]

James Hemming offered the 'objectives of social studies' early in the book:

> to combine the material of History, Geography and Civics, together with relevant material from other subject fields, into a single integrated background course, through which the child can come to appreciate the inter-relatedness of all the elements of his environment and to feel himself to be clearly associated with the

past and present struggles and achievements of mankind, and to have a personal contribution to make towards future progress.

Hemming went on to give a score of examples of 'project work' which would fulfil these objectives. The more geographically inclined ones included: 'A ride around Extown', 'The sea', 'Where is the school?' and 'Men and mountains'.

Geographers, by now, a coherent and active force in schools, viewed these developments with some suspicion. Would the full range of geographical ideas be taught if they allowed themselves to be subsumed into a larger grouping? What would happen to all the physical and scientific aspects of geography, if they were under a 'social studies' umbrella? Was this a subtle attempt to keep the subject as something appropriate for the non-academic?

As is the norm in curriculum politics, the most vociferous spoke out first and considered negotiation and co-operation only as a fall-back option. The GA had little enthusiasm for being involved with social studies but it was the Royal Geographical Society (now in a post-Hinksian era) which came into the fray first with a resounding opposition to the idea in a 1950 memorandum.[34]

> Social studies represent an attempt to compress several branches of learning into one. The result is exactly what happens when a lemon is squeezed; the juice is removed and only the useless rind and fibres remain. The attempt may be attributed, first, to the influence of American theories, which however, have since lost ground in the United States and also in Canada; secondly to the pressure of subjects in school curricula; thirdly to a new and rather dangerous conception of education; and fourthly to the necessity of training teachers quickly. It is felt that 'social studies' will destroy the value of geography as an important medium of education.

The sound of drawbridges being cranked up behind subject-based high walls can be resoundingly heard here, though there was concern about the squeezing not only of geography, but of a whole suite of non-vocational subjects. The writers of the paper (does the voice of Sidney Wooldridge seem to ring through?[35]) seemed strangely unconscious of the fact that the arguments about the 'compress (of) several branches of learning into one' had also been levelled at geography itself in the past, not least by Principal Murray, whose 1942 words are reported earlier in this chapter.

Beyond the resounding rhetoric of the peroration quoted above, some more substantial points emerge. The 'new and rather dangerous conception of education' emerges to be 'those whose adherents regard education as the adjustment of the child to its social environment and not the development of the child's individual potentialities within the environment'.

The report also puts its finger on some dubious thinking from the

1943 Norwood Report[36] which had characterised the 'secondary modern type of child' as follows:

> He is interested in things as they are; he finds little attraction in the past or the slow disentaglement of causes or movements ... because he is interested only in the movement he may be incapable of a long series of connected steps; relevance to present concerns is the only way of awakening interest, abstractions mean little to him.

It is at least heartening to find geographers resisting the idea that a general 'dumbing-down' of the curriculum was necessary, as the Norwood extract seems to advocate.

At about the same time as the RGS report was published, Neville Scarfe weighed in with a critical survey of how 'social studies' contributed to education in the USA.[37] 'There seems little point in muddling haphazardly oddments from various subjects into disconnected units', he concluded.

A more eirenic and dispassionate approach to the issue was taken a little later by Reg Honeybone in a wide-ranging and thoughtful paper which reflected its title, 'Balance in geography and education'.

> I do, however, suggest that just as it is important to examine the implications of Social Studies, it is equally important to examine the implications of our own teaching of geography ... let us not, in our enthusiasm for our subject, forget that there are other fields of knowledge and other methods; or that where geography abuts on to other subjects, we should take every opportunity to ensure that there is active collaboration by the other members of the school staff.[38]

In the end the momentum of the 'social studies' movement in England and Wales foundered as it came up against the entrenched positions of the subject associations and the powerful forces of curriculum tradition. It encapsulated a lively modernist approach to current affairs and sought to develop citizens who were well informed even if they were not academically able. But the movement was made up of an amalgam of people with different interests (and from different educational ideologies) who themselves could not seem to agree fully on principles or methodology. Most of them also had major preoccupations in other matters.

Was the structure of subjects a better way to induct pupils into knowledge, or should the amalgam of subjects found in real-life situations be replicated in teaching through topics? Geographers found themselves in an ambiguous position, since they often deployed the 'synthesising role' argument to buttress their own claims for a place in the curriculum. Must geography now find a new rationale? The matter was never debated in clear philosophic terms, but became a matter of power plays and pragmatic arguments. Since the subject specialists were already in employment, and they were more numerous, the defence of their corner was a marginally easier position and they were, in England, in the end, successful. The 'social studies' enthusiasts failed to produce a convincing intellectual argument as to the superiority of their way of wanting to do things.

In Scotland, on the other hand, where the debate was also undertaken, the balance of persuasive argument went the other way: 'Modern Studies' was established as an extra examination subject at 'O'-level Grade by 1960 and at 'Higher Grade' by 1966.[39] Geography, however, has continued to co-exist alongside Modern Studies in the years since.

SEPARATE OR INTEGRATE?

The same pedagogical issue – should there be separate subjects or integrated approaches – has raised itself in different forms in later years as other movements have emerged.[40] 'Inter Disciplinary Enquiry' (IDE) a style of social studies curriculum in which the pupils called the tune about what they wanted to study and teachers were enjoined to follow and then improvise useful work from such ideas, was favoured by Charity James and the educationists of the Goldsmiths Curriculum Laboratory. It had a brief vogue in the 1960s and developed some innovative classroom practices before collapsing under its own lack of structure.[41]

Ivor Goodson has written of the attempt in the 1970s by Sean Carson, the Rural Studies LEA adviser of Hertfordshire, to both transform the nature of his own subject and enhance it by the advocacy of Environmental Studies as an A-level subject.[42] This was a bold initiative and a matter in which Carson clashed with geographers and biologists in a series of high-profile meetings and conferences. Goodson's account of the affair is something of an apologia for Carson[43] but it does reveal some of the fine-grain of curriculum politics at a particular stage in time and is full of interesting detail about the issue and its context.

The Hertfordshire Environmental Studies (later, Environmental Science) initiative was a project which ultimately failed through its inability to convince traditional-subject-dominated examination boards that it had a coherent base as an examinable subject of study and should be given an extra place at the A-level table. If Carson had aimed less expansively, perhaps at classes below the examination level, the idea might have prospered in a time when school curricula initiatives were relatively unfettered by government edicts. The integrated approach to environmental work he sought had more chance of initially gaining a foothold on its own merits in the lower forms of secondary schools than on the fortress walls of pre-university study. It may well have been an over-ambitious strategy, rather than a deficient basic idea which eventually scuppered the enterprise.

More recently, the attraction of inter-disciplinary work has revived in a different form through the creation of 'Humanities' curricula. This

THE MOST INFLUENTIAL EDUCATOR
OF THEM ALL?

It might be argued that Charles Warrell made a greater contribution to the geographical and environmental education of children than any other teacher of the 1950s and 1960s, though he did so without hardly stepping inside a school.

Warrell, a former primary-school head teacher, who had trained at Culham College, Abingdon early in the century, turned to writing post-1945 and developed the I Spy-movement through inexpensive paper-back books and, later, regular columns in the Daily Mail and the News Chronicle. At one stage there were over half a million members of the I-Spy tribe, of which Warrell was 'Big Chief'.

The aim of the I-Spy movement was to heighten young people's awareness of the world around them by encouraging them to record their sightings of birds, animals, castles, churches and a myriad of categories which encompassed environmental landmarks and activities. Each I-Spy book had an introduction which discussed the general scope and nature of the particular category being considered and the items to be observed were clearly described and illustrated. A tick for each item seen earned points; when a sufficient number were amassed, the 'young brave' could apply to Big Chief I-Spy at his Fleet Street tepee, (address; Wigwam-on-the-Water, EC4) for a coloured feather to stick in a headband. The assiduous I-Spyer could obtain a host of trophy feathers.

Big Chief I-Spy instilled the belief that to cheat was unthinkable; children were to be scrupulously honest in keeping the records of their sightings in their books. They walked, cycled, cajoled parents to make car journeys and travelled by bus and train to complete the more elusive sightings. The movement was a popular expression of the post-war mood which valued environmental experience and education and encouraged young people to explore the countryside.

Warrell held 'pow-wows' all over the country, attended by thousands of children. By the time he retired, 18 million copies of the I-Spy books had been sold; the original series remained in print until the mid-1980s. Big Chief I-Spy remained available for sightings for a long period; he lived to be 106, dying in 1995.

term is frequently used in secondary schools as an administrative umbrella term to cover a loose-knit faculty structure in which geography, history and religious education are being taught in separate departments. But there are also a number of schools which have integrated the material in these three subjects for teaching purposes. The movement to do this has grown mostly from the 1980s, and there have been some outstanding examples of successful work, pioneered by dynamic departments and inspirational individuals.[44] The individuals invariably pass on to other schools (and other things), however and prove difficult to replace.

The question arises, more generally, as to whether such an integrated style can be competently handled by teachers who are not deeply knowledgeable (let alone trained specialists) in the wide variety of material which they may be handling. The exceptional, highly skilled and motivated teacher may rejoice in the curricular scope provided; for others, it is too easy to get lost in the undergrowth. In the 1990s these arguments echo some of those deployed in the past controversies about the 'integrated day' in primary schools, and 'social studies'.

'Humanities' was beginning to displace separate geography and history on the timetable in some schools in the 1980s, but concern about lack of curriculum structure attracted the attention of HMI. One particular HMI report at a crucial time expressed disquiet about the quality of work achieved and in particular about the way in which the process of work was sometimes valued to the exclusion of any product.[45] Any possible further movement towards integrated Humanities teaching was restricted by the choice of separate subject formulations for the National Curriculum in 1988.

NOTES

1. Max Beloff 'The road to war', in R. Smith (ed.), *Against the Odds* (RAF Museum, Hendon, 1990), pp. 10–32.
2. W. G. V. Balchin, 'UK Geographers in the Second World War: a report', *Geographical Journal*, 153, 2 (1987), pp. 159–80.
3. The 'Baedaker' raids on cathedral cities were so called because, it is said, Hitler used the famous travel guidebook to determine where he might hurt British pride by destroying heritage landmarks such as cathedrals and historic houses.
4. J. Murray, 'Inaugural address to the 1942 conference of the Geographical Association', *Geography*, 27, 4 (1942), pp. 117–21.
5. H. J. Mackinder 'Geography, an art and a philosophy', *Geography*, 27, 4 (1942), pp. 122–30.
6. D. Stoddart, 'To claim the high ground; geography for the end of the century', *Transactions of the Institute of British Geographers NS*, 12, 3 (1987), pp. 327–36.
7. M. Williams, 'Editorial: Can the centre hold?', *Transactions of the Institute of British Geographers NS*, 12, 4 (1987), pp. 387–90.
8. A. Garnett 'Comment: "The Pioneers": some recollections', *Transactions of the Institute of British Geographers NS*, 12, 2 (1987), pp. 240–1.
9. Report of the Consultative Committee on Secondary Education with special reference to Grammar Schools and Technical High Schools (Spens Report) (HMSO, London, 1938).
10. *Children's Charter*, a documentary film (Crown Film Unit, 1945).
11. A. B. Archer and H. G. Thomas, *Geography: First Series*, 4 vols (Ginn, London, 1936).

12. O. Garnett, *Fundamentals in School Geography* (Harrap, London, 1934). The quotation is taken from pages 31–2 of the 1934 edition.

13. For a full description of the provisions and implications of the 1944 Act, see Chapter 11 of S. J. Curtis, *History of Education in Great Britain* (University Tutorial Press, London, 1967).

14. Besides David Elleray (Harrow) and Kevin Stannard (Eton), acknowledged earlier, I owe thanks to Malcolm Bailey and Sue Cole (Charterhouse) who searched out much useful information about the history of geography in their school and informed me of it.

15. A. J. Herbertson, 'The major natural regions: an essay in systematic geography', *Geographical Journal*, 2 (1905), pp. 300–12.

16. See P. Vidal de la Blache, *Principles of Human Geography*, trans. Millicent Todd Bingham (Constable, London, 1926); Jean Brunhes, *Human Geography*, trans. E. F. Row (Harrap, London, 1952); L. Febvre, *A Geographical Introduction to History*, trans. E. G. Mountford and J. H. Paxton (Kegan Paul Trench Trubner, London, 1932).

17. R. C. Honeybone, 'Balance in geography and education', *Geography*, 39 (2) (March 1954), p. 97.

18. Thomas Pickles, *Geographies for Senior Forms*, a series of 11 books, (Dent, London, 1935).

19. D. M. Preece and H. R. B. Wood, *Modern Geography*, a series of six books (University Tutorial Press, London, 1938).

20. W. E. Marsden. 'Geography text-book publishing from the 1930s to the 1960s', *Geography*, 73, 4 (1988), pp. 327–43.

21. See Keiran Egan, *Educational Development* (Oxford University Press, Oxford, 1984). Egan propounds a theory of development which considers appropriate content as well as mind maturity. He suggests that children first go through a period in which stories are important, then a period (usually between 9 and 13 years of age) in which they enjoy acquiring information, thirdly a stage in which they are interested in looking for principles, rules, laws and generalisations, and finally (the sign of a mature mind) a stage in which they enjoy puzzling about the exceptions to the rules and laws about which they have previously learnt.

22. G. M. Hickman, 'The sample study: a method and its limitations', *Journal of Geography*, 49 (1950), pp. 151–9; B. S. Roberson and I. L. M. Long, 'Sample studies: the development of a method', *Geography*, 41 (4) (1956), pp. 248–59.

23. A. E. Frye, *Elements of Geography* (Ginn, London, 1895), an American textbook, contained studies of 'Tibbu: the Congo Boy', 'Hans, the Holland Boy', etc. The book was re-cast for British audiences by A.J. Herbertson as *An Illustrated School Geography* (Edward Arnold, London, 1898), but the emphasis on particular examples is diminished.

24. J. Fairgrieve and Ernest Young, *Human Geography* (George Philip, London, 1920).

25. David Wright interviewed E. W. Young in the series 'Authors and their books', in *Teaching Geography*, April (1977), pp. 173–5 and the article contains more biographical details about Young.

26. E. W. Young and J. E. G. Mosby, *Our World* (later retitled as *Our Changing World*), a series of four books: *Our Town and Beyond*; *Our Neighbours Overseas*; *Our Changing World*; *Our World and Ourselves* (Edward Arnold, London, 1950).

27. E. W. Young and J. H. Lowry (eds), *A Course in World Geography*. There are seven books in the original series: *People in Britain*; *People Round the World*; *Regions of the World*; *The British Isles*; *The World*; *Europe and the Soviet Union*; *North America*. Books 8 and 9 (East Africa; Central Africa) were written principally for students studying in African schools, though also used in the UK. A Book 10, a re-working of Book 4, was added later (Edward Arnold, London, 1957).

28. David Wright's interview with E. W. Young, *Teaching Geography*, see note 25 above.

29. J. G. Rushby, M. Dybeck and J. Bell, *Study Geography*, a series of five books (Longman, London, 1967).

30. R. C. Honeybone and M. G. Goss (eds), *Geography for Schools*, a series of five books: *Britain and Overseas*; *The Southern Continents*; *North America and USSR*; *Europe and the British Isles*; *World Geography* (Heinemann, London, 1956). The significance of the series is discussed in more detail on pp. 20–3 of D. Hall, *Geography and the Geography Teacher* (Unwin, London, 1976), a book which ranges widely and interestingly over many geographical and educational issues, with a focus on the 1960s and 1970s.

31. I. L. M. Long and B. S. Roberson, *Teaching Geography* (Heinemann, London, 1966).

32. Egan, *Educational Development*.

33. James Hemming, *The Teaching of Social Studies in Secondary Schools* (Longman, London, 1950).

34. 'Geography and social studies', a memorandum prepared for the Council of the RGS by its Education Committee, published in *The Geographical Journal*, June (1950), pp. 181–5. The fact that the Geographical Association reprinted the Memorandum in *Geography*, 35 (3) (Sept. 1950), pp. 181–5 indicates that the GA probably gave broad support to the sentiments expressed.

35. S. W. Wooldridge 'On taking the ge- out of geography', *Geography*, 34 (1) (1949), pp. 9–18.

36. Board of Education, *Curriculum and Examinations in Secondary Schools*, Report of the Secondary Schools Examinations Council, chaired by Sir Cyril Norwood (HMSO, London, 1943).

37. N. V. Scarfe, 'Geography and social studies in the USA', *Geography*, 35 (2) (June 1950), pp. 86–93.

38. R. C. Honeybone, 'Balance in geography and education', *Geography*, 39 (2) (1954), pp. 91–101.

39. Modern studies in Scottish schools began as an amalgam of geography and history with some current affairs added, but post-1968 there has been a considerably greater emphasis on sociology and politics. The aims and objectives of geography and other 'social subjects' in Scotland were set out in Curriculum Paper 15, *The Social Subjects in Secondary Schools* (Scottish Central Committee on Social Subjects, 1976). A recent survey of the state of geography in Scottish schools is published in the series 'Effective learning and teaching in Scottish secondary schools, *Geography: A Report by HMI*', Scottish Office Education Department, 1995. My thanks to Alastair Robinson (University of Strathclyde) for drawing my attention to these documents and for providing me with other information about geography in Scottish schools. See also L. Hunter, 'Geography in the Scottish school curriculum', in E. Rawling and R. Daugherty (eds), *Geography into the Twenty-First Century* (Wiley, London, 1996), pp. 235–46.

40. The matter is covered comprehensively in M. Williams (ed.), *Geography and the Integrated Curriculum: A Reader* (Heinemann, London, 1976).

41. Charity James, *Young Lives at Stake* (Collins, London, 1968).

42. I. Goodson, *School Subjects and Curriculum Change* (Croom Helm, London, 1988).

43. It is intriguing that, in the first edition of *School Subjects and Curriculum Change*, Goodson pays tribute to Carson and acknowledges the use of his private papers in a foreword, but omits this subsequently (see the edition published by Falmer Press, 1993). Even more interesting, is that Carson himself, whilst an adviser in Hertfordshire had earlier encouraged and supported the formation of the Hertfordshire Geography Teachers Association.

44. Work of this kind is currently encouraged and supported by The Humanities Assocation, which publishes a newsletter, *Humanities Now!* The Association does not have permanent headquarters but the current honorary secretary (2000) is Deidre Smith, c/o Wirral LEA, Hamilton Building, Conway Street, Birkenhead, L41 4FD.

45. Her Majesty's Inspectors, *A Report on Humanities Work in 20 Secondary Schools* (Department of Education, London, 1989).

8

The New Model Army,
1960–75

FROM BODIE TO MADINGLEY

As the 1960s passed, school geography was ripe for a new initiative. It came through the enterprise of two young Cambridge lecturers and their use of a base in the East Anglian countryside. Richard Chorley and Peter Haggett were in the unlikely surroundings of a Californian ghost-town in the summer of 1962 when they first discussed the idea of running a course for British schoolteachers; their vacation teaching at Berkeley and Denver was to be followed by a series of memorable annual summer courses based at an elegant Elizabethan mansion a few miles west of Cambridge, Madingley Hall.

> The road to Madingley began at Bodie, an abandoned mining town in the northern part of the Owens Valley ... during the Labour Day weekend of September 1962. In the late morning of the Monday we sat in the shade of the saloon bar (sadly, deserted many decades before) and turned to look forward to plans for the following summer ... school geography in Britain was in something of the doldrums.[1]

As they explained later, it was not because they thought university academics should tell schoolteachers what and how to teach but because they were excited about the new work which they were doing and wanted to share it with a wider audience. What teachers made of it was entirely for them to decide.

Sometimes the most mundane administrative decisions have far-reaching consequences. In choosing participants for their courses at Madingley, Chorley and Haggett decided not to give the usual priority to any applications which might come from older and more senior teachers, supposing that the under-forties and the newly qualified might be those who would be most interested. The conferences proved more successful than they dared hope.

The somewhat disparate set of lectures from the first course in 1963 were published as *Frontiers in Geographical Teaching*.[2] Most of the contributors were young members of the Cambridge University

Department of Geography or recent graduates of it. In the very first of the chapters E. A. Wrigley (later to achieve eminence as a demographer, rather than a mainstream geographer and to become President of the British Academy) argued the case against regional geography, which he called 'a concept overtaken by the course of historical change', and asserted that many contemporary developments in geographical techniques and methodologies were linked to the social and physical sciences.

> One aspect of this which appears to be of singular importance is the application of statistical concepts and devices to many new areas of study ... they help with one of the subject's most intractable methodological problems ... the recurring worry about the best way to accommodate in a single discipline a physical and a social side.

In one bound, so to speak, they were free; as subsequent lecturers in the course revealed in various ways, a quite fresh set of methodological tools were being fashioned, experimented with and utilised to invigorate and also re-unite the different aspects of the subject. The new techniques of the physical and social sciences were being brought to bear on the distinctive dimension of geography – space. Geography would thus gain clarity, precision, utility, it was argued; more importantly, equipped with these techniques, its general theorising could be liberated from the weakening credibility of determinism (and later more sophisticated derivatives, such as 'possibilism', which still preserved deterministic elements).

As the world changed, so the growth of a supra-national culture became more apparent. Clearly, the 'control' of the physical world appeared to have less effect on life than at the turn of the century. What was remarkable about life in Manchester, Amsterdam and Tokyo was not its national distinctiveness but the homogeneity of industrial, office, commuting life. Dick Chorley coined an aphorism for the time: 'Papua New Guinea is getting more and more like Luton every day.' The traditional search for regional differences needed replacement by a new concern to find recurring instances, patterns, even, as Schaefer had called them, 'laws'.[3] Geographers would use quantitative precision and theory to solve spatial conundrums, not remain imprisoned in qualitative reflection and discussion.

A second book from a later conference, *Models in Geography*,[4] a mammoth 800-page tome was published in 1967 and elaborated the themes at greater length and with a strengthened framework of ideas. The books, like the conferences, contained ideas of baffling abstruseness and exciting novelty in about equal parts (see Figure 8.1). The young geographical wizards laid out an enticing but winding yellow brick road of conceptual frameworks, quantitative techniques and theoretical models which appeared to lead to a distant shining city of spatial Oz. The Madingley conferences swiftly enrolled an eager band of followers, some of whom were disenchanted by the present lack of challenge and

UNIVERSITY OF CAMBRIDGE
BOARD OF EXTRA-MURAL STUDIES

SYLLABUS
of a
RESIDENTIAL COURSE
entitled
THEORY IN GEOGRAPHY:
NEW TEACHING PROBLEMS
to be held at
MADINGLEY HALL, CAMBRIDGE
23–30 July, 1966

PROGRAMME

Saturday, 23 July

5.15 p.m.	Introduction: Aims and Objects of the course	The Directors
8.15 p.m.	The teaching of geomorphology	Mr Chorley

Sunday, 24 July

2.00 p.m.	Analysis of transport networks	Mr Haggett
5.00 p.m.	Networks: Some practical operations*	Mr Haggett
8.15 p.m.	Correlation structures in geomorphology*	Mr Chorley

Monday, 25 July

9.00 a.m.	Demography and geography	Dr Wrigley
11.00 a.m.	Analysis of population records*	Dr Wrigley
2.15 p.m.	Harmonic analysis of periodic data in geography**	Dr Rayner
5.00 p.m.	Maps and information theory	Dr Board
8.15 p.m.	Rethinking school geography	Mr Bryan

Tuesday, 26 July

9.00 a.m.	Diffusion models in geography*	Dr Board
11.00 a.m.	Geographical climatology	Dr Beckinsale
2.15 p.m.	Data collection and analysis in urban areas**	Mr Morley
8.15 a.m.	Teaching global temperatures*	Dr Beckinsale

Wednesday, 27 July

9.00 a.m.	Multivariate data analysis in geography**	Dr Cox
2.00 p.m.	Location theory and decision making	Mr Chisholm
8.15 p.m.	Weber's least-cost location model*	Mr Chisholm

Thursday, 28 July

9.00 a.m.	Hardware models in geography**	Dr Morgan
5.00 p.m.	Climatic geomorphology	Dr Stoddart
8.15 p.m.	Studies of drainage density*	Dr Stoddart

Friday, 29 July

9.00 a.m.	What price the Arctic?	Dr Jackson
11.00 a.m.	An exercise in economic hydrology*	Dr Jackson
2.15 p.m.	Problems of teaching the new geography in schools+	Mr Bryan
5.00 p.m.	Models in geography+	The Directors

The Course will disperse after breakfast on Saturday, 30 July.

* Demonstration exercise.
** Lecture plus demonstration session (Double period).
+ Discussion period.

Figure 8.1:
Programme of the 1966
Madingley Hall geography
conference organised by
Richard Chorley and Peter
Haggett (*Source*: author)

excitement in school geography, others who themselves were young graduates who had become aware of new intellectual stirrings in the subject during their recent time at university. A New Model Army of teachers sprang to the colours flown by Chorley and Haggett in East Anglia just as eagerly as their predecessors had done for Cromwell 300 years before.

The impact of the Madingley conferences was remarkable and the spread of the ripples from them was swift. The time was ripe for such an initiative, but part of the success stemmed from the genuine dialogue fostered by the young academics who led the sessions. Lectures were almost invariably coupled to workshops in which practical examples were presented and hammered out. The Madingley conferences opened up a new intellectual life for a key cadre of young geography teachers of the time. It was given all the more sharpness by the clear hard scientific methodology and positivist thinking which underlay the ideas.

It was postulated that the interaction and movement of people could be replicated by analogy with physical phenomena; human geography was social physics, with people seen to be attracted by the 'retail pulling power' of towns just as iron-filings were attracted by magnets. The river could be profitably considered as a quantitative system and process, rather than primarily as a landform – What?, Where?, How Much? and At What Speed? became the dominant questions to ask in hydrology and geomorphology rather than the identification of obsequent and subsequent tributaries. The ideas of geographers in other European countries and in North America (some past, some present) newly infused British academic thinking. The geometry of Christaller's hexagons in central place theory, of Kansky's analysis of transport networks, of Hagerstrand's diffusion waves generated the precisely sculptured outline of a newly revealed world.

Though *Frontiers* and *Models* were tough books for teachers to absorb, in a few short years they became the influential testaments of a religion which proselytised with the same Puritan zeal as had the men of the Lord Protector. The old regional monarchy, scarcely able to land any solid intellectual punch in the face of this offensive was seen to be tottering; the new spatial Commonwealth was soon proclaimed.

THE CHALLENGE TO THE 'OLD GUARD'

John Everson and Brian Fitzgerald, two young teachers who had attended early Madingley conferences, formed the London Schools Geographical Group (LSGG) in 1966 to promote these ideas. The group began its existence as an informal forum for the exchange of lesson plans, most of which derived from ideas picked up at Madingley conferences. Some proved quite unworkable in schools, but others were found to stimulate classes and began to change favourably attitudes to geography amongst pupils, especially the more able ones.

The LSGG was a short-lived though influential ginger group which was at first challenged, but then quickly embraced by the Geographical Association. It had metamorphosed into the Models and Quantitative Techniques Committee of the GA by late 1967; a major landmark was the January 1969 issue of the GA's journal, *Geography*, which was guest-edited by Richard Chorley and which laid out some of the embryonic educational possibilities of the new ideas.[5]

In an accompanying commentary, Professor Stan Gregory of Sheffield (who himself had recently written a text about the use of statistical method in geography) commented prophetically 'Geography has reached its own particular Rubicon; to refuse to cross it could cut us off from contemporary scientific thought for many decades to come.' Another paper in the same issue by Derek Thompson indicated a daunting passport needed for this brave new world – a 'Bibliography of Academic Reading'. In the next decade, this bibliography continued to be updated and published on a regular basis. It was an important initial instrument in disseminating the unfamiliar ideas –with books starred for their merit and relevance – and a sign of how much purely academic reading was taken on board by teachers anxious to project the 'New Geography'.

As several older practitioners pointed out,[6] there had been other 'New Geographies' before this, but the term was indiscriminately applied, for a time, as a handy way of describing what was an eclectic set of lively teaching ideas. Ultimately, the novelty, originality and classroom efficacy of the ideas were as significant as their dependence on spatial analytic theory.[7]

At the same time as successfully infiltrating the Geographical Association, Madingley attenders were also circulating their attempts to turn the 'New Geography' into school practice – duplicated exercises and worksheets which sought to simplify and identify the essence of such concepts such as central place theory, Von Thunen's model of concentric rings of land use and the ideas of Weber and Losch about industrial location. It was the first stage of a powerful 'underground' publishing movement which sought to short circuit traditional channels of publication for a time and challenge the domination of more traditional materials.

MOVING INTO THE MAINSTREAM

In 1967, whilst on a routine school visit to sell books, a publisher's representative saw some of the worksheets which Everson and Fitzgerald were producing at Haberdashers' Aske's School for Boys, Elstree and carried them back to his superiors at Longman. Within a few weeks, Marilyn Sayers, newly appointed as editor for geography schoolbooks there, had taken a brave gamble and commissioned a textbook, based around the apparent obscurities, formulae and strange unworldly diagrams of the worksheets. It was designed for sixth forms, but educated as many teachers as sixth formers in its considerable publishing life.

Settlement Patterns[8] was bold by being produced in paperback as well as by being innovative geography. Peter Haggett, in the foreword, said:

> The major changes in geography courses at many British and most American and Swedish universities have yet to be passed on to schools ... this book lays the basis for more wholesale change in the future.

The authors, in their introduction, offered their perspective on this from the school context:

> Many changes are slowly penetrating school geography in a piecemeal and unco-ordinated fashion. Teachers are beginning to realise that much of what is taught in our schools is purely repetitive and lacks intellectual stimulus and challenge to the student. Basic to these changes, we feel, is an ability of the student to appreciate fundamental concepts in geography, those concerned with space, location and interactions through time ...

> The student is encouraged to learn concepts through discovering them for himself ... in much of the work the teacher will find himself actively participating with his students in the formulation of the group's ideas in a particular field.

In other words, a radical change in pedagogy as well as in content was intended. The book put into 'proper' print for the first time many of the ideas which had been circulating on the underground-duplicated-worksheet network.

Though designed for sixth forms, many of the sales of *Settlement Patterns* (which peaked as late as seven years after publication) were to teachers keen (or at least feeling obliged) to acquaint themselves with what was going on. No doubt some of its success was due to the fact that some examination boards were also readjusting their syllabuses to take account of the 'new geography'. It did not look like any other geography textbook in existence – it had pages of lists, tables, complex calculations and formulae and strange-looking geometrical diagrams – not all of which yielded immediate comprehension. Yet it threw out bold ideas and stimulating class exercises in equal measure. The book was a key influence on rising stars and a focus for much discussion.

One significant common factor between the Chorley and Haggett books and *Settlement Patterns* was that both owed little to previous publications in geography, save a handful of obscure journal articles – in this sense the books were the product of a genuine revolution in thinking rather than the usual evolution. The change was not wholly driven by the geographical academy, however. Everson and Fitzgerald acknowledge, importantly, the influence of one major non-geographic text of the time, Jerome Bruner's, *The Process of Education*.[9] Bruner, a noted American psychologist, had been earlier involved in a conference in which eminent scientists had debated educational issues at Woods Hole, Massachusetts, and some of their ideas now informed his own views.

The Process of Education was a slim book of fewer than 100 pages – perhaps that was the secret of its sucess – but it was written with great clarity and packed full of salient thinking which challenged dominant Piagetian ideas in relation to how quickly and how early children learn. Bruner's beliefs about the possibility of the 'acceleration of learning' were to be highly influential in the decades to come. For geography, in particular, his belief that children's ability to hypothesise long preceded their facility with words had implications about the kind of geography offered in primary schools. It opened up the potential of simple maps as an alternative non-verbal means of communication for the very young.

The discovery (and subsequent adoption) of Bruner's thinking led the school geographers involved in 'new geography' to other educational sources – and in absorbing these, the justification for new approaches was given an extra dimension. This exploration of educational theory provided a broader and stronger base for the advancement of 'new geography' in schools than the justifications often advanced in the higher education sector at the time. David Gowing and Trevor Bennetts, writing in 1973 on 'Objectives in the geography curriculum' for instance,[10] draw on the philosophers of education Hirst and Peters, the psychologists Bloom and Bruner, the sociologists of education Musgrove and Kerr, and the curriculum theorists Skilbeck and Satterley, to support their arguments.

Another to mine educational theory to advantage was Norman Graves, who succeeded to the Headship of the Geography Department of the London Institute of Education in the early 1960s. Though Graves stood urbanely apart from the more zealous of the 'new geography' advocates, his writing incorporated much of the new educational territory through several decades and his *Geography in Education* was an influential guidebook for teachers and teacher-trainers in the 1970s.[11]

NEW IDEAS AT SEVEN-PLUS

The curriculum model of development predicated by Haggett in his introduction to *Settlement Patterns* appeared to be one in which change emanated from the top and spread downwards; however, the ideas of the academic spatial analysts were by no means uncritically adopted in schools and there are examples, in this period, of the diffusion of ideas working in more complex ways.

John Cole of the Department of Geography in the University of Nottingham was a man of individual initiatives and unusual breadth of interest. He had already published a best-selling popular paperback[12] in addition to his more academic work when in 1965 he began an innovative low-key publishing venture in his own department under the title *Bulletins of Quantitative Data*. In reality, the Bulletins were much more wide-ranging than their title suggested and some were hardly

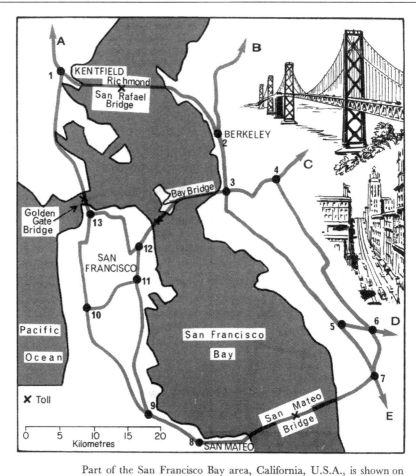

Part of the San Francisco Bay area, California, U.S.A., is shown on the map. Four of the longest bridges in the world are here. The map shows the four bridges as well as some fast main roads.

1 Can you make a journey by road starting at 12 and returning to 12, passing over each of the four bridges once and once only?
2 A bank is robbed at 11. At which bridges should the police put up traffic controls to prevent the robbers reaching (a) escape road A, (b) escape road B, (c) all escape roads A–E?

51

Figure 8.2:
Page from *New Ways in Geography* by J. P. Cole and N. J. Beynon, 1968 (reduced in size)
(*Source*: Blackwell)

quantitative at all; No.8 was the first British publication on geographical games, a methodology which was to play an important part in developing a practical and motivating study of geographical processes and change in the 1970s (see below). Cole had become aware of the needs and interests of his two young sons as they passed through primary school. One of his undergraduate students, John Beynon, had a father who was a primary school head teacher and so there was a convenient laboratory available for the testing of ideas. Cole explored the very fundamentals of 'the new geography' with elegant simplicity, as he turned his mind to this level. What emerged was the *'Seven-Plus' Geography* project, first published in

June 1966, in duplicated form as one of the Nottingham Bulletins.[13]

The introduction to the exercises reveals some interesting evidence on the origins of Cole's work. He quotes the Swedish geographer, Torsten Hagerstrand (and many of the other early 'new geographers' were influenced by Hagerstrand's university department at Lund),[14] Balchin and Coleman's seminal article about graphicacy[15] and 'a stimulating talk on the teaching of geography in a primary school by Mr R. S. Barker at the Geographical Association Conference in Nottingham in 1965'. Ron Barker was a genial and hard-working Suffolk primary school head teacher who gave long service to committees of the Geographical Association. So the diffusion of ideas was sometimes bottom-upwards.

Cole's pamphlet contained painstakingly hand-drawn maps for the exercises and supplementary pages which showed the structure and the conceptual framework and analysis of the material presented in ways which were quite new for the primary sector. The thinking behind the material chimed with Jerome Bruner's ideas about letting young children handle abstract concepts as long as they were in appropriately simple form.

The exercises eventually found their way into a more orthodox print form as *New Ways in Geography*[16] and almost single-handedly the four-book series revived some interest in geographical work in primary schools. The books remained in print for over 20 years, selling nearly 400,000 copies (some of them also to secondary schools though they were not intended for that sector). They also broke new ground in pioneering the supplementary provision of disposable workpads to be used in conjunction with the textbooks and half a million of these were sold (see Figure 8.2).

CONFERENCES PAMPHLETS AND MAGAZINES

The ideas of spatial analysis, models and quantitative techniques disseminated effectively in the general expansionist climate of the 1960s and 1970s. There was a population boom and so a need to expand the teaching force rapidly. Many young teachers found paths to rapid promotion; in geography, the espousal of new ideas was seen to be an advantage, particularly as they seemed to offer more intellectual fibre and sinew than before. Some more senior teachers regretted the shift away from 'real geography' and felt (if only intuitively) that a move towards a more theoretical and quantitative approach was not in the best interests of all pupils. But the limitations of positivist thinking in the geographical sphere were, as yet, unexposed, and its deficiency in dealing with human agency and in examining wider social issues challenged only in a mild way. For the time being, it provided intellectual vigour and excitement and a whole new intoxicating environment for many younger geographers to explore.

Conferences, formal and informal helped to spread the new ideas;[17] a group of teachers and lecturers met annually at Charney Manor in Oxfordshire to argue informally both geographical and educational issues and devise new approaches: Her Majesty's Inspectors, under the leadership of John W. Morris, turned the focus of their annual vacation 'long courses' towards an examination of the new ideas and gave them tacit approval (see Figures 8.3 and 8.4); there was a three-line whip on all geography HMI to attend one early in-service course about the 'new geography' held at Maria Grey College, Twickenham. Everson and Fitzgerald found themselves recruited into the Inspectorate at an unprecedentedly early age, where their capacity to influence was greatly increased.

One participant at these conferences was Richard Aylmer, then a teacher at Bloxham School near Oxford. Aylmer was an unusual man, a humorist whose droll approach pricked some hot-air filled balloons of rhetoric (see Box) as well as representing a more critical approach to some of the new ideas. His entrepreneurial instincts stretched from making hardware models to producing attractive ties and scarves for teachers with the interlocking hexagonal patterns of central place theory as their decoration.

He also became an influential second-wave underground publisher, producing, from his home, a stream of A5-size duplicated booklets under the generic title *Setwork*. These had a ready-made market as they were neatly tailor-made for modules of the Oxford and Cambridge Board A-level Geography syllabus – which had been reorganised to take account of new ideas during a brief period when Peter Haggett was Chief Examiner. The Oxford and Cambridge Board examinations were taken by many of the independent and grammar schools and had a high proportion of able students as candidates. Thus successful innovators shrewdly operated the levers of power. Aylmer's booklets were the precursor of other modular-style pamphlets which supported further A-level change in the 1980s, most notably in respect of the '16–19' project.[18]

In the early 1970s a second and more organised phase of 'underground press' emerged. At one of the DES Doncaster courses Neil Sealey, a young lecturer at Luton College of Technology, put forward the idea of a monthly magazine specifically to disseminate teaching materials, new methods and techniques, and to act as a forum for discussion of the new ideas. So came into being *Classroom Geographer*.

Sealey, took a novel line as a journal publisher. Editorialising in his second issue, he said:

> There is no editorial board as such, and while some submissions may lack clarity, logic, brevity, be mistaken, or be generally of poor quality, it is not proposed to use editorial judgement to decide this. Rather, it is hoped that readers, and thus the contributors, will set their own standards and use the space provided for letters and articles to correct mistakes and redress balances.
>
> This may seem an unusual approach, but it is also very easy for editors to be mistaken, and for censorship to replace quality

Figure 8.3: Cover page of *Geography in Education*, HMI pamphlet, 1960 (reduced in size) (*Source*: HMSO)

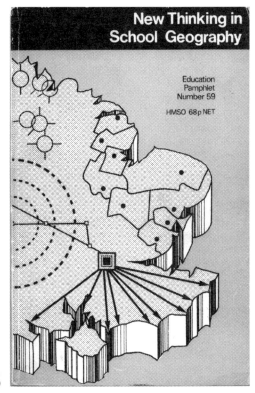

Figure 8.4: Cover page of *New Thinking in School Geography*, HMI pamphlet, 1972 (reduced in size) (*Source*: HMSO)

SONG OF THE CYNIC
(An old geography teacher's lament)
Tune: The Vicar of Bray

Verse 1

In Stamp and Beaver's golden days
When loyalty no harm meant
A zealous regional man was I
And so I got preferment
To teach my flocks I never missed
Regions laid out in text books
And damned were those that did resist
And they received my vexed looks

Chorus

And this is work that I'll retain
So long as I'm assured, sir
That it is in my syllabus
And favoured by my Board, sir.

Verse 2

When model men obtained the crown
And games came into fashion
The regional men I hunted down
Christaller was my passion
Von Thunen's rings, I found would fit
And so would correlation
Provided the data was fudged a bit;
So much for quantification!

Chorus

And this is work that I'll retain
So long as I'm assured, sir
That it is in my syllabus
And favoured by my Board, sir.

R. G. Aylmer

Note: L. D. Stamp and S. H. Beaver's *The British Isles* was the standard reference work for teachers from the 1940s to the 1960s.

---

control. It is not expected that contributors will submit rubbish. Genuine mistakes are often common ones and their publication, and the discussion of them can be of benefit in the long run.

Though organised entirely by volunteers, *Classroom Geographer* was a brilliant and unconventional publishing venture, appearing as regularly as clockwork each month for seven years. Operating from the garage of their small terraced house in Luton, Sealey and his wife Yvonne, edited, typed, duplicated, collated, stapled, bagged-up and posted an engagingly friendly and lively magazine to an eager audience. The circulation reached 2,000.

The pages proved a venue for many short articles with a practical flavour as well as for a vigorous set of letter-writers. Simple classroom-friendly geographical games and simulations, a good many of them devised by the students of Rex Hall, a geography lecturer at Worcester College of Education, were a feature of most issues. They were a testament to the growing and widespread interest in this new approach, which had become one of the pedagogical spearheads of the drive towards understanding world processes and changes. Games had become linked almost accidentally to the new mathematical approaches, but they caught the imagination of many teachers who were looking for a relief from note-giving and note-taking, and wanting a more participatory atmosphere in their classrooms.[19]

By its very accessibility and informality, *Classroom Geographer* also encouraged the floating of tentative, experimental ideas and the flying of intellectual kites. One such kite was John Bale's prophetic article 'How to overturn a discipline again';[20] another was David Wright's use of the concept of the model to present geographical education's progress as a meandering river (see Figure 8.5).[21] This was an intriguing idea (also espoused by John Paterson[22] and much earlier, in a slightly different way, by Douglas Freshfield[23]) which unfortunately never attracted the attention of the discipline's philosophers who wrote in the weightier academic journals.

The efficacy of the magazine, while Sealey ran it, was apparent from the respect and affection in which it was held. Eventually, in 1979, he departed to a post in his home islands, the Bahamas, and the magazine passed into other hands, gradually losing its particular magnetism and its regularity in the process.

There were other informally printed magazines of influence also at this time. *Profile* was a student-edited magazine from St Paul's and St Mary's Colleges, Cheltenham, which often attracted lively contributors from outside its own walls; the *Bulletin of Environmental Education* (BEE) was dynamic and quirky and emanated from the Education Unit of the Town and Country Planning Association. Here Colin Ward and Tony Fyson promoted work on the built environment, not solely confined to geographical perspectives, and coined the term 'streetwork' to match 'fieldwork'.

The Geographical Association reacted somewhat cautiously to all this for a few years, though its series of pamphlets called *Teaching Geography* was a barometer of change. Whereas No. 3 in the series offered help on 'The use of a revolving blackboard', 'The use of screen and blackboard together' and 'Producing a slide set for fieldwork', the new wave engulfed it a few issues further on. No. 11 in the series concerned hypothesis testing, No. 14 the techniques of network analysis and No. 23 the use of the rank correlation co-efficient.

It was not until 1975 that the GA responded firmly to the pedagogical ferment; then it introduced a new magazine *Teaching Geography* to supplement its long-established journal *Geography*. This, under the skilled editorship of Patrick Bailey, a lively and likeable teacher-educator

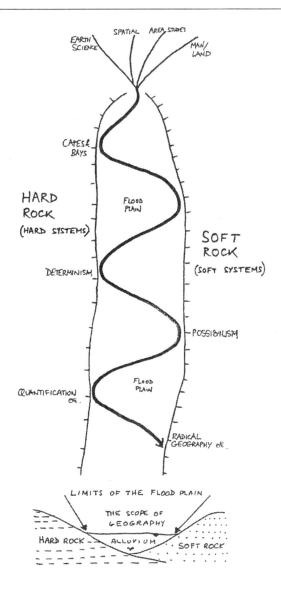

Figure 8.5:
'The river of geography' – a model devised by David Wright in *Classroom Geographer*

The dynamic aspect of geography ... is indicated by the meanders of the river ... Each swing of the meander brings the river against either 'hard' or 'soft' systems. Erosion takes place and the influence of the former swings is still present in the load carried by the river. Thus the ideas, for example, of 'capes and bays geography' – hard facts – are still one vital ingredient, especially in school geography ... most of the load from earlier erosion is quickly deposited in the stream bed ... while the vital elements remain as part of the heritage of geography and constitute a part of forward movement.

How far the 'meandering river' model can be a predictive model is open to question. Could a 'braided stream' be the next development – in which the different elements of geography go their own way for a while before reuniting? Or will a delta develop, with separation into 'adjectival geographies' preceding submergence in an 'integrated studies ocean'? Or is this meandering river above a waterfall, and rejuvenation will overtake us with unpredictable consequences? ...

who was to play a major role in GA affairs over the next 25 years, immediately began to have an impact and to offer practical help and resource information to teachers.

Teaching Geography has gone on, under successive editors, Eleanor Rawling, Jan Kelly, David Boardman and Elisabeth Barratt-Hacking, to play a significant role in transmitting new ideas. Its older sister *Geography* (founded in 1901 as *The Geographical Teacher*) now caters for and reaches a more limited, scholarly audience. (In 1989, in the wake of National Curriculum developments, a third major journal, *Primary Geographer*, joined the stable of GA publications, aimed particularly at the many non-specialist teachers who teach geography in primary schools. It has perhaps the highest design standards and 'readability' of all geographical educational publications.)

The development of three regularly published journals (plus a newsletter) is an indication of the GA's increased commitment to publishing since the 1970s: its publications officers and managing committee, though voluntary workers, have no sinecure. Its current annual catalogue of publications grows more extensive year by year with total annual sales approaching a quarter of a million pounds: all its design and production work is now of high quality, more than matching that of many commercial publishers.

MAKING A DIFFERENCE IN SCHOOLS

We need to return to the Madingley story, however. Ten years on from the first of the summer conferences run by Chorley and Haggett, much of geography in British schools had been influenced, if not transformed.

Some gifted teachers, such as Ken Briggs at Canon Slade Grammar School in Bolton and Vincent Tidswell at Hereford College of Education produced texts for schools on particular topics[24] which digested the new approaches and re-cycled them for appropriate levels of school work; Briggs' sixth-form geography magazine for a time contained work by his students of such dazzling precocity that some university lecturers would have been taxed to fully appreciate the content.

Individual school geography departments embraced the ideas with varying expertise and enthusiasm. At Farnborough Grammar School, Geoff Dinkele, and his colleagues Stephen Cotterell and Ian Thorn, developed a notable department which was a hive buzzing with interactive approaches and stimulating ideas and which led to one of the first co-ordinated and coherent series of text books for schools using the new approaches.[25] Working in a relatively unfavoured environment, Brian Greasley and his colleagues in the geography department of the Manor Comprehensive School in Cambridge, produced a parallel series demonstrating that the approach need not only be for high flyers.[26]

It was not only the 'spatial analysis' approach which was making the difference, though there is no doubt that some of the intellectual muscle of that movement rubbed off on to teachers and their pupils. The

'Madingley' style (in schools, at any rate) had also to do with using the ideas and insights of educational theorists and with the injection of innovative pedagogical techniques, some of which had first come to prominence from overseas.

TRANSATLANTIC INFLUENCES

One particularly strong influence in Britain in the 1960s and 1970s was the work of the American High School Geography Project (AHSGP), a phenomenon which was as important by its status as myth as it was in its actual outcomes. The Project had its origins through the Russian achievement of putting men into space in the early 1960s. This stirred the American government to want to compete and to improve the quality of its education programmes. This was to be done through increased funding for curriculum improvement. The AHSGP ran for nine years from 1961 to 1970, financed by over two and a half million dollars of money from the National Defence Education budget[27] – big money, even by American educational standards.

Its most inspirational and effective work was done in the second half of its life, whilst under the direction of Nicholas Helburn, an academic geographer who was seconded from the University of Colorado. Helburn had a deep understanding of educational issues and empathy with students. Coming into post following an abortive attempt to create a library of videos of 'Masterteachers' at work, Helburn changed the tack of the project and enlisted the help of several academic colleagues at other US universities. A set of six units for secondary (high) schools were devised and created: *The Geography of Cities*; *Manufacturing and Agriculture*; *Cultural Geography*; *Political Geography*; *Habitat and Resources*; *Japan*. These incorporated many ideas from the high-riding school of spatial analysis but also had a strong participative and enquiry-based approach. 'We certainly felt that we represented Science with a capital S', wrote Helburn later, reflecting on the Project's relative lack of focus on behavioural issues and perspectives, yet the pedagogical power of the ideas gave them a wide appeal.[28]

News of the project filtered through tantalisingly slowly to Europe during the late 1960s. AHSGP took a strict line about limiting the availability of pilot trial materials, and so much of what became known about it in Britain was through hearsay and was fragmentary. More substantial news (though not actual curriculum materials) was disseminated by British visitors who visited the Project's headquarters at Boulder, Colorado.[29]

The units produced by AHSGP were highly structured in their published form and rigorous in their pedagogic and conceptual approach (see Figure 8.6). Each classroom step was set out clearly, and comprehensive teachers' guides (which even indicated when and where the teacher should use chalk and blackboard) supplemented sets of class texts. The texts needed to be explicit, since in American schools

Overview of Teaching Times, Objectives, and Strategies for the Unit

Integral Activities	Time in 50 min. class periods	Media and Procedures	Major Ideas and Skills	Possible Home Assignments	Related Optional Activities or Readings
1 Different Ideas About Cattle	3	Students view slides of different uses of cattle around the world and discuss these uses in the context of the total cultures involved.	Customs that seem strange to Americans make sense when one understands their function in the total culture of a people.	Readings: "What's a Cow to the Nuer?" "Bullfight" "Cattle in India"	
2 A Lesson from Sports	2 to 3	Students examine and discuss the origin and diffusion of sports.	As an idea spreads through time and space its content often changes.	Readings: "Football" "Basketball" Library research Write essay	Games Illustrating the Spread of Ideas Readings: "Origins of the Olympic Games" "Home Away from Home"
3 Expansion of Islam	5 to 7	Through readings, discussion, and mapwork students follow and account for the spread of Islam.	Many factors jointly influence the diffusion of a culture and the consequent change of landscape.	Any sections of the narrative	"Letters from the Padres" "Corn and Custom" "The Long Road" "The Muslim Town"
4 Canada: A Regional Question	3 to 4	Students read about and discuss two adjacent cultures in Southeastern Canada, then try to draw a boundary between the two cultures.	Common traits in a cultural heritage can be used to distinguish culture regions.	Reading: "Canada: A regional Question"	
5 Culture Change: A Trend Toward Uniformity	2 to 3	Students view slides of several American and foreign cities. They discuss and account for the similarities and differences they see.	Ideas are being exchanged among the various areas of the world at an accelerating rate, resulting in a certain cultural uniformity.	Readings: "The Traditional Chinese City" "The Muslim Town"	

Figure 8.6:
Unit Summary page of 'Cultural Geography', Unit 3 of American High School Geography Project (reduced in size)

geography was at a low ebb at the time, and it was often being taught by teachers without any geographic training. Yet the influence of AHSGP in the USA was not widespread because it was seen by many teachers as too alien and removed from what they knew. In Britain, however, a more 'prepared' young workforce was eager to use it.

The tragedy was that the European publishers of the material then sought to operate a misguided policy of selling only complete units of the material (which included 30 of everything, expensively produced). Given the transatlantic mark-up costs, this put the glossy AHSGP units well beyond the total annual budget of the geography department of an average British school. Consequently, much material circulated only at second-hand or by illicit copy. 'Portsville' (an urban growth simulation) 'Metfab' (an industrial location game), 'Rutile and the Beach' (a role-play about environmental issues) and other curriculum activities, famed by repute remained elusively inaccessible to most.

In the final event, the ideas behind AHSGP, if not the actual materials, did have wide international influence.[30] It was honoured more elsewhere than in its country of origin, and its impact in Britain was indirect. However its thinking about approaches to geographical education pervaded many articles in the teaching magazines of the period and was personably mediated by Helburn in international conferences and tours. In particular, its thorough and coherent approach to the planning of whole curriculum units had immediate effect on some important comparable British initiatives which were starting.

CURRICULUM PROJECTS BRITISH STYLE

The drive to improve the curriculum had also begun in Britain in a mild way. A Conservative Minister of Education, Sir David Eccles, set up, in 1962, the innocently named Curriculum Study Group to advise him, an act which, in hindsight can be seen as the first impetus to open the door into the hitherto 'secret garden' of the curriculum in England and Wales. The CSG was transformed into the Schools Council in 1964, and the new body given sums of money for, on the one hand, curriculum research and development and, on the other, the improvement of public examinations. The Schools Council was a well-meaning body but overloaded with committees; many of the appointees to these committees came through their prominence and influence in teaching unions and whilst representative of the profession, they did not exactly form the cutting-edge of innovation and reform which was hoped for by government.

The Schools Council way of working was to set up 'projects' in particular subjects and second teachers and/or lecturers from their teaching posts for a few years to a project base, hoping that they would do some new thinking or produce some new materials which would be favourably received by other teachers. Many of these early projects were naive in the extreme in their strategies of both development and dissemination; their laboriously baked bread, cast hopefully upon the waters, turned soggy and regularly sank without trace.

Geography, perhaps fortunately as things turned out, did not receive any awards in the first round of projects; by the time that money was made available to the subject – in 1970 – some lessons had been learnt. Two projects were created – at Avery Hill College of Education in south-east London (*Geography for the Young School Leaver*) and at the University of Bristol (*Geography 14–18*). In the long term, though both were successful, neither of the titles turned out to be accurate.

THE AVERY HILL PROJECT

The *Geography for the Young School Leaver* project ('GYSL' as it later became more usually known) was enjoined to cater for the lower-ability pupils who were now required to stay on to the age of 16, because of the Raising of the School Leaving Age in 1967. There was something of a curriculum vacuum across the board for these 'ROSLA kids' as they were sometimes inelegantly known; could geography help to fill the gap by producing material of interest and relevance to a group who were unlikely to stay on a day beyond the statutory requirement and who had little chance of going on to higher education?

One of the co-directors of GYSL visited Boulder during AHSGP's final stages and was influenced by the quality of the teaching materials being produced there. The GYSL Project adopted a similar approach by concentrating on the production of a rich variety of high-quality resources (the worksheets were designed by students from the Royal College of Art) and putting these together in large project boxes.[31] Three somewhat controversially themed units were developed, with topics linked, at least in part, to local experience: 'Man, Land and Leisure'; 'Cities and People'; and 'People, Places and Work'. 'Teachers' Guides' thoroughly explained the structure of 'Key Ideas' which were a high-profile part of the scheme.

The big brightly coloured GYSL boxes were disseminated most successfully by a series of conferences in which a hard-sell was made to Local Education Authority Advisers, people who held the strings of large purses and who could place scores of boxes into the schools of their district if they thought it would bring about curriculum improvement. Hardly an authority in England and Wales did not succumb to the persuasive combination of the eloquence of the Project directors and the quality of the materials. One team of outside evaluators called GYSL 'the jewel in the crown' of the Schools Council[32] and it was certainly one of the most widely disseminated projects ever funded by them.[33]

Rex Beddis, one of the leading geography educators of the 1960s and 1970s[34] and one of the Project's co-directors[35] commented later:

> The project team had the difficult task of acting as agents of change ... whilst at the same time judging (the project's) relevance to the curriculum needs of lower-ability pupils ...

> Some teachers remained unwilling to concede the desirability of a conceptual geography – perhaps more than one would like to admit ... Nevertheless ... the geographical world seemed to have weathered reasonably well the storms of a changed geography, the raising of the school leaving age and the pressures for a curriculum relevant to the needs of the decade.[36]

The other co-director of the project, Tom Dalton, showed, in a later book how, though the ideas of the project were seen as pathfinders of change in one school, they could be seen as retrograde in another. In the case-study of the latter, it was the very structure of 'Key Ideas' and the gathering of empirical data as a work task which was viewed with suspicion. Teachers committed to the belief that educational process was more important than 'product' in teaching and that the needs of pupils at this age were not helped by dividing work into subjects did not favour GYSL – but they were very much a minority.[37] GYSL is regarded (by the educational community as a whole and not just by geographers) as the epitome of a funded project that 'worked'.

GYSL owed something, but by no means everything to the 'new geography'; the more fiercely quantitative elements and quest for precision were damped down, but the search for models and the reference to theories and ideas shone through in the rich materials resource-base. There was also an important extra dimension – a beginning of the conscious exploration of 'attitudes and values' within geographical topics. It was the size, profusion and attractiveness of the materials which perhaps had the biggest pulling-power; the 'big box' approach won the day. GYSL spread through the classrooms of the land with rapidity and some schools which had never been very strong in geography were transformed by the instruments put in their hands.

THE BRISTOL PROJECT

The '14–18' project team[38] based at Bristol set off on a very different track. Their first year was largely a reconnaissance of their constituency (the average and above-average pupil) and their early material mostly circulated in duplicated form to emphasise its provisional nature. Despite providing a thought-provoking publication aimed at teachers,[39] they quickly discovered that those responsible for examination-oriented classes had little time for the consideration or discussion of innovative or experimental materials; if any lasting impact was to be made it would have to be by changing the examination itself.

So, concentrating first on the 14–16 age group, the project set out on the rather tortuous path to get a new geography O-level syllabus put into the system.[40] The ideas behind the syllabus had a more direct line of ancestry to Madingley than GYSL; models and hypothesis testing were prominent and there was a requirement to be confidently numerate in order to handle data-response questions as well as key formulae. The written paper (worth 50 per cent of the total marks for the examination) included problem-solving questions, and decision-making exercises and allowed the use of an atlas. Its rubric was quite revolutionary:

> Some of the questions probably contain information about places which neither you, nor the other candidates, have studied in detail. This should not prevent you from answering these questions; it is not your factual knowledge of these places which the examination is trying to test, but your ability to use skills and ideas and to interpret and apply information. The use of an atlas is permitted in the examination room.

A dozen keen pilot schools, nervously licensed by the Schools Council, set out to test the examination in 1974, but it soon proved its practicability and gained a place in the portfolio of possible geography examinations open to all schools. Its recognisable descendant was readily identifiable as a survivor in the current, more restricted, range of exams available at GCSE available 25 years later. So too is a syllabus and examination (both are administered by OCR) which is called 'Avery Hill' – a surprising outcome, perhaps, given the original intentions of that project. But the success of GYSL materials soon spread them beyond the confines of their original target audience; it was not long before GYSL advocates sought a new O-level examination for those 'more able' pupils whom teachers might want to have the same stimulation and enjoyment from geography as their 'less able' colleagues.

In the same way, the Bristol project saw the benefit of producing good classroom materials to support their innovative O-level examination, and this is turn encouraged teachers to spread the ability level of those who might take it. (It was, in any case, difficult for a school to prepare students for two quite different O-levels at the same time.)

So, in the end the projects, starting from either end of the ability spectrum, met in the middle and crossed over as they searched for 'customers' to justify their success. Both the Avery Hill and Bristol projects refined and made practical new ideas and teaching strategies in school geography in the 1970s and geographical education was served well by their respective approaches.

The Bristol project ran out of time and money before it had turned its thoughts to reforming A-level and so the Schools Council funded another project *Geography 16–19*. This was based at the London Institute of Education in the period 1976–85.[41] The '16–19' project effectively replicated the work of the Bristol project by the considerable achievement of installing a new geography A-level on to the books.

The examination required knowledge of case-studies rather than global distributions; it encouraged the linkage of physical and human geography topics, used predominantly an enquiry-learning approach and was much less book-ridden and memory-based than its competitor A-levels. Some criticised it for its relative soft-pedalling of physical geography and some university tutors felt that '16–19' pupils 'knew less about the world' than those trained under more traditional regimes, but pupils voted with their feet and '16–19' had risen to the top of the candidate entries table for geography A-level by 1990.

A fourth Schools Council project catered for a younger age. *Place, Time and Society*[42] was based at the University of Liverpool School of Education and aimed at the 8–13 age group. It produced some interesting teachers' booklets which explored inter-disciplinary themes and teaching ideas, and some attractive materials on a much smaller scale than GYSL, but these were never disseminated with quite the same vigour and 'streetwise' knowhow that GYSL used. With a non-specialist audience not quite as ready to take them on as in the secondary sector, the materials were used patchily, and on the whole, only by those who were committed geographers or historians already – not by the generality of primary school classteachers. It deserved a better fate.

Fig. 13.7 (left) The growth of London   Planning ahead

Fig. 13.8 Suggested sites for New Towns in the south-east of England

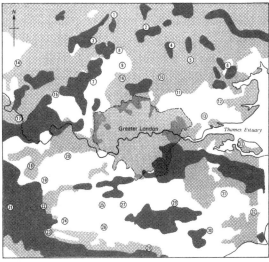

Planning New Towns

This problem was soon appreciated by the planners and the obvious need was for this growth outside the Green Belt to be planned and controlled so that it did not get out of hand like the pre-war growth had done. It was decided to focus this growth in New Towns sited in the country beyond the Green Belt which would provide their own employment and thus cut down the number of commuters.

Fig. 13.8 shows the sites of thirty-three proposed New Towns with their distances from London and areas of good agricultural land.

15 Imagine that you have been appointed to a Royal Commission on New Towns with the task of choosing eight of the proposed thirty-three New Towns for definite development.
(a) Each member of the class should choose or be allocated a site and list the relative advantages and disadvantages of it. They should then present a short report to the rest of the Commissioners.
(b) The entire Commission should then vote on which eight proposed town sites should be chosen.
(c) These eight sites should be marked on a large wall-map copy of Fig. 13.8.
(d) Then compare your list with the eight actually chosen which are listed in Fig. 13.15 at the end of this chapter. How many of them coincide?
(e) On the basis of your own Commission's conclusions, write a detailed criticism of the actual sites chosen in Fig. 13.15.

Figure 8.7:
Page from Book 3 of *Oxford Geography Project*, 1974 (reduced in size). (*Source:* Oxford University Press)

Key to suggested sites

1 Sandy, Beds.	13 Basildon, Essex	24 Liphook. Hants.
2 Royston, Herts.	14 Bicester, Oxfordshire	25 Cranleigh, Surrey
3 Flitwick, Beds.	15 Princes Risborough, Bucks.	26 Billingshurst, Sussex
4 Quendon, Essex	16 Hatfield, Herts.	27 Crawley, Sussex
5 Great Dunmow, Essex	17 Wallingford, Berks.	28 Plumpton, Sussex
6 Kelvedon, Essex	18 Silchester, Hants.	29 Ashurst, Kent
7 Hemel Hempstead, Herts.	19 Hook, Hants.	30 Robertsbridge, Sussex
8 Stevenage, Hertfordshire	20 Bracknell, Berks.	31 Headcorn, Kent
9 Welwyn, Herts.	21 Micheldever, Hants.	32 Ham Street, Kent
10 Harlow, Essex	22 Alton, Hants.	33 Queenborough, Kent
11 Ongar, Essex	23 Petersfield, Hants.	
12 Woodham Ferrars, Essex		

155

A SUMMARISING SERIES

The most influential series of geography textbooks of the 1970s was a series which emerged as a result of a chance meeting in Wright's Bar in Houghton Street, the tiny cafe which is next door to the London School of Economics. LSE hosted the Geographical Association's annual conference for many years and it was the place where publishers sought contacts and if they were fortunate, potential authors.

Martin Cuss of Oxford University Press accosted John Rolfe, newly appointed Head of Geography at Haberdashers' Aske's School for Boys, Elstree (formerly the base of Everson and Fitzgerald) one conference day in 1972 and guilelessly asked him 'Anything on the stocks, John' as they sipped coffee together. Rolfe happily acknowledged that he had a young department full of vitality and ideas. From this chance conversation, the idea for a textbook series was born which would sell

A 'GEOGRAPHICAL' ANALYSIS OF SOME GEOGRAPHICAL TEXTBOOKS FOR 11-16 YEAR OLDS

Date of 1st publication	Author	Title & publisher	Size (in ins)	Colour	Text (%)	Iustrations (%)	Activities (%)
A 'The regional geography era' (1920 - 1950)							
1928	Fairgrieve & Young	Human geography II (George Philip)	7.5 x 5.5	B & W	87	8	5
1935	Pickles	The British Isles (JM Dent)	7.5 x 5.5	B & W	64	29	7
1938	Preece & Wood	F'ndations of Geog I (Univ Tutorial Press)	7.5 x 5.5	B & W	57	40	3
B 'The sample studies era' (1945 - 1975)							
1951	Young & Mosby	Our changing world (Edward Arnold)	9.5 x 7.25	B & W	59	38	3
1958	Honeybone & Roberson	Geog for Schools II (Heinemann)	8.0 x 5.25	B & W	40	33	27
1971	Graves & White	Geog of British Isles (Heinemann)	10.0 x 7.5	B & W	47	38	15
C 'The new geography era' (1970 - 1985)							
1979	Greasley et al	Basic geography 3 (Harrap)	11.0 x 8.5	2-colour	18	47	35
1974	Grenyer et al	Oxford Geog Project 3 (OUP)	9.5 x 9.0	2-colour	17	56	27
1985	Beddis	A new geog of Britain (OUP)	11.0 x 8.5	Occ full colour	27	63	10
D 'The National Curriculum era' (1990 - ?)							
1992	Lambert	Jigsaw pieces (CUP)	11.0 x 8.5	2-colour & full col	38	47	15
1992	Waugh & Bushell	Connections (Stanley Thornes)	11.0 x 8.5	Full col	26	54	20
1994	Kemp et al	Access to geog 4 (OUP)	11.0 x 8.5	Full col	30	53	27

Figure 8.8:
Analysis of the use of space in a variety of geography textbooks (*Source*: author)

over half-a-million copies and be the best-seller of its own times – the Oxford Geography Project.

It is significant that 'OGP', as it came to be known[43] – not a funded project like GYSL or Bristol in spite of its name, but a series of textbooks and workbooks – was a team effort in comparison to some of the charismatic solo accomplishments of the past. It was the communal classroom experiences of the Haberdashers' geographers working in a school with more than its share of bright pupils, which shaped the series. It was designed as a trilogy of books for 11–14 year olds in the first instance, but was later used by a wider range of abilities in the 11–16 age range.

OGP had a distinctly different flavour from its predecessors and like *Settlement Patterns*, this was because of pedagogy as much as content. 'We feel convinced that the structure that we have provided is a significant advance on anything that has preceded it' the authors boldly claimed in their preface. Though it was not in full colour, 80 per cent of the space in the books was given over to pictures, graphs, diagrams and work activities, rather than text. Models, and concepts abounded. There were over 40 interactive simulation and game ideas in Book 3 alone (see Figure 8.7). An average OGP page was as far removed from Fairgrieve and Young or Pickles as you could get (see Figure 8.8).

OGP's success in sales confirmed the fact that the ideas generated in Madingley had spread wide and far; modified along the way, injected with pedagogical insights, given new twists, it was a sign that geography had come of age.[44]

NOTES

1. R. J. Chorley and P. Haggett, 'From Madingley to Oxford', foreword to W. Macmillan (ed.), *Remodelling Geography* (Blackwell, Oxford, 1989), pp. xv–xx.
2. R. J. Chorley and P. Haggett (eds), *Frontiers in Geographical Teaching* (Methuen, London, 1965).
3. Fred K. Schaefer (1953), 'Exceptionalism in geography: a methodological examination', *Annals of the Association of American Geographers*, 43 (1953), pp. 226–49; reprinted in P. J. Ambrose (ed.), *Analytical Human Geography* (Longman, London, 1969), pp. 57–83.
4. R. J. Chorley and P. Haggett (eds), *Models in Geography* (Methuen, London, 1967). The book was also divided, re-packaged and sold successfully in separate parts.
5. *Geography*, 54 (1) (1969). The edition included papers about problem-solving in geography, a Monte Carlo simulation model, the use of operational games in the classroom, a model for land-use analysis, the use of hypothesis-testing in field-work, and a description of comparable developments in the USA. The issue also included examples of classroom lessons and the results of a questionnaire to teachers about the new ideas.
6. C. A. Fisher, 'Whither regional geography?', *Geography*, 55 (4) (1970), pp. 373–89.
7. The 'spatial analytic' approach is both described and thoroughly critiqued in Chapter 3 of A. Holt-Jensen, *Geography: History and Concepts* (Sage, London, 1999).
8. J. A. Everson and B. P. Fitzgerald, *Settlement Patterns* (Longman, London, 1969).
9. J. S. Bruner, *The Process of Education* (Vintage Books, New York, 1959).
10. D. Gowing, 'A fresh look at objectives' and T. H. Bennetts, 'The nature of geographical objectives', in R. Walford (ed.), *New Directions in Geography Teaching* (Longman, London, 1973), pp. 152–74.
11. N. J. Graves, *Geography in Education* (Heinemann, London, 1975).
12. J. P. Cole, *Geography of World Affairs* (Penguin, London, 1959). The book went through many editions and revisions and remained in print for over 20 years.
13. J. P. Cole (ed.), *The Seven-Plus Geography Project: Bulletin of Quantitative Data*, No. 5 (Department of Geography, University of Nottingham, 1966).
14. See W. Bunge, *Theoretical Geography* (University of Lund Press, Lund, 1966). Bunge was an American geographer whose first book was highly influenced by spatial analysis; it was remarkably different from his later maverick radical utterances and publications. A similar

Odyssey can be traced in the life of David Harvey by comparing his *Explanation in Geography* (Arnold, London, 1969) with his *Social Justice in the City* (Arnold, London, 1973).

15. W. G. V. Balchin and A. Coleman, 'Graphicacy should be the fourth ace in the pack', *Times Educational Supplement*, 1965, 5 November edition, also reproduced in J. Bale, N. J. Graves and R. Walford (eds), *Perspectives in Geographical Education* (Oliver & Boyd, Edinburgh, 1973). See also W. G. V. Balchin, 'Graphicacy', *Geography*, 57 (2) (1972), pp. 185–95. The term 'graphicacy' was coined by Balchin and Coleman to describe the ability to read and make maps and diagrams and they suggested that graphicacy should be taught formally and given equal status in education alongside oracy, literacy and numeracy (the traditional 'Three Rs'). The idea has proved a durable one for primary school geography teachers.

16. J. P. Cole and N. J. Beynon, *New Ways in Geography*, Books 1–4 (Blackwell, Oxford, 1968). There was also an associated teachers' guide and workpads for each book.

17. 'Long courses' organised by the Department of Education and Science at Maria Grey College, Twickenham and Doncaster College of Education and staffed by HMI were the original diffusion sources for the work; the series of annual informal weekend conferences at Charney Manor, Oxfordshire, supplemented this but also continued well after the DES courses were abandoned, the victim of financial cutbacks in education. For the fruits of some of the Charney Manor Conferences, see R. Walford (ed.), *New Directions in Geography Teaching* (Longman, London, 1973); R. Walford (ed.), *Signposts for Geography Teaching* (Longman, London, 1981); R. Walford (ed.), *Viewpoints on Geography Teaching* (Longman, London, 1991); R. Walford and P. Machon (eds), *Challenging Times: Implementing the National Curriculum in Geography* (Cambridge Publishing Services, Cambridge, 1994).

18. M. Naish, 'Geography 16–19', in D. Boardman (ed.), *New Directions in Geographical Education* (Falmer Press, Brighton, 1985), pp.99–115.

19. For an introduction to geographical games, see R. Walford, *Games in Geography* (Longman, London, 1969).

20. J. Bale, 'How to overturn a discipline again', *Classroom Geographer*, December 1978. Bale went on to carve out a distinctive career at the University of Keele, both as an innovative geographical educator, and as a pioneer in studying and writing about the geography of sport. See J. Bale, *Sports Geography* (E. & F. N. Spon, London, 1990); *Sport, Space and the City* (Routledge, London, 1993).

21. D. R. Wright, 'Dimensions and traditions of geography: an attempted synthesis', *Classroom Geographer*, October 1980. Wright contributed many stimulating pieces to geographical magazines and journals on a variety of subjects during his time at Keswick Hall College of Education, Norwich, and at the University of East Anglia. Together with his wife Jill, he has also become an originator, deviser and consultant for several popular atlases.

22. J. Paterson, 'Some dimensions of geography', *Geography*, 64 (4) (1979), p. 276.

23. Douglas Freshfield in his Presidential address to the Geographical Association in 1902 said, 'Our advance is not unlike that of a devious stream. At one point, seeking the points of least resistance, we are working a channel in the fossilised beds of the ancient universities, at another we attack the soft places in the more modern strata of the School Boards.' *Geographical Teacher*, 1 (2) (1902), p. 86.

24. See K. Briggs, *Introducing Transportation Networks* (University of London Press, London, 1972); *Introducing Towns and Cities* (University of London Press, London, 1974); *Beginning the New Geography* (University of London Press, London, 1979); W. V. Tidswell, *Pattern and Process in Human Geography* (University Tutorial Press, London, 1973).

25. G. W. Dinkele, S. Cotterell and I. Thorn, *Reformed Geography*, a series of five books (Harrap, London, 1976). Dinkele went on to be the Geography Inspector for Hampshire (1982–95); in that period, his bulky, termly newsletter for all schools in the county, was an astonishing melange of ideas, activities, resources, jokes, aphorisms, tips and advice. Though never published or publicised beyond the county, each copy reflected the life and preoccupations of geography teachers in a revealing and heartening way.

26. B. Greasley *et al.*, *Basic Geography*, a series of three books (Harrap, London, 1978).

27. See American High School Geography Project, *Geography in an Urban Age: Units 1–6*

(Collier-Macmillan, London, 1970); D. J. Patton (ed.), *From Geographic Discipline to Enquiring Student* (Association of American Geographers, Washington, DC, 1970); R. B. McNee, 'Does geography have a structure?', in R. J. Chorley (ed.), *Directions in Geography* (Methuen, London, 1973), pp. 285–313.

28. Nicholas Helburn, 'Reflections on the High School Project', in J. Huckle (ed.), *Geographical Education* (Oxford University Press, Oxford, 1983), p. 21.

29. N. J. Graves, 'The High School Project of the American Association of Geographers', *Geography*, 53 (1) (1968), pp. 68–73; B. P. Fitzgerald, 'The American High School Geography Project and its implications for teaching in Britain', *Geography*, 54 (1) (1969), pp. 56–63; J. Rolfe, 'The completion of the American High School Geography Project', *Geography*, 56 (3) (1971), pp. 216–20.

30. Angus M. Gunn (ed.), *High School Geography Project: Legacy for the Seventies* (Centre Educatif et Culturel, Montreal, 1972).

31. The units of *Geography for the Young School Leaver* were published by Thomas Nelson & Sons.

32. B. Macdonald and R. Walker, *Changing the Curriculum* (Open Books, London, 1976).

33. D. Boardman, 'Geography for the Young School Leaver', in D. Boardman (ed.), *New Directions in Geographical Education* (Falmer, Brighton, 1985); D. Boardman, *The Impact of a Curriculum Project: Educational Review*, Occasional Publication, No. 14 (University of Birmingham, 1988).

34. Rex Beddis was appointed Humanities Adviser to schools in Avon County Council, following his time at GYSL. He went on to write several major geography textbooks for schools, including *A New Geography of Britain* and the well-produced and influential *Sense of Place* series for Thomas Nelson, before an untimely early death.

35. Tom Dalton was the other co-director, and Trevor Higginbottom and Pamela Bowen were the other senior members of the project staff.

36. R. Beddis, 'Geographical education since 1960: a personal view', in J. Huckle (ed.), *Geographical Education* (Oxford University Press, Oxford, 1983), pp. 10–19.

37. T. H. Dalton, *The Challenge of Curriculum Innovation* (Falmer Press, Brighton, 1988).

38. The project was personably led by Dr Gladys Hickman, with Harry Tolley, John Reynolds and, later, John Hancock as Senior Research Associates.

39. G. M. Hickman, J. Reynolds and H. Tolley, *A New Professionalism for a Changing Geography* (Schools Council, London, 1973).

40. Sheila Jones and John Reynolds, 'The development of a new O-level syllabus', *Geography*, 58 (3) (1973), pp. 263–8.

41. The project was originally directed by Michael Naish and the Senior Associates included Frances Slater, Ashley Kent, Clive Hart and Eleanor Rawling. See M. Naish, E. Rawling and C. Hart, *The Contribution of a Curriculum Project to 16–19 Education* (Longman/SCDC, London, 1987).

42. The *Place, Time and Society 8–13* project was directed by Professor Alan Blyth. Gordon Elliott was the geographer on the staff of the project. A series of 15 resource boxes (including tapes, slides, booklets and worksheets) on various topics and teachers guides were published by Collins–ESL Bristol from 1975 onwards. Those of geographical significance included *Rivers in Flood*; *People on the Move*; *Villages and Towns*; *Points Patterns and Movement*; *People and Progress*; *The Geography of Hunger*.

43. J. Rolfe, A. Kent, C. Rowe, N. Grenyer and R. Dearden, *Oxford Geography Project*, three vols and teachers' guide: *The Local Framework, European Patterns, Contrasts in Development* (Oxford University Press, Oxford, 1974).

44. Another lower secondary school series based around concepts (rather than themes or places) which also had success at this time was: M. Walker, E. Walker and T. Wilson, *Location and Links* (Blackwell, Oxford, 1973).

9

Radical Responses, 1975–85

If David Wright's vivid metaphor of school geography as a flood plain is adopted (see Figure 8.5) it can be said that the meander of the spatial analytic river reached its fullest extent in the mid-1970s. By then, some notable academic voices were diverging from the general acclaim and reservations about its suitability for all pupils were beginning to be expressed in schools.

David Harvey, geographical guru for many young geographers in the 1960s, moved away from the spatial analytic positions held in *Explanation in Geography*,[1] published in 1969 to a more committed socio-political position in *Social Justice in the City*[2] four years later. Harvey had, in fact, pre-figured his change of position a year earlier, in a little-known, co-authored, school textbook, which was almost certainly the first to expound an openly Marxist philosophy.[3] A more open consciousness to radical ideas was also espoused by David Smith, professor of geography at Queen Mary College, London, who urged geographers to speak not of differences but of inequalities in the world.[4] The term 'welfare geography' was coined.

The critique of spatial analysis was that its attempt to be objective, scientific and thus value-free was a myth; and that its theories and models usually presumed a 'billiard-ball universe' of unhelpful simplicity. It mirrored the political ideology in which it operated – a capitalist system – by focusing attention on the surface questions of management, planning and control of space, not on the deeper questions of class, ownership of land and social justice.

A higher-education journal, *Antipode*, was founded in 1970 to propagate 'welfare' and 'radical' ideas; its founder, Richard Peet, gathered some key contributions together in *Radical Geography* a few years later.[5]

Richard Reiser, a young LSE geography graduate who went to teach in London's East End, offered one of the sharpest schoolteacher criticisms of the prevailing new orthodoxy:

> Spatial analysis with its odd-shaped bag of tools (seeks) data virtually irrespective of social and historic content on which to perform its new-fangled technical wizardry. The very content of the

world is abstracted into quantitative geographical space, allowing status-quo views of the world to pass for scientific observations and analyses.[6]

Some geographic educators, notably John Huckle working at Bedford College of Education (now part of De Montfort University), began to espouse radical ideas at teachers' in-service courses and some 'welfare geography' approaches began to appear in school textbooks, though with less overt left-wing political overtones than in higher education. Norman Graves devoted parts of his 1979 GA Presidential Address to a discussion of 'humanistic geography' and to examining phenomenology as a philosophic antidote to positivism;[7] his colleague at the London Institute, Frances Slater, campaigned for a greater recognition of 'attitudes and values' in geography teaching.[8] Questions about the ethnocentricity of textbooks and images of other countries began to be raised. The scene was set for a new debate, and a particular article in a non-mainstream journal was the accidental spark which set it off.

THE START OF THE TRAIL

The 1981 Lent Term issue of the Cambridge Journal of Education carried a 20-page article by Dave Hicks, newly created Director of the Centre for Peace Studies, at St Martins College, Lancaster.[9] Hicks had been a geography teacher in Gloucestershire and East Anglia between 1964 and 1974 but had then become Education Officer of the Minority Rights Group, before setting up the new Centre at Lancaster. He had completed a PhD at Lancaster in 1980 based on research which he had conducted and material which he had used in the school classroom. The article, a summary of the key parts of his PhD thesis, was called 'Images of the world; what do geography textbooks actually teach about development?'

Hicks explained that in his research he had recently been concerned in examining the following questions:

> what images of the world, especially of the 'third world' do we have in Britain?
> how do such ethnocentric images manifest in the curriculum generally and in teaching materials in particular?
> what part might the 'relevance revolution' in Geography have to play in all this?
> what images of world development do geography textbooks in the UK actually convey?

He went on to assert:

> whereas awareness of these issues may be fairly high amongst some teachers in multi-ethnic inner-city areas, elsewhere it is certainly not.

185

At a workshop in Oxford someone said that they had previously thought that bias was 'something to do with playing bowls', whilst in Cumbria I was asked what 'multi-cultural' meant.

I was also warned that if I went around challenging the cultural assumptions of the status quo by exploring ethnocentric and racist bias in education I would be labelled both a Red and a subversive. If that is the case I am proud to be a subversive.[10]

Hicks went on to explore the historical context of images found in British geography textbooks (see Chapter 4) and reviewed existing research (mostly North American) about ethnocentric bias in teaching materials. He also gave a positive answer to a self-posed question 'Should we expect geography to be concerned about contemporary issues such as world development?'

He drew attention to what he called the 'relevance revolution' (another name for welfare and radical approaches) which he asserted had occurred in some parts of academic geography in the 1970s, the beginnings of a backlash to the positivist and theoretical tenets of the spatial analysts.

Its essential nature is humanistic: the development of a humane human geography, or putting the 'human' back into the subject. It is a 'people geography' about real people and **for** people in the sense of contributing to the enlargement of human being for all – especially for the most deprived.[11]

It is also about who gets what, where and how. This 'geography of concern' will thus focus on all issues of human welfare and justice ... suffice to say that it gives adequate legitimation for the study of contemporary issues in the school curriculum.

The major part of the article was concerned with a survey which Hicks had done on school textbooks. One aspect which attracted particular attention was a diagram in which he classified a range of popular contemporary school textbooks on two scales (see Figure 9.1). One scale was related to the supposed 'geographical paradigm' on which the book was judged to be based; it ran between Radical–Liberal–Status Quo. The other scale was related to the supposed 'perspective' of the book and was calibrated between Racist–Ethnocentric–Anti-racist.

Some of the evidence for Hicks' classifications was revealed in the article by quotations from the books under scrutiny. His study had been thorough, but, of course, the overall judgement about the books was a subjective one.[12] Some authors found themselves unfavourably classified in print, without a chance to respond or explain concerning their books. There is little doubt that Hicks' intentions were impeccable and the article was generous to textbook writers in other places. But unconsciously it set some precedents for later debates when the

TABLE 5

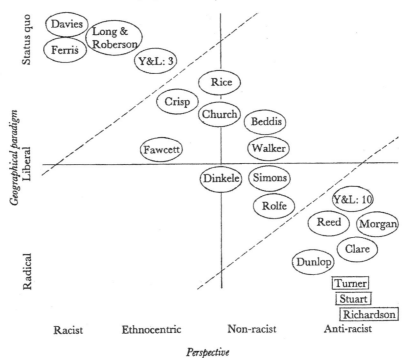

Images of the World: A Preliminary Map

Figure 9.1:
Diagram from David Hicks'
article about supposed racism
in textbooks, in *Cambridge
Journal of Education*, 1981
(*Source*: CJE)

temperature on the issues raised in the article was raised (many would say justifiably) and judgements about attitudes and intentions thrown about with abandon.

At the conclusion of his article Hicks urged that:

1 We urgently consider how to bring the 'relevance revolution' into school geography...

2 Educational publishers need to develop checklists and guidelines on ethnocentric bias in geography textbooks a) to use themselves and b) to be used by authors

3 Educational publishers need to commission new textbooks to rectify the deficient images already noted in this survey.

4 Teachers and study groups need to make known praise or blame for textbooks and make their comments and criteria known to publishers and colleagues.

This article (adaptations and extracts of which were subsequently printed elsewhere) was notable in seeking to link the concerns of what was coming to be known as 'welfare geography' to what was taught in schools.[13] It brought into prominence some key issues and also set the scene for a major controversy in the world of geographical education.

THE REPORT THE SCHOOLS COUNCIL REJECTED

In the year following Hicks' article, 1982, the Schools Council made headlines in the educational press when they declined to publish a report which they had themselves commissioned in the previous year. The report, designed to highlight the problems of assessment in a multi-cultural society, with special reference to geography, was one of a series on different subjects commissioned by a Schools Council project team. The Geography Report was commissioned from Dawn Gill, then Head of Geography at Quintin Kynaston School, in St John's Wood, London, a school with many ethnic minority pupils on its school roll.

The Schools Council project's 'leading officer' Geoff Bardell maintained later that:

> Miss Gill received detailed and critical comments on her work ... and was asked to take on board some/all of the criticisms ... some two months later the steering group received a virtually unchanged report and reluctantly reached the decision not to recommend publication.

Gill had chosen to interpret her brief widely, taking on board not only examination issues but also issues concerning geography syllabuses in general. She concluded that many syllabuses were inherently racist in the way in which they tackled matters. Her criticisms included the accusations that geography syllabuses failed to discuss colonialism and its effects fully: that developing countries were exclusively seen as 'problems': that other countries were defined by what 'they' could provide for 'us'; and that there was an undesirable Eurocentricity in much of what was studied.

The Schools Council admitted that there was much of value in the report but felt that it was too partial in coverage and too negative and critical to influence examination boards into making changes – which had been the original purpose of the exercise. The decision not to publish precipitated the report (and Gill herself) into national prominence.

The Education Officer of the Commission for Racial Equality (CRE), Gerry German, ascertained that Gill had kept the copyright on her own work and then shrewdly offered to make the report freely available to those who wished to see it. A press conference, radio appearances and a flurry of correspondence in the educational press made the report something of a *cause célèbre* and it was given further publicity at a conference in March 1983 at the London Institute of Education which

Figure 9.2:
Cover of a collection of papers
produced for the first ACDG
conference

was backed by the CRE and the Multi-Ethnic section of the Inspectorate of the Inner London Education Authority.[14]

The conference was advertised as 'Geography and education for a multi-cultural society'. The bulky set of documents which every delegate received had several constructive papers, and resource lists but bore the more stark and enigmatic title 'Racist society; geography curriculum'. The cartoon on the cover of the papers seemed to make a sharp comment on the state of British geography teaching (see Figure 9.2).

The focus of Gill's criticism was on the immensely successful Geography for the Young School Leaver project (see Chapter 8), whose well-produced materials were widespread in London schools. Gill criticised particular resource sheets in the material of the project for their approach and their implicit Eurocentric bias : accusations of racism were made in forthright terms.[15] GYSL co-directors and classroom users were not slow to respond. The conference erupted into surprisingly angry scenes as assertions and justifications were hurled across the floor.

Gill's criticisms were penetrating, but her final conclusion was quite a moderate one. Her concern at this point was that resources like the Dallas sheet might be used 'without questioning the underlying assumptions'. This is a point which might well have been acknowledged and accepted in a calmer context. Many schoolroom resources stem from particular attitudes and viewpoints not shared by the teacher or the school (newspaper articles being an obvious example); in the hands of skilful teachers, such attitudes are exposed and discussed and the resource evaluated as well as put to use. But the widespread success of GYSL in geography classrooms was its undoing; it tended to make those suspicious of it act in a confrontational manner.

The GYSL team subsequently invited Gill and some of those who supported her on the issue to a consultation meeting about the materials and also to the 1984 national conference of GYSL teachers, held at Homerton College, Cambridge. But a further dispute then ensued about whether or not the GYSL team had acknowledged the materials as 'racist' and whether or not such material should go on being published and circulated. Following the conference Dawn Gill and Ian Cook (an academic geographer who had been drawn into the argument) circulated a letter to conference members, accusing GYSL of lack of action to correct perceived inadequacies and saying: 'We have no alternative but to withdraw from co-operation with the project.' They likewise refused an invitation to participate in the development of techniques for teaching the existing syllabus more effectively saying 'Cosmetic alterations will not alter the inadequacies of this syllabus.'

GYSL did, in fact, eventually withdraw the material which was under criticism, but maintained that, 'Our line has always been that teachers are intelligent beings, capable of using such materials with care.' They acknowledged gaucheries and language deficiencies in some of their early work sheets while stoutly resisting a charge of racism.

The issue was complicated by the wider issues which Gill and her colleagues now brought to the analysis of the materials. A set of six newer textbooks from GYSL was seen as 'part of a subtle system of indoctrination' and the 'fostering of capitalist ideology to the exclusion of alternatives'.[16] 'The current system of power relationships – globally and nationally – is presented as natural and inevitable. The books fail to encourage critical questioning of these power relationships, thus they support an inequitable status quo in world affairs.'

The argument was broadening out into a number of much wider and more fundamental educational issues: Should schools support or criticise the society in which they exist? Are they to accept broadly the system in which they are governed and administered, or to be 'reconstructionist' in their philosophy, possibly seeking to bite the hand that feeds them? Should the individual classroom teacher have a free hand to advocate 'reconstructionist' ideas, whatever the school's ethos may be? Should all geography teachers be 'reconstructionists'?

One notable non-sponsor of the London conference had been Michael Storm, the Geography Inspector of ILEA, a long-established writer and commentator on Third World topics.[17] Storm had observed the wrangling with concern but kept his own counsel; he now sought to disentangle matters of fact from matters of opinion in the debate and argued that Gill's analysis was oversimplified. 'The necessary dialogue is not advanced by stereotyping (teachers) as misguided simpletons or malevolent National Front recruiting agents', he wrote:

In reply, John Huckle, pushed the context ever wider:

> Dawn Gill and others ... are seeking to raise awareness of the political or ideological role of much that currently passes for geographical education in schools ... geographical education is inevitably political education and its goals are not served by 'professionals' who either remain unaware of structuralist explanations of society and inequality, or reject them and then fail to give them any mention in the classroom.[18]

Huckle had been a discerning commentator from the left on geographical educational issues for some years and had provided a probing but less overtly aggressive view about what went on in school classrooms. He nevertheless wrote openly of the need to progress 'towards a socialist approach to school geography' in a thought-provoking set of essays which he edited at the time.[19]

CHANGING TIMES

The central thesis of Huckle's book was that:

> the new geography was a conservative and adaptive response to prevailing social realities and that subsequent developments in geography and education now allow geography teachers to make a more constructive contribution to human development and social justice

The times, however, were not propitious to advance such a stance with a Conservative government near the beginning of a continuous 18-year spell in power, and now taking a greater interest in educational issues. (Huckle did find a way of espousing some of these ideas in practical form in sets of materials developed both for schools and teacher-education in later years.[20])

The heavy political baggage which came to surround the Gill report and the subsequent imbroglio with the GYSL camp was counter-productive in producing immediate educational change. Many teachers who acknowledged the cogency and legitimacy of some of Gill's criticisms of school materials did not necessarily share the radical and Marxist-inspired analysis of education which accompanied them. The highly politicised context recruited some enthusiasts to the cause, but the strident and indiscriminate tone of later criticisms alienated other possible supporters. The original basic concerns (notably the need to develop multicultural perspectives in geography teaching) became bound up in complex ideological arguments which did little to advance day-to-day work in schools.

Other factors contributed to an eventual loss of impact of these viewpoints as the 1980s proceeded. The whole tide of educational thinking was swinging away from radical 'progressivism'. The liberal educational establishment which had dominated thought and action from the Plowden Report onwards found itself being uncomfortably wrong-footed by a Conservative government led by a powerful and crusading Prime Minister, Margaret Thatcher, who had herself once been Minister of Education.[21] The opinions and influence of parents, school governors and employers were sought and used to balance those of professionals. The quest for 'traditional values' was hoisted high on the agenda and this presaged a return to emphasising 'the basics' , a concern for standards, (exemplified by more rigorous testing of children) and eventually the creation of a National Curriculum (see Chapter 10). In time this was adopted as enthusiastically by Labour and Liberal Democrat politicians as by the majority ruling-party Conservatives; a remarkable tri-partisan volte-face, following the mild espousal of reconstructionist ideals in national policy during the previous 25 years. Educators, faced with lay challenge to their philosophies and practices (and some hard evidence about their relative ineffectiveness) sometimes reacted with strategies perilously close to those of King Canute.

This, allied to a shrinking school population (which in turn meant that there were fewer promotional opportunities for young teachers), provided a much less favourable climate for change than in the expansionist times of the 1960s and 1970s. Quite apart from any merits of their case, circumstances were not favourable for those who wanted change and reform.

TAKING THE WRONG TURNING?

Gill and her colleagues also took some curious strategic options. Having set up a new organisation, the Association for Curriculum Development in Geography (ACDG) in the immediate aftermath of the 1983 London conference, the nucleus of a coherent group of like-minded idealists was identifiable. The ACDG proceeded to produce some issues of a lively journal *Contemporary Issues in Geography and Education*, which was generously and sympathetically reviewed, even by those who had reservations about its ideological stance.[22] The first two issues concentrated on 'Geography and education for a multi-cultural society' and provided provocative and stimulating reading.

But the journal brooked no viewpoints other than those which it endorsed as ideologically pure, even to the point of eschewing advertisements for books which it had not specifically endorsed. A greater contrast to the editorial policy of *Classroom Geographer* could not have been envisaged. The journal successively began to search for other targets, to change its format, and to become more 'academic'. In doing so, it lost its raison d'etre and its 'zing'.

As a volunteer editorial team laboured to produce it, its frequency became ever more erratic. Originally intended to be thrice yearly, only eight editions were published in eight years. A letter in February 1991 to the remaining band of dwindling subscribers regretted that it was no longer possible to publish, through lack of finance (a substantial ILEA grant having eventually run out).

> We regret particularly that we have to discontinue publication at a time when the need for a radical educational journal in Geography is especially acute ... we will continue to work as individuals towards the aims which we held as a collective and hope that you feel that the work which we have done over the past few years has not been entirely wasted.

SECONDARY IMPACTS

The ACDG rose and fell as mercurially as a November firework, yet its influence was not entirely extinguished. It is tempting to speculate what might have happened had the ACDG become involved with the well-established GYSL project (as invited to do) and with The Geographical Association, whose much larger membership and substantial infrastructure of committees and salaried administrators could have provided fertile ground for a group with enthusiasm and purpose. (A similar situation had occurred 20 years earlier on the emergence of a group concerned to promote spatial analytic ideas: the leading lights of the London Schools Geographical Group were taken on board by the GA as a newly constituted Models and Quantitative Techniques Committee. This provided a platform for them to have reasoned dialogue with critics, establish credibility with a wider audience and eventually disseminate 'new ideas' with success to an audience which had been initially sceptical.)

The GA was, in fact, moved to respond to the impact of Gill's speaking, writing and lecturing. It set up its own Working Party on Multi-Cultural education in 1984, which, after a year's work, produced a Report which was published and extensively circulated.[23] There is no doubt that the cogent criticisms of the ACDG and its analysis of both

The Report of the Geographical Association Working Party

Synopsis

The Working Party believes that:-

1. it is unhelpful and inadequate to make a response such as 'This is not my problem because I don't have any black/Irish/Muslim, etc. pupils in my school';

2. there is a distinctive part for the geography teacher to play in educating for life in multi-cultural Britain;

3. geography teachers, through their concern to develop a multi-cultural perspective for pupils, should be concerned to give controversial issues full consideration in their programmes of work and to facilitate rational and informed debate and discussion about them;

4. teachers should subscribe to a GA originated statement which seeks to oppose racist practices in schools and classrooms;

5. teachers should be prepared to examine thoroughly their own classroom practices and resources and ensure that there is representation of different cultural viewpoints;

6. teachers should seek to develop strategies of teaching and learning which exemplify multi-cultural realities in practical ways. For example:

   if the diversity of races and cultures across the world is to be considered it should not be in hackneyed stereotypes or rooted in the picturesque;

   more than one source of information should be used in teaching about our own and other cultures wherever possible;

   a move to increase experiential (in additional to informational) teaching should be encouraged;

   the development of good relationships between pupils and between teachers and pupils in the classroom can be the most effective demonstration of how the outside world should be.

Figure 9.3:
Synopsis of the GA's report on Multi-Cultural Education, 1985 (*Source*: GA)

textbooks and pedagogies played an important part in shaping the deliberations of that Working Party (see Figure 9.3), whose conclusions were circulated widely.

Accompanying the Report were checklists for teachers (as Hicks had suggested), a set of teaching examples and an extensive bibliography. The Working Party also drew up an Anti-Racist Statement which the GA adopted in June 1984 as its official policy. Many teachers felt that the GA document brought a calmer tone to the rather frenetic arguments which had characterised the 'GYSL affair'.

Beyond this a wider debate in geographical education was being stimulated. Starting tentatively with general issues of multi-culturalism, it extended into the harder-edged debate about racism and anti-racism. Through the 1980s, the consciousness of many geography teachers was raised on the issue and this helped to stem the more insensitive expressions of cultural bias which had previously disfigured some classrooms.

Prompted and made uncomfortable by Gill's diligent exposes, publishers and authors became much more aware of the reasons for the criticisms which she and her colleagues in ACDG were raising.[24] Whilst extreme radical conclusions were not generally accepted, the general analysis which lay behind them often was. The radical critics had the ability to lay bare the inadequacy of much that was being unconsciously perpetrated with good intentions. The relative status visibility and portrayal of ethnic minorities in books, pamphlets and worksheets was assessed. Techniques for the analysis of publications were developed and demonstrated. Author's guidelines were amended. Associated issues (particularly those concerned with gender bias) were raised and brought into full public debate at geography teachers' conferences and in-service sessions.

Thus the apparent demise of an organisation, a journal and a movement cloaks an ultimate success. Though Gill's full-blooded reconstructionist philosophy for geographical education was not widely adopted, the essence of most of her criticisms had its effect. They led to the start of various houses being put in better order in subsequent years.

DEVELOPMENT EDUCATION

The impetus for the multi-cultural debate in geography had come through the post-war emergence of an increasingly multi-cultural Britain but also indirectly through the refocusing of teaching about other countries and, in particular, other countries in 'less-developed' parts of the world. It is prudent to put a term like 'less developed' in inverted commas, since in some ways countries with lower Gross Domestic Product (GDP) than so-called 'developed' countries may nevertheless have better development (or at least better maintenance) of kinship, happiness, social harmony and environment. To judge countries by their standard of living is a prevalent occupation in a materialistic age but not the most revealing one.

Geographical education became aware of this paradox as teaching about other countries moved away from picturesque case-studies to fuller analyses of a country's economic health, fuelled by the rising tide of data that was becoming available from the United Nations and other agencies. Wide-focus charities, such as Oxfam, Christian Aid and Cafod grew in size and, in the 1970s and 1980s, developed specific education sections; they were supplemented by more specialist agencies (such as Population Concern). There was an associated growth of 'Development Education Centres' around the country (often wholly or partly funded by the charitable agencies) which provided resource banks for teachers and also ran campaigns and developed curriculum materials themselves.[25]

This led to a greater profile for such studies in schools and inevitably a move towards considering issues in economic development as well as teaching descriptive material about areas. In turn this has thrown up matters for debate about classroom pedagogy. How far should particularly controversial matters (such as population limitation by birth control in poor countries) be addressed in the classroom? Is there a particular set of values and attitudes which can (or should) be inculcated to pupils in relation to world problems (such as the possible abandonment of debt repayments in less-developed parts of the world)? Should children become actively involved in campaigns about particular issues (saving whales, relieving flood disasters) through their geography lessons?

These questions (in relation to both development and environmental issues) became matters for debate in the 1970s and 1980s without there being any very clear resolution of them (until the advent of the National Curriculum). Sir Keith Joseph, when Minister of Education in the mid-1980s, espoused the idea of 'balance' in the presentation of all issues, a point which was first codified by Section 45 of the 1986 Education Act which required teachers to ensure a 'balanced presentation of opposing views'.[26] But practice in relation to teaching about (and the teaching of) attitudes and values in schools still varies widely and remains very much the province of the individual teacher.[27]

In the later decades of the century, the question of 'the affective domain' as it has been labelled by the psychologist Benjamin Bloom and his co-workers,[28] at least has become more consciously a matter for debate and discussion amongst teachers, whereas, in the years before, attitudes were conveyed in a blithely unconscious way by many teachers, who had little worry that their own views might or might not be reasonable to pass on to their pupils.

WHICH VALUES?

The question of whether and how the teaching of values is done has grown to be a thorny one throughout the state educational system, and not least in geography lessons. In a society which some would now call predominantly 'post-modern' in outlook, the idea that any view expressed in a classroom is as good as another has gained a foothold through a cherishing of participative methods (good in themselves) reinforced by a libertarian tolerance.

In past times a series of predominant values were transmitted almost implicitly and accepted by pupils, parents and teachers with much less questioning than today. Teachers espoused moral principles ('public values') with more certainty and inculcated them into pupils, backed up by the support of church, home and community. In a more fragmented and disjunctive world, our state education system now searches rather hesitantly to find a set of values acceptable to all and is very much more tentative transmitting them. A recent set of 'ten common values for today' proposed for schools by the Qualifications and Curriculum Authority met with a very mixed response.[29]

Value-clarification rather than value-transmission tends to be the more favoured stance (though it might be argued that the most effective way to be a value-transmitter is to pretend to be a value-clarifier). Value-clarification is based on extensive involvement of pupils in participatory activities, and the growth of greater discussion and debate in classrooms is welcomed by transmitters and clarifiers alike. But the 'acceptance of all different points of view' as legitimate has been hoisted into place as a pluralist goal in education by some, despite the practical paradoxes which may result.

Consequently, some geography teachers may now find themselves on contested ground in seeking to persuade classes that it is 'right' or 'our duty' to adopt certain attitudes or take certain actions to the physical world or to our fellow humans. 'Grand narratives' of ordered progression towards a better future and of the 'integrated self' are now distrusted in some academic circles. Particularly in regard to issues of citizenship and environment there is a gulf between postmodernists and those who espouse the traditional principles of the nation state. Though postmodernist writing may have its finger on the pulse of many contemporary developments, it may also be essentially too incoherent and negative ever to provide much influence, let alone any satisfactory answers.

Most school students in Britain at present still take (consciously or unconsciously) their ultimate line about the value of life and of the natural world from the nation's historic Judaeo-Christian cultural heritage, which has been at the heart of much geography teaching in schools for centuries. Such explicit transmission of values was done openly in the past, even if not always fully appreciated. In a society where explicit value-transmission has given way to more guarded 'discussion' of values, it is difficult to know if hidden and implicit value-transmission now holds sway in most classrooms or if a genuine relativism is being fostered. If it is relativism that prevails, the time may eventually come when students have little notion of what might be an appropriate sustaining attitude to the world, to their local environment, their own community and even their own bodies – or even a desire to care about it.

Teachers in religious denominational and independent schools and colleges may have a more clearly defined task, since the historic origins and traditions of such institutions are usually made clear and attendance of pupils is by the positive choice of parents. The ethos of these establishments can be clearly determined and publicised. (There has been an increase in the number of state schools seeking to become 'church schools' in recent years.[30] More recently, the Muslim community has sought permission from government to develop schools with a distinctive religious ethos.) In these situations it is still possible to advocate and uphold a distinctive set of values for a community, and avoid a post-modern, relativist outlook becoming the eventual common denominator accepted by both teacher and pupils.

OTHER MOVEMENTS

Besides the growth in 'development education', in the 1970s and 1980s, there were other inter-disciplinary movements which impinged on geography teaching. The World Studies Project, was set up in 1973 and financed by The One World Trust, an educational charity and an offshoot of the Parliamentary Group for World Government. It ran for six years under the gifted directorship of Robin Richardson with the intention of supporting and promoting 'world studies' in schools – a diffuse concept, but one which included both 'world understanding' and 'child-centredness'.[31] Its reputation grew as it produced a host of lively teaching ideas[32] as well as providing a powerful and practical advocacy for interactive classroom strategies.

From this emerged, in 1980, the World Studies 8–13 Project,[33] jointly financed by the Schools Council and The Joseph Rowntree Trust. The aim, said the project in its defining paper, was not to see world studies as a new subject but rather as a dimension in the curriculum which embraces:

(a) awareness of contemporary global issues such as world inequality, human rights, peace and conflict, social change
(b) understanding other cultures than one's own
(c) the need for the curriculum to include a global perspective.
    In doing so, it notes that children will have to cope with a future very different from today, a future that will be greatly influenced by the outcome of current world issues which increasingly impinge on all our daily lives.

Clearly there was much that was geography here, but also ambitiously much beyond it.

World Studies 8–13 found supporters in those counties of Britain where there were middle schools (usually taking pupils for four years between 8 and 12 or 9 and 13 years of age), since it offered an appealing inter-disciplinary mix of geography, history and religious education, mid-way between the 'theme' work of primary schools and the more specialised work of the secondary sector. The geographical elements of the work were lively but almost always human-based. The role of the physical environment was less visible; if geography had become metamorphosed in world studies, it would have gained much pedagogically, but pupils would almost certainly have lost the understanding of physical processes in the landscape.

David Hicks and Robin Richardson were significant and continuing influences in the sphere of world studies for a decade and their work was complemented by another initiative at the University of York, the Centre for Global Education, run by David Selby and Graham Pike.[34]

Another initiative in the mid-1980s was for 'peace education' in schools. In 1980, The Centre for Peace Studies was founded at Lancaster, one of the key genesis points for several of these curriculum developments.[35]

As the government became more and more concerned about the diffuse developments going on in schools, this and associated cross-disciplinary movements attracted increasing critical attention from Ministers, HMI and civil servants. Events of the late 1980s would soon create an adverse environment for such developments.

THE COMING OF TECHNOLOGY

One other factor conspired to blunt the mainly liberal and radical initiatives of the 1980s; it was a rival spring of activity which commanded as much interest and, in the end, much more political power and money – the coming of Information Technology.

Geographers had long been in the vanguard of developing new teaching aids and so it was not altogether surprising that the potential use of computers became a preoccupation for some geographers before it raised much more than a glimmer of interest in other subjects.

An early group of university geographers combined with schoolteachers to write articles and produce a pioneer book on the topic in the early 1980s[36] and an early valuable initiative was a 'package exchange' organised through the GA, which existed to disseminate programmes and software to a growing audience. It was not long before collaborations with the National Council for Educational Technology (and its successors, who have operated under different names)[37] were initiated and teaching exercises and ideas spawned through a specialist section in *Teaching Geography*.

The power of computing and the spread of knowledge through telecommunications (eventually leading to the Internet) had a close technical ally in the avalanche of visual material coming from space agencies. From the late 1970s onwards, remotely sensed photographs from satellites offered wonderful new images of the world, as well as giving a renewed impetus to the understanding of weather patterns and forecasting. There was also a rapid growth in the development of computer-generated Geographical Information Systems (GIS) for use in planning and commercial development.

In the light of this, the prime interest of many geography departments turned to the acquisition of technical resources in order to explore this, literally, new world which had been revealed. Publishers added new 'media' divisions to their operating companies and new sections to their catalogues; as the 1980s passed, many geographers in schools, and their pupils, began to be attracted more and more by the rapidly expanding frontiers of information and communications technology. The impetus for geography at the end of the century seemed to be gathering its energy from the banks of visual display units in a new phenomenon, the school computer room, and from the promised coming of a 'world-wide web' of knowledge.

NOTES

1. D. Harvey, *Explanation in Geography* (Arnold, London, 1969).
2. D. Harvey, *Social Justice in the City* (Arnold, London, 1973).
3. D. Harvey and M. Merry, *People Poverty and Wealth* (University of London Press, London 1972).
4. David Smith, *Human Geography: A Welfare Approach* (Edward Arnold, London, 1977).
5. R. Peet (ed.), *Radical Geography* (Methuen, London, 1978).
6. R. Reiser, 'The territorial illusion and the behavioural sink', *Antipode*, 5 (1973), pp. 52–7. Also reprinted in Peet, *Radical Geography*.
7. N. J. Graves, 'Contrasts and contradictions in geographical education', *Geography*, 64(4) (1979), pp. 259–67.
8. Many of Frances Slater's distinctive views about geographical education are thoughtfully distilled in *Learning Through Geography* (Heinemann, London, 1982).
9. D. Hicks, 'Images of the world: what do geography text books actually teach about development?', *Cambridge Journal of Education*, 11(1) (1981), pp. 15–35. Shorter versions of this are: D. Hicks, 'Bias in geography textbooks', Working Paper No.1, Centre for Multicultural Education, University of London Institute of Education, 1980; D. Hicks, 'The contribution of geography to multicultural misunderstanding', *Teaching Geography*, 7(2) (1981), pp. 64–7.
10. In the education world, the term 'subversive' had been given a new (and somewhat cosmeticised) layer of meaning through the use of it by two American authors, Neil Postman and Charles Weingartner in 1969 in their best-selling book written in 'popular' style, *Teaching as a Subversive Activity* (Penguin Education, London, 1970). Postman and Weingartner, who called themselves 'simple romantics who believe in the improvability of the human condition through education', said that their aim was to 'help all students develop built-in shock-proof crap detectors as basic equipment in their survival kits'. They saw the teacher as the catalyst for a new creativity, leading a new questioning 'to face the challenges of accelerating change within society' and thus effectively the teacher was 'an agent for subversion'.
11. Hicks is here quoting from Smith, *Human Geography*.
12. Curiously, one book (book 3) in the series, *A Course in World Geography*, by E. W. Young and J. H. Lowry, was judged to be at the racist end of the spectrum, whereas Book 10 of the same series by the same authors was placed almost at the opposite end. It is impossible to know if this was a matter of great change of attitude in a short time by the authors or a flawed analysis of the books.
13. It should be noted that though this article (through its comprehensiveness and its survey report) became the focus for later discussion earlier articles had already drawn attention to some of the issues raised. See for instance: D. R. and J. A. Wright 'Materials for development education', Chapter 4 in *The Changing World in the Classroom* (UNESCO, Paris, 1974). Author not named, 'Teaching about the Third World: a report of a

symposium', *Geography*, 60(1) (1975), pp. 52–8; W. E. Marsden, 'Stereotyping and Third World geography', *Teaching Geography*, 1(5) (1976), pp. 228–31; M. Storm, 'Multi-ethnic education and geography', *Schooling and Culture*, 3 (1978); J. A. Binns, 'How we see "them" – some thoughts on Third World teaching', *Teaching Geography*, 4(4) (1978).

14. The Geography Section of the ILEA Inspectorate was more circumspect about events and decided to keep a watching brief.

15. Gill's first published critique of GYSL was in 1981, Dawn Gill, 'Geography for the young school leaver – a critique', *Bulletin for Environmental Education*, Aug./Sept. (1981), pp. 35–9. One worksheet which became the focus of later criticism concerned the problems of Dallas, Texas. The worksheet (numbered 4.2 in the Cities and People Unit) said:

> Dallas is a visual mess – fine new buildings jostle rundown shacks, unsightly parking areas blot the town, festoons of garish advertising defile the walls, and raw, unfinished or abandoned building sites proliferate
>
> The crime rate is also a disgrace and has been growing at three times the rate of population increase
>
> Nineteen per cent of the population is negro and economically deprived – though by most American standards the 'deprived' negro is well off

Gill's criticism was:

> Are criminal behaviour and skin colour necessarily related? If not, why the juxtaposition of these statements? Although economic conditions are mentioned there is no attempt to link explicitly the incidence of crime with that of economic or social deprivation, with relative powerlessness or the acquistiveness associated with low social status in a consumer oriented society. In fact, skin colour is presented as the only relevant factor, because although the American negro is economically deprived 'by most American standards the "deprived" negro is well off'. What does this phrase mean? One of the consequences of using this resource sheet in the classroom without questioning the underlying assumptions and the juxtaposition of these statements may be that racism is fostered unintentionally.

16. The *Geography and Change* series (Nelson, London, 1982). The series was designed to explore the GYSL themes in a broader global context and the project was funded by the Overseas Development Administration, a Government department. Books were produced on *Tourism, Developing Cities, Food Farming and Famine, Patterns of Underdevelopment, Peru, the Middle East.*

17. M. Storm, 'Multi-ethnic education'. Storm was also one of the contributors to the symposium, reported in January 1975 issue of *Geography*, 1978.

18. J. Huckle, writing in the *Guardian*, 21 February 1984.

19. J. Huckle, *Geographical Education: Reflection and Action* (Oxford University Press, Oxford, 1983).

20. *Global Environmental Education Programme* (four modules) (WWF/Richmond Publishing, London, 1987); *Reaching Out* (World Wildlife Fund, London, 1994).

21. The Inner London Education Authority, whose Chairman, Frances Morrell, had chaired the 1983 London Institute conference with gusto, and which was home to many radical educational initiatives, was itself abolished in 1987.

22. *Contemporary Issues in Geography and Education* (Association for Curriculum Development), vols 1–8 (1983–90). Each edition was themed: 'Geography and education for a multi-cultural society' (Issues 1 and 2, 1983/84); 'The global economy: trade and multinationals' (vol. 1, no. 3, 1984); 'South Africa: apartheid capitalism' (vol. 2, no. 1, 1985); 'Confronting the ecological crisis' (vol. 2, no. 2, 1985); 'War and peace' (vol. 2, no. 3, 1987); 'Gender and geography' (vol. 3, no. 1, undated, 1988?); 'Anarchism and geography' (vol. 3, no. 2, undated, 1990?).

23. R. Walford (ed.), *Geographical Education for a Multi-Cultural Society* (Geographical Association, Sheffield, 1985).

24. Michael Storm, 'Geography and anti-racist teaching', *ILEA Geography Bulletin*, 25 (1987), pp. 6–10.

25. The Birmingham Development Education Centre has been particularly active in developing

classroom materials and teacher guides over the last three decades, led by Scott Sinclair and Roger Robinson.

26. The Education Act of 1996 aims to ensure that children are not presented by their teachers with only one side of political or controversial issues. Section 406 of the Act requires school governing bodies, head teachers and LEAs to forbid the promotion of partisan political views in the teaching of any subject in schools; and to forbid political activities by pupils under age 12 while in school. Section 407 requires them to take all reasonably practical steps to ensure that, where political or controversial issues are brought to pupils' attention, they are offered a balanced presentation of opposing views.

27. See J. J. Wellington (ed.), *Controversial Issues in the Curriculum* (Blackwell, Oxford, 1986).

28. B. S. Bloom *et al.*, *Taxonomy of Educational Objectives: Handbook, The Cognitive Domain* (Longman, London, 1956); D. R. Krathwohl, B. S. Bloom and B. B. Masia, *Taxonomy of Educational Objectives: Handbook 2, The Affective Domain* (Longman, London, 1964).

29. Final Report of the National Forum for Values in Education (Schools Curriculum and Assessment Authority, London, 1997).

30. See, for example, 'Parents lead demand for church school status', an article on the front page of the *Daily Telegraph*, 2 June 1999.

31. D. Hicks, 'World Studies, 8–13: A Short History, 1980–89' (St Martin's College, Lancaster, 1990).

32. R. Richardson, *Learning for Change in World Society: Reflections, Activities and Resources* (World Studies Project, London, 1979); R. Richardson, M. Flood and S. Fisher, *Debate and Decision: Schools in a World of Change* (World Studies Project, London, 1980).

33. D. Hicks and S. Fisher, *World Titles, 8–13: A Teachers Handbook* (Oliver & Boyd, Edinburgh, 1985); D. Hicks and M. Steiner, *Making Global Connections: A World Studies Handbook* (Oliver & Boyd, Edinburgh, 1989).

34. G. Pike and D. Selby, *Global Teacher, Global Learner* (Hodder & Stoughton, London, 1988).

35. D. Hicks (ed.), *Education for Peace: Issues, Principles and Practice in the Classroom* (Routledge, London, 1988).

36. I. Shepherd, Z. Cooper and D. Walker, *Computer-Assisted Learning in Geography* (Geographical Association and Council for Educational Technology, London, 1980).

37. It was for a time known as the Micro-Electronics Support Unit (MESU) and is now the British Educational Council for Technological Advancement (BECTA).

10

The Notion of a National Curriculum, 1985–90

HOW IT ALL BEGAN

Prime Ministers do not often make speeches about education; their flights of rhetoric are usually reserved for more general national or international themes.[1] Ministers of Education have usually been somewhat minor figures in the Cabinet and on the front bench.[2] James Callaghan, however, leader of the short-lived Labour government between 1976 and 1979, chose to concentrate on educational issues when making a speech at Ruskin College, Oxford, in 1976 and the speech is often counted as the starting point for a course of events which led to the establishment of a National Curriculum for Schools in England and Wales 12 years later.[3]

The background to the speech was a paper specially prepared by the Department of Education and Science (the so-called 'Yellow Book' – never published) which was sharply critical of many aspects of education in the new comprehensive schools (These had, since the 1960s, mushroomed in many LEAs with government approval, following a circular, known as 10/65, issued by the Ministry of Education. In the generally egalitarian spirit of the time, the aim was to have comprehensive schools, in which pupils of all intellectual abilities were educated together, replace the 1944 tripartite division of grammar, secondary modern and technical schools.) The DES paper was a first note of reservation; it broadly confirmed the main thesis of the writers of the recent polemical pamphlets known as 'The Black Papers'.[4] This suggested that schools had become over-concerned about social matters (such as deliberately mixing a wide range of academic abilities in classes to prevent social stigmatisation) and were not doing enough to promote and raise academic standards. The Schools Council was singled out for its 'mediocre performance'.

Callaghan took the opportunity to voice unease; there were 'complaints from industry that new recruits from schools do not have the basic tools to do the job that is required' : vacancies for students in science and engineering were not taken up while humanities courses were full: unease was being felt by 'parents and others about the new informal methods of teaching'; the schools were not pulling their weight and adjusting their standards upwards quickly enough in a rapidly changing world. Callaghan stated the aims of education as being ' to equip children to the best of their ability for a lively constructive place in society and also to fit them for a job of work. Not one or the other, but both'. Then came the fateful words, 'It is not my intention to become enmeshed in such problems as whether there should be a basic curriculum with universal standards – although I am inclined to think there should be.'

The speech provoked a number of government initiatives which included a series of 'consultative meetings' around the country, though these scarcely did anything positive except give those who had a particular bee in their bonnet a chance to sound off in public. But at least the meetings showed a desire to engage with some pressing issues. The 'Great Debate' about education had begun.

For over 70 years the Ministry of Education (and its handmaiden, Her Majesty's Inspectorate of Schools [HMI]) had pumped out reports, consultative and guidance documents for professional consideration. These documents often carried pearls of wisdom and glimmers of far-sighted vision, but there was no mechanism for implementing their ideas, if local authorities chose not do so. Thus various radical and innovative curriculum schemes were mooted, and formed the basis for discussion amongst the educational cognoscenti but their impact was always limited by what the average head and classroom teacher thought was practicable in their school.

Educational theorising about the curriculum grew in intensity and in stature in the years following the Second World War and the work of the philosopher of education P. H. Hirst in defining knowledge into 'forms' and 'fields' provided the focus for discussion in many places in the 1960s.[5]

For a period, HMI advocated a curriculum based on 'areas of experience' rather than subjects[6] but their proposals remained a discussion point in teacher-training courses, rather than a practical recipe for action. Only rarely did visionary heads attempt to overturn the whole structure of teaching through traditional subjects and put a new formulation in its place.[7] Though sometimes vibrant experiments carried through by talented administrators and teachers which attracted much attention, they did not prove to be practicable models for other schools.

Disillusionment with an era of expansion and teacher-led innovation was spreading. It was not only the right-wing authors of the 'Black Papers' but the Fabian Society which argued 'the curriculum is too important to be left to teachers'.[8] Government feeling was growing that leaving curriculum innovation to schools, even to the funded Schools Council projects, was not delivering effective and relevant education (whatever that was) in a widespread or a fast enough way. Thus, following the Callaghan speech, a spate of documents preparing the ground for more proactive intervention from Whitehall began to appear.[9] Just the whisper of the notion of a 'National Curriculum' was heard.

Where did geography stand in all this? Unsure of its curriculum position and nervously waiting on the periphery of the 'great debate' for the most part. Though much had happened to reinvigorate the subject internally in the previous two decades, to many of those outside its boundaries a traditional 'capes and bays' image still prevailed. It seemed ominous that geography was omitted from the 12 subject areas discussed by HMI in their review of the 11–16 curriculum[10] and even more alarming that, in a later document HMI's assertion that 'there was a strong case for maintaining some study of history in the final secondary years' was not matched with a comparable case for extending the study of geography.[11]

GEOGRAPHERS GET TO GRIPS WITH CURRICULUM POLITICS

As the 'Great Debate' got underway, the prevailing view amongst geographical educators was that, if there were moves towards some kind of curriculum core, it would be best to campaign for as small a prescription as possible so that geography would have room to manoeuvre. The assumption was that geography would be outside any kind of likely 'basic formulation' of study which might come to be required. Even if grudgingly admitted to the circle of main subjects for secondary study in the 1920s, it had never basked in the favoured approbation of government civil servants or attained any leverage in the corridors of educational power, and it was unlikely to start doing so now, went the thinking.

Geography was known to be a popular optional choice in schools when a free-market operated, however, and it was thought that this could be exploited to the subject's advantage. But the emergence of the Technical and Vocational Educational Initiative (TVEI) – money for schools to develop new courses in technical and vocational areas – was an element in cutting down choice and was already casting doubt on the long-term hopes for this strategy. The emphasis from the centre was on education as a preparation for job opportunities; light weighting was given to the curricular role of the arts, the humanities, the social sciences and other subjects which contributed to the general education of the pupil.

The principal threads of the argument were evident in the first of the DES publications which moved from being a discussion to a policy document.[12] There was only a passing reference to geography and that in the 32nd paragraph of a 35-paragraph report where it was named as one of a group of subjects which were considered 'also important in the preparation for adult life'.

But the document was not fully thought through. There seemed to be only the most tenuous links between the six major aims promulgated for education in one part of the document (one of them was 'To help pupils understand the world in which they live, and the interdependence of individuals, groups and nations') and the list of subjects suggested as an essential and protected core curriculum in another.

The Geographical Association had come to realise the need to be 'streetwise' as far as curriculum politics were concerned in the late 1970s, and a newly formed Education Standing Committee was in a good position to consult wisely and formulate a response. Its chairman and secretary composed a brief but robust response to the DES publication, seeking to analyse and criticise the thinking behind the whole document as well as to argue for a more prominent position for their own subject.[13] Somewhat to their surprise they were subsequently invited to Elizabeth House, the headquarters of the DES, to discuss their paper with a senior civil servant, in the presence of the Staff Inspector for Geography from HMI. A few months later a revised DES document was published[14] and the place of geography had become marginally more visible. A lesson in curriculum politics had been learned.

The experience was a formative one in a new period of GA activity during which the Association learnt to be vigilant about the increasing stream of government pronouncements, to become aware of their deeper political implications, and to respond to them with alacrity.

The GA published two brief codifications of the subject[15] which were circulated in their thousands to senior staff in schools as part of a campaign to have the potential contribution of geography to the curriculum better understood by non-geographers. Regular meetings between GA officers and HMI were established. Closer links with the Royal Geographical Society and other geographical groups in the UK were developed, initially through an ad hoc liaison committee, and then through the founding of the Council of British Geography (COBRIG) in 1988, which provided a forum for all major geographical bodies in Britain.

THE FIRST MINISTERIAL SPEECH DEVOTED TO GEOGRAPHY

After several abortive attempts, the GA persuaded the then Secretary of State for Education, Sir Keith Joseph, to be the main speaker at a specially convened one-day conference held at King's College, London in June 1985 – the first time that a government minister had ever devoted a major speech wholly to geographical education. Joseph was different from many of his predecessors in that he had a genuine interest in educational matters, rather than seeing the ministerial brief merely as a staging-post to preferment or retirement.

An austere, thoughtful and highly intellectual man, he infuriated some teacher unions by his belief that throwing money at problems did not necessarily improve matters, but he grasped several key educational nettles without flinching during his time of office. It was characteristic of him to meet an audience of subject-specialists and to debate issues with them on terms of their own choosing. His speech went some way towards clarifying the issues and challenges which geography would face if it were to claim a place in the curriculum. Abandoning a prepared format, he engaged in discussion with his audience for half an hour afterwards, enjoying the cut and thrust of academic argument with relish, demonstrating his breadth of relevant reading and ultimately winning considerable respect.[16]

He left behind a provoking series of seven questions for the GA to answer, if geography was to justify its place in the school curriculum.[17] If this was a rhetorical flourish, the GA called his bluff, since, within weeks, a provisional response was on his desk[18] and later, after a series of teachers' conferences held around the country, a fuller and more measured reply was made.[19]

By the time *A Case for Geography* was finally published, however, a new Secretary of State had taken office. Sir Keith Joseph's unconventional stance on educational matters was now replaced by a more orthodox but also more urgent approach to educational issues. The new Minister, Kenneth Baker, was mindful of the fact that his Prime Minister, Margaret Thatcher, wished to make some major educational reforms whilst still in office. It was not long before he unexpectedly revealed on a television programme that he planned a package of radical measures to be made statutory in a new Education Reform Act.

GETTING THE BILL ON THE STATUTE BOOK

The GA sent a 'bridging letter' to the new incumbent in August 1986, seeking to keep open the dialogue initiated with his predecessor. The letter also defined elements of the GA's emerging policy towards a National Curriculum:

1 understanding geography should be a fundamental part of every child's education (it was currently not so in many primary schools)
2 geography had powerful integrating qualities in itself 'with strong links in both the sciences and the arts' and should not be seen as just a humanities subject
3 direct observation and investigation of the environment was an important part of geographical work and should be undertaken by every pupil
4 geography could be a vehicle for the study and discussion of controversial social and environmental issues and therefore should be studied up to the age of 16 by all.

The GA sought a meeting with Mr Baker, a request to which he readily acceded. The Minister seemed anxious to give prominence to the subject-associations in discussions about the curriculum, perhaps because of some uneasy initial encounters with the teacher unions. It also confirmed the view that his own inclination was towards a traditional subject-based national curriculum, rather than any of the alternative formulations being suggested by philosophers and curriculum theorists.[20] Some who were unexpectedly sidelined fulminated about their inability to influence or even contribute to curriculum discussion when the chips were down.[21] Baker calculated that such encounters would be confusing and unproductive and that a framework based on traditional subject categories was most likely to win the allegiance of parents, as well as of teachers.

By the time a GA delegation visited Elizabeth House, the unprepossessing home of the Department of Education and Science near Waterloo Station, in June 1987 the die concerning the shape of the National Curriculum had been cast. The typescript of *A Case for Geography* made a timely arrival on the Minister's desk during the deliberation period.

But other factors also had influence. Baker, whilst Minister of Technology, had been responsible for an initiative which put computers into schools; on his visits he had been impressed by the use being made of them in geography classes. The supposed bias and possible indoctrinatory effects of Peace Studies and World Studies were disliked by Baker, who felt that geography, as a longer-standing and more traditional subject, offered a 'safer' delivery of world knowledge and issues. (The Association for Curriculum Development in Geography had almost vanished across the horizon by this time and no public utterances or articles came from its officers during the vital months leading up to the Education Act.) Also, Baker had studied history at Oxford, and was strongly inclined to a separate subject formulation for his own discipline. When the GA team arrived at the door of his room, he greeted them with a beaming smile and began the meeting with a reassurance that geography would find a distinctive place in the National Curriculum plans which he was about to announce.

What kind of place was less clear, however? Would the subject have parity with history? Would there be geography for all from 5 to 16? Would it perhaps be included only in a wider requirement for 'humanities'? The initial consultation document, published on 24 July 1987 created a furore for many reasons, and not least because it suggested specific allocations of time to subjects. These amounted to a required National Curriculum taking up 90 per cent of available time in a school year. For geographers there was particular relief in finding the subject specifically named. The proposals for years 4 and 5 of the secondary phase caused concern, however; here the proposal was for History/Geography or History-or-Geography for 10 per cent of the time. Some saw this as an omen which presaged a future loss of identity and as a confirmation of the unfortunate belief that geography and history were interchangeable rather than complementary.

A 'leak' from Elizabeth House in the autumn suggested that DES officials might be considering the introduction of 'humanities' rather than geography and history (a formulation regarded with suspicion by many geographers – see Chapter 7) but the Minister's own preference for separate formulations prevailed and when the published Bill appeared early in 1988 geography and history appeared as separate entities. Even the hybrid formulations of the Consultation Document had been dropped. So too, more ominously, were any proposed time allocations. The proposals were for geography to be studied (along with other 'foundation' subjects) 'for a reasonable time' in each year for all students between the ages of 5 to 16.

Behind the somewhat unexpectedly broad formulation of a ten-subject curriculum in which geography was somewhat surprised to find itself, there lay an interesting political battle in the Cabinet as Baker later revealed in his memoirs:[22]

> At our meeting on 3 March, the Prime Minister warned against over-elaboration of the Curriculum and said that she wanted to concentrate on the core subjects of English, Maths and Science. In the debates that took place between us both before and after the Election this proved to be the central issue. I believed that if we were to concentrate just upon the core subjects then schools would teach only to them and give much less prominence to the broader range which I thought was necessary. (p. 193)

The basis of Baker's views is made little more explicit than that but one of his advisers was the Chief Inspector of Schools, Eric Bolton, and he may well have been influential in helping to define the position. Baker argued his case tenaciously through several Cabinet meetings despite sustained challenge from the Prime Minister. The question of time and possible overload became critical factors in the discussion. Baker believed that a ten-subject[23] curriculum could be fitted into the school timetable taking 80/85 per cent of the teaching time 'but, of course, for brighter children it would be less'.

The question came to a head in a Cabinet Committee in October 1987 when the minutes recorded that art and music should not be compulsory subjects, that the main curriculum should take up only 70 per cent of the time and that attainment targets for all subjects other than the three core ones should be dropped. Baker challenged the minutes in a personal memorandum to Mrs Thatcher, a step almost without precedent. He suspected (rightly) that the Minutes had been adjusted to reflect the views of the Prime Minister.

A private meeting with the Iron Lady followed. Baker told her, 'If you want me to continue as Education Secretary, then we will have to stick to the curriculum [of ten subjects] that I have set out in the White Paper. I and my Ministerial colleagues have advocated and stoutly defended the broad curriculum.'

In a rare, almost unique act, the Prime Minister withdrew her opposition and allowed that of a Cabinet colleague to prevail. Geography remained a specified subject of study.[24]

LATE NIGHT SKIRMISHES IN PARLIAMENT

The campaign for the successful incorporation of geography into a National Curriculum programme still had some battles to win, however.

The Labour Party's decision to support the general framework of Kenneth Baker's proposals largely removed the matter from the forefront of House of Commons debate on the Reform Bill, which had many other aspects; however, it was well known that the more independent spirit of the House of Lords might well cause parts of the Bill to be substantially amended on second reading. Educational lobbies therefore focused their efforts on members of the Upper House.

In a lengthy and historic debate which went to several late-night sittings, a successful lobby for strengthened religious education and school assembly provisions won the curriculum limelight; pressures to have classics and home economics included in the foundation subject list were also eloquently applied, but resisted. In the shadows, however, were some interesting episodes which had implications for geography.

Lord (formerly Sir Keith) Joseph, now happily maverick on the government back-benches, proposed a wrecking amendment to his successor's plans, which would have abolished the concept of a centrally directed national curriculum altogether. A small group of cross-party geographer/explorer peers, mobilised through the Royal Geographical Society to see that the interests of geography were safeguarded, were, for some time, in a quandary about how to vote on the amendment. Should they support it and thus strike a blow for curriculum independence? Or oppose it on the basis that ground gained was best held on to? The amendment was not pressed to a vote.

Another amendment monitored anxiously was one proposed by Lord Somers, which would have transferred history (but not geography) to the list of core subjects. When the amendment was finally called (at 2 a.m.) the proposer had either fallen asleep or gone home, as no one rose immediately to speak to it. The amendment therefore fell. Thus, on a nuance of Parliamentary procedure, a dangerous corner for the national future of geography in schools was navigated safely.

WORKING TOWARDS A WORKING GROUP

The Government avoided defeat on almost all of its original proposals, despite having only narrow majorities in the House of Lords on some issues. The Education Act became law in July 1988 – destined to be, along with the Acts of 1902 and 1944, one of the three most significant Education Acts of the century. But then there was an unexpected turn of events. The educational world had presumed that there would be a simultaneous setting-up of 'Working Groups' to fill out the fine-grain of the stark single-word definitions of subjects of study contained in the Act. Attainment Targets and Programmes of Study were to be defined and developed by these groups for all core and foundation subjects. It soon transpired however, that, for reasons more logistical than conspiratorial, Working Groups would be set up sequentially, with Science and Mathematics leading the way. In a letter to the GA, the Secretary of State rationalised the decision by saying that he did not think it mattered that the Groups would not meet at the same time as it would not be helpful if Working Groups were 'over-burdened with the need for consultation'.

During the course of the Bill through Parliament many special-interest groups had sought the inclusion of their own concerns in the specified National Curriculum proposals; the usual Ministerial response had been to justify the proposals already outlined but assure the groups that their views would be taken into account when detailed plans were made. Now it emerged that since the ten Subject Working Groups were not to exist simultaneously, the way in which they could liaise with each other to consider cross-curricular themes would be limited.

The National Curriculum Council (a new body set up by the Act to replace the discredited and abolished Schools Council) was asked to convene groups to advise on particular cross-curricular themes, though it was not clear how such 'advice' would be implemented. Three of the six groups eventually established were concerned with topics of special interest to geography; economic awareness, citizenship and environmental education.[25]

There was initial dismay amongst geographers at not being one of the initial Subject Working Groups created. It was thought that geography in schools, seeing itself as characteristically synthesising and wide-ranging, would need to be heavily involved in linking with other subjects and in consulting about some of the cross-curricular issues. In the absence of an offical Working Group, the GA recruited small specialist teams to keep a watching brief on the work of the early-established Working Groups, to give evidence to them on behalf of geography, and to respond to the Interim Reports which they might produce. This proved to be an important, demanding and time-consuming task.

It was particularly important in respect of the Science Working Group – whose Final Report was published before the offical Geography Subject Working Group was even formed. The Science proposals seemed, in their proposed Programmes of Study, to claim for their own a large amount of what was usually taught in physical geography lessons, particularly in relation to climatology and meteorology and in aspects of earth science. A swift move by the Minister (almost certainly prompted by the known severe teacher shortages in science subjects) reduced the proposed extent of the Science National Curriculum for some pupils, but elements of earth-science themes remained in the truncated proposals.[26]

In the autumn of 1988, it began to be appreciated that the delay in setting-up the official Subject Working Group in Geography might have some advantages. Helpful indicators of the way to proceed (and not to proceed) were emerging from the experiences of the first Working Groups. It was discovered that the Minister was likely to make his own excisions and amendments to the Group's finished work and that the style and form of the formulations was as important as their intentions. Successful curriculum achievement required a sophisticated study of the 'art of the possible'.

On the other hand, it later proved difficult to have dialogue about or to amend the formulations of the Subject Groups who reported early, given that their Reports had already been 'accepted' and were in the hands of the Minister.

During the Spring of 1989 short-lists for membership of the Geography Working Group were drawn up by DES officials, advised by HMI. There were then selection interviews at Elizabeth House, conducted by one of the Ministers of State for Education in informal style; probing questions on curriculum issues were posed among the inconsequential conversation and atmosphere that surrounds a typical English summer afternoon tea-party.

Those who survived this bourgeois inquisition were nominated to be members of the Group, which met for the first time on 18 May 1989.

GEOGRAPHICAL EDUCATION IN WALES

Although a separate Welsh curriculum was not envisaged the distinctiveness of Welsh educational needs was acknowledged in the instructions to the Curriculum Working Groups set up in the wake of the 1988 Education Reform Act. A separate Welsh Department had been set up by the Board of Education as early as 1907, and a Central Welsh Board of Examinations (later to become the Welsh Joint Examinations Board) created in 1911.

Though no substantial differences in the curriculum of England and Wales were apparent following 1907, the creation of the Welsh Department signalled the acknowledgement and encouragement of Welsh language education in the schools of the Principality. S. J. Curtis[27] observes that 'Emphasis was also placed on the study of Welsh history, traditions and institutions' but does not mention geography.

The proposals which eventually emerged from the 1988 Act did, however, suggest a distinctive geography curriculum for Wales. Though much of it was common to the proposals for England,[28] it was published in a separate document by the Welsh Office.[29] A substantial study of Wales was specifically enjoined in Key Stage 3: there was no comparable requirement in the English version of the curriculum. An extra problem was that the addition of Welsh language as a subject meant that the Welsh geography curriculum was likely to have marginally less time than in England.

The proposals were mediated to teachers by the newly-formed Curriculum Council for Wales (a body equivalent to the National Curriculum Council formed in England). The CCW professional officer for geography, Anne Whipp, shrewdly monitored events across the border and worked to produce advice and guidance materials which seemed more 'teacher-friendly' than those originated in England. The curious situation arose in the 1990s that some English teachers preferred to use the Welsh guidance materials in equipping themselves for the new geography curriculum.

NOTES

1. However, Tony Blair, Prime Minister of the Labour Government elected in 1997 after 18 unbroken years of Conservative rule, said that his priorities in government would be 'Education, education, education'.
2. Who, at a distance of years, can recall either the face or the distinctive policies of such post-Second World War senior education ministers as Florence Horsbrugh, Fred Mulley, Mark Carlisle, Edward Short?
3. J. Callaghan, 'Towards a national debate', *Education*, 22 October 1976, pp. 332–3.
4. The original 'Black Papers' were a series of pamphlets (designed as a polemical antithesis to Government 'White Papers') which were later republished in a collection: C. B. Cox and A. E. Dyson (eds), *The Black Papers on Education* (Davis-Poynter, London, 1971).
5. P. H. Hirst, *Knowledge and the Curriculum* (Routledge & Kegan Paul, London, 1974).
6. For a full plan of these ideas see Her Majesty's Inspectorate, *The Curriculum, 5–16* (HMSO, London, 1985).
7. Some of the new community secondary schools in Leicestershire adopted such approaches, with Countesthorpe College notable for both its radical pedagogy and its curriculum structure. Another school prominent in this approach was Sheredes School, in Broxbourne, Hertfordshire between 1969 and 1975. For a description of this approach and a consideration of the idea behind it see M. Holt, *The Common Curriculum* (Routledge & Kegan Paul, London, 1978).
8. A. Corbett, *Whose Schools?* Fabian Research Series no. 328 (Fabian Society, London, 1976).
9. Department of Education and Science, *Educating Our Children*: Four Subjects for Debate (HMSO, London, 1977). Department of Education and Science, *Education in Schools: A Consultative Document* (HMSO, London, 1977), popularly known as 'The Green Paper'; Department of Education and Science, *Primary Education in England: A Survey by HMI* (HMSO, London, 1978); Department of Education and Science, *Aspects of Secondary Education in England: A Survey by HMI* (HMSO, London, 1979).
10. Her Majesty's Inspectorate, *Curriculum 11–16: Working Papers* (HMSO, London, 1977) popularly known as 'The Red Book'. The Staff Inspector for Geography, Trevor Bennetts, worked hard to get a geography supplement produced, subsequently.
11. Her Majesty's Inspectorate, *A View of the Curriculum* (HMSO, London, 1988).
12. Department of Education and Science, *A Framework for the School Curriculum* (HMSO, London, 1980).
13. R. Daugherty and R. Walford, 'A framework for the school curriculum', *Geography*, 65 (1980), pp. 232–5.
14. Department of Education and Science, *The School Curriculum* (HMSO, London, 1981).
15. Geographical Association (GA), *Geography in the School Curriculum 5–16* (GA, London, 1981); *Geography in the School Curriculum 16–19* (GA, London, 1983).
16. R. Walford, 'Sir Keith speaks to the GA: a report', *Teaching Geography*, 11 (1985), pp. 20–3.
17. K. Joseph, 'Geography in the school curriculum', *Geography*, 70 (1985), pp. 290–7.
18. P. Bailey and J.A. Binns, 'A case for geography: a response to Sir Keith Joseph', *Geography*, 72 (1987), pp. 327–31.
19. P. Bailey and J.A. Binns, *A Case for Geography* (GA, London, 1987).
20. See for instance, the radical formulation proposed by David Hargreaves, then Chief Inspector of ILEA, in D. Hargreaves, *The Challenge of the Comprehensive School* (Routledge & Kegan Paul, London, 1982).
21. J. White, 'An unconstitutional national curriculum', in D. Lawton and C. Chitty (eds), *The National Curriculum* (London Institute of Education, London, 1988).
22. Kenneth Baker, *The Turbulent Years: My Life in Politics* (Faber & Faber, London, 1993).
23. The original ten-subject curriculum proposed consisted of: English, maths, science ('core subjects'), design and technology, a modern foreign language, history, geography, music, art, physical education ('foundation subjects').
24. It is ironic that the thrust of the education policies of the Labour Government post-1997 has been to marginalise the 'foundation subjects' for which Baker fought and return to a curriculum position in which the core subjects are stressed to the exclusion of almost all else, as Mrs Thatcher would have wished.

25. The groups eventually reported through a series of pamphlets published by the National Curriculum Council under the title *Curriculum Guidance*. Some of these were considered helpful by teachers but they were left to be taken at face value and no statutory need to observe them was ever decreed.

26. Later revisions (see Chapter 11) reduced the earth-science component of Science even more, so that now the National Curriculum 'environmental' work to be done in schools is mostly in the Geography Orders.

27. S. J. Curtis, *History of Education in Great Britain* (University Tutorial Press, London, 1967).

28. Department for Education, *Geography in the National Curriculum: England* (HMSO, London, 1995).

29. Welsh Office, *Geography in the National Curriculum: Wales* (HMSO, London, 1995).

11

The Butcher, the Baker, the Curriculum Fudge-Maker, 1990–2000

GETTING TO WORK

The establishment of a National Curriculum Working Group for Geography by the government represented a key moment in the history of the discipline. The membership of the Group eventually chosen consisted of: the head of geography in a Welsh secondary comprehensive school; a recently retired primary head-teacher; two LEA advisers; two teacher-educators; an ex-teacher, now co-ordinator of a geography curriculum project; and a strong lay representation – the managing director of a large travel firm, a former chairman of a steel-manfacturing company, a member of the Countryside Commission and a university professor of geography.[1]

It was the presence of this latter element that was novel to curriculum discussion in school geography and the complement of lay members was completed by the Chairman chosen for the Working Group, Sir Leslie Fielding, the newly appointed Vice-Chancellor of the University of Sussex. Sir Leslie had spent much of his life in the British Diplomatic Service, spoke several languages, and had travelled the world extensively. Although by training a historian he professed a strong lay interest in geography and claimed proudly that he had once taught for a spell in a primary school in the West India Dock Road, in the heart of London's old Docklands.

He brought his diplomatic skills to his Chairman's role, jockeying the Working Party along in its set tasks, subtly setting its course direction and providing an iron hand (usually) in a velvet glove. (The cover slipped once as he pointed out in a moment of crisis, 'Look, do you people want to finish this job? If not, make no mistake, the government will get some others who will – and it may not be to your liking'.) In retrospect, it may be seen that his skills of negotiation, persuasion and manipulation of the Group's agenda were a major influence.

Duncan Graham, the Chairman of the National Curriculum Council, in his book which purports to describe the inside story of the making of the National Curriculum thought that the Geography Group worked more successfully than most of the others

Members of the group worked well together under the doughty chairmanship of Sir Leslie Fielding ... and as far as one could see there were no internal tensions' ... All that one heard was good news.[2]

The Geography Group may not have experienced the cataclysmic (and very public) divisions which affected the History Group, but Graham's latter comments are a matter of misunderstanding or else deliberate euphemisms, compared with what actually went on in the 12 months of the Group's existence.

The Department of Education and Science provided published Terms of Reference for the Group which set initial parameters and emphasised concern that it should particularly address questions related to a European dimension and to general environmental matters. Other government views were mediated , though not prescriptively, by the DES Secretariat, who staffed the group's work. At the head of these was a senior civil servant who acted as the eyes and ears of the Secretary of State during the meetings, and laconically but sharply pointed out political considerations. An industrious and task-oriented administrator acted as senior secretary to the group and the Staff Inspector of Geography (HMI) was also present as an 'Assessor' (though in practice a key participant). A struggle for power between DES and HMI was played out both within and beyond the Group as discussion took place.

The Working Group was given a year to complete its task, and its members were expected to find the time for meetings whilst continuing their own regular work. Some 50 days of meetings were scheduled (some as day meetings, some as residential conferences in which discussion and drafting sessions were mingled with visits to schools and visits from delegations of other bodies). Between the regular meetings, members received huge parcels of documents prepared by the secretariat for consideration and further work.

The Government's Task Group on Assessment and Testing (TGAT) had already prescribed a shape for the curriculum Reports of the Working Groups. There would be a number of Attainment Targets (ATs) for each subject, made up of Statements of Attainment (SOAs) at ten levels of study, level 1 being that presumed as the average condition of a child's knowledge when entering school at the age of 5. Programmes of Study (POSs) would develop these SOAs into a teaching framework. Geography chose to develop its Programmes of Study not year by year but in relation to the four Key Stages of schooling identified by TGAT – Key Stage 1, 5–7 years; Key Stage 2, 7–11 years; Key Stage 3, 11–14 years; Key Stage 4, 14–16 years. The terminology of 'Key Stages' has become common parlance in education since.

Those subject groups which had reported early had created a considerable number of Attainment Targets (Science had 17 initially, and Maths 13) but realisation about the difficulty of testing such a large number of ATs caused subsequent revision to smaller numbers for other groups. The Geography Working Group eventually reached a formulation of 7 ATs, each with a number of subject 'strands' that could be identified as sub-sections.

The final formulation was:

AT 1 *Geographical Skills* (especially in using maps and doing field-work)
AT 2 *The Home Area and Region*
AT 3 *The United Kingdom within the European Community*
AT4 *The Wider World*
AT 5 *Physical Geography* (atmosphere; hydrosphere; lithosphere; biosphere)
AT 6 *Human Geography* (population; settlements; communications and movements; economic activities – primary, secondary, tertiary)
AT 7 *Environmental Geography* (the use and misuse of natural resources; the quality and vulnerability of different environments; the possibilities for protecting and managing environments).

Examples of particular topics that could be used in the classroom were given alongside the specific Statements of Attainment in each AT in the Final Report of the Group[3] although it was recognised that these could not be made part of the draft or final Statutory Orders.[4]

The Report also provided a detailed rationale for its work in accompanying chapters to the proposals. These began with an assessment of the present situation (and its supposed deficits) and included chapters on specific topics such as mapwork, field-work and information technology.

WHAT WENT ON INSIDE THE GROUP

Given the wide constituency of membership and the need to provide concrete proposals, the discussions within the Working Group would serve as a unique focus for the major issues which geography had come to face as it had grown in strength as a school subject. From the first day that the Working Group assembled, the question of what exactly geography *was* emerged as a recurrent theme of conversation. Educators, academics and laity found themselves going back to basic, even instinctive, formulations, as they sought to convince each other of what they thought was at the heart of geography. Allied to this was the issue of whether the essence of school geography could or should match the essence of the geography taught in institutions of higher education – questions that had echoed through the years.

An early initiative served to sharpen the point and highlight some divergence of view. The Chairman accepted a suggestion that members should circulate – for the enlightenment of each other – one or two pieces of writing that they considered the epitome of geography. Almost everyone took the opportunity to do so. Major statements about the discipline from academics such as Goudie and Stoddart[5] were not unexpected contributions; more intriguing and just as stimulating, however, was the nomination of such pieces as a poem by Philip Larkin ('Here'), a children's story by Roald Dahl ('The fantastic Mr Fox'), a description of teaching in a country village school (by Sybil Marshall) and paragraphs from a Cambridge college admissions prospectus.

Such variety was also reflected in the viewpoints expressed in early discussions as the Group sought a framework on which to build the Attainment Targets. The relative under-emphasis of place studies in current British school curricula was remarked on,[6] and the possible primacy of place studies, thematic studies and skills as organising frameworks were advanced from different quarters. The eventual production of the 'cube' diagram (see Figure 11.1) to express the heart of the subject (in which areas, themes and skills were presented as equal and potentially integratable partners) was a simple but profoundly argued final solution.

Figure 11.1:
Cube diagram developed by the National Curriculum Working Group

There was also animated discussion about whether the heart of school geography was, or should be seen as, a body of knowledge or a *way* of learning. This opened up deep philosophical crevasses about the nature of the subject and the desirability or otherwise of 'academic' geography (a study for a small elite) and 'school' geography (potentially a study for all pupils) dancing to the same tune.

There was a greater degree of agreement on the need to see physical and human geography as equal partners in the geography curriculum. In the 1960s and 1970s, some schools (particulary if studying geography through the medium of the GYSL project and the 16–19 project materials) had almost cast all physical geography adrift in following the excitements and controversies of economic and social issues. There were also a minority of schools following 'humanities' schemes of work in which human geography was usually much more prominent than physical geography. The view emerged in the Working Group that these represented an emasculated experience of geography and their problematic nature was highlighted by an HMI Report placed before the Group, which reported only 50 per cent of 'humanities' lessons as being satisfactory, compared with an overall average of 80 per cent for all GCSE lessons inspected over the previous two years.[7]

The need to see geography taught as a separate subject in secondary schools was agreed on a basis of experience, (recalling the debates of the 1950s and 1960s – see Chapter 7), inclination and evidence, including an examination of 'social studies' taught in countries overseas. (Members of the group made several visits to European countries to consult with government officials, curriculum managers and teachers.) In this respect, the Group's own views matched those of successive Secretaries of State for Education who felt that combined or integrated courses 'usually combined history and geography to the detriment of both'.[8]

A further concern for schools endorsed unanimously by the group was the need to see geography as a unity and a subject which synthesised ideas. In higher education, it was observed, fragmenting tendencies had been apparent in the recent past with 'adjectival' geographies much in evidence and many academics seemingly preoccupied with their own specialisation. (Shades of the debate between Principal Murray and Mackinder in 1942!)

The Working Group was inclined to a holistic view of the subject in which the interaction of physical and human environments was constantly expressed and explored in school work. The balance of physical and human studies was buttressed in the Final Report by a linking Attainment Target discreetly (though tautologically) called 'Environmental geography'. In reality this sought to encourage the study of environmental issues and controversies, but its title was 'damped down' in order not to excite government concern. It was an opportunist move, capitalising on the mood of the age, and fuelled by the belief that school geography should be concerned with 'big issues' of the contemporary stewardship of the earth and the possible scenarios for its future.[9]

BAKER – PROVIDING THE GIVEN FRAMEWORK

Kenneth Baker suggested to the group at the start of its work that it had the opportunity to plan a definitive geography curriculum 'from scratch' and without any external constraints. To this end, it was pointed out, the question of assessment would be divorced from the curriculum planning exercise, so that it should not unduly influence the deliberations. In actual practice the divorce between curriculum planning and assessment caused major technical difficulties[10] that might, with hindsight, have been avoided. But the national framework of assessment (which was being determined by the Schools Examination and Assessment Council [SEAC] – one of the two bodies which were successors to the Schools Council) was itself subject to bewildering change during the lifetime of the Group; even a group of psychics could not have guessed the eventual framework which was to eventually emerge and so it would have been unprofitable to have allowed assessment issues to have dominated discussions.

The TGAT ten-level framework already put in place was much more suitable for Science and Maths than for other subjects. Its complexities complicated the task and led to a fateful decision – the inclusion of *content* in the Statements of Attainment for each level. This course of action followed the model already published in the Science report, but created potential problems for teaching groups in which students might not be all at the same level.

It gave rise to an interesting debate both within and without the Group because it led to the criticism that content-laden SOAs did not provide progression of knowledge but merely accumulation of knowledge. Is accumulation part of progression, i.e. is knowing more about something an advancement of understanding – a step up a ladder or merely a further step along a path? Defenders of the formulation which included content argued that, in any case, as the levels went higher, a sophistication of concepts was implied as well as a growth in knowledge.

The issue also led to keen argument within the group about the importance of specifying content in a geography curriculum and eventually revealed a key difference between a minority who envisaged that a curriculum could be based on 'geographical enquiry' and the rest. The matter was made more complex because government advice was to concentrate on a curriculum which clearly set out geography's distinctive contributions; most Group members doubted that the development of 'enquiry skills' (however significant as a teaching approach) could be justified as distinctive to geography. The disagreement rumbled on through the group's life, caused more by the restrictions of the brief than by any fundamental intellectual chasm. The Final Report affirmed a belief that geography *did* have a content base and that enquiry skills were important but not distinctive to geography.

THE LAY INFLUENCE

With a complement of five out of the twelve members, the lay presence in the Working Group was a powerful, as well as a new, influence on geography curriculum discussions. Sceptical comments about their presence or possible contribution came from some professional educators outside the Working Group, but one suspects that these were largely a production of sour grapes. The value of the lay members was that they took none of the current educational wisdom at face value, they questioned every issue on its merits, and they pointed to particular weaknesses to which professionals had perhaps been too close to see properly. The lay team acted as a provocative antidote to prevailing orthodoxies.

Part of this significance derived from the clear DES directive that the status quo in schools was broadly unsatisfactory and that there were weaknesses (notably in the realm of world knowledge) that needed to be remedied. The lay members had a strong belief that geography was essentially about place and that it should equip pupils with practical knowledge and understanding of the modern world – the need to have more 'locational knowledge' and more concentration on 'the study of places and areas' were themes repeatedly expressed. Some saw the laity as leading the Working Group inexorably backwards; but looked at another way, their presence might be judged to have led to a timely rediscovery of the roots of the subject.

PLAYING CURRICULUM POLITICS

Kenneth Baker had pre-defined discussion in an important way by plumping for a base of traditional subjects. His assumption was that this would be most comfortable for parents and employers and also probably command the greatest consensus amongst teachers. Subject groups would define their own boundaries. This fudged the issue of skills or content which might be genuinely common to more than one subject. Thus, the Geography Working Group was discouraged from developing a skills AT which would include general library and enquiry skills because it would not be sufficiently distinctive to geography. It was of little consequence to argue that it would be more educationally coherent to allow overlap, because the 'division of spoils' philosophy was already operating on curriculum territory.

Despite representations from the geographic community, the Science Working Group defined the boundaries of their domain as a far-flung empire. Some of this colonialism extended to parts of the earth sciences usually taught by geographers in schools, notably in geomorphology (landforms), climatology and meteorology. The Geography Group responded by showing their concern over such tactics and drawing the (new) Secretary of State's attention to it in their Interim Report. John McGregor, the new incumbent Minister (Baker having been quickly promoted to Chairman of the Conservative Party following his successful piloting of the Education Act through Parliament), responded with comforting ambiguity, and softened the line, suggesting that, in this case, both science and geography should define their territory as they wished, leaving schools to decide their own solution to the content overlap. This half-answer assuaged fears temporarily but showed up the disadvantages of the single-subject development process, the serial organisation of groups and the discouragement of consultation. The imperial ambitions of science were tripped up late in the day when their curriculum was cut back in the earth-science sphere, through perceived overload.

Linkage with the History Working Group (whose meetings overlapped with geography for some of the time) was also discouraged. One member of the Geography Group, used to making common cause with historians in her 'topic work' in primary education, sought unauthorised consultation with members of the History Group and was admonished by the Chairman for doing so. The final Reports of the Geography and History Groups differed in quite radical ways. Some members of the Geography Group positively welcomed the chance to distance geography from history and stress the scientific elements of geography as important; some members of the History Group showed similar tendencies in wanting to stress links with English.

It is possible to read these subject-conscious strategies as protectionist stances, an abhorrent hindrance to curriculum free-trade. But the planning of the National Curriculum by separate groups did at least have the merit of being practical, whatever its other faults. There was a lot to be said for 'going to the summit' in a solo expedition. Cross-curricular links were not excluded for ever by this process; they could emerge in higher profile once the basic building blocks of the curriculum had been established. The Working Groups were at such full stretch over the limited time of their existence that extensive inter-subject consultations and debates would probably have prevented any end-product from appearing at all.[11]

Some bemoan the fact that the idealism of whole-curriculum planning was sacrificed to a realistic quick-fix arrangement through separate subjects. But flawed though it undoubtedly was, working in separate-subject groups represented a first step to a whole curriculum that otherwise might never have been completed.

GOVERNMENT INFLUENCES

The conclusion drawn by some outside the process is that the Working Group was 'manipulated by the Chairman' to educationally unsound conclusions,[12] and thus by proxy was putty in the hands of a Machiavellian set of civil servants and ministers. The hypothesis is too melodramatic. The government had an agenda it wished to see implemented, based on a dissatisfaction with the status quo in schools. It required professionals on the Working Group – who had enjoyed curriculum freedom for almost all the century – to be prepared to re-examine some of their cherished positions. The strong lay contribution was the catalyst for this.

What emerged from both DES and lay pressure was a wish to move the curriculum ethos from child-centred and reconstructionist emphases (often strongly apparent in the 1970s and still powerful in the 1980s) to more conservative emphases of vocational relevance and a desired transmission of cultural heritage (exemplified, in geography's case by a concern about providing a base of world knowledge). Mrs Thatcher made the point in an interview, given during the life of the Working Group, when she was still Prime Minister:

> It is obvious you must have some history and some geography, you are not a complete person unless you have that general knowledge.[13]

To oppose this view would have been openly conflicting with the Terms of Reference; in fact, the need to restore a knowledge base was acknowledged unanimously by the members of the group, the differences between them being related to how this should be prescribed and how much it should be emphasised. The DES Assessor (and the Secretariat) also had a trump card to play – in the last resort, would things be 'acceptable' to the Minister? The DES Assessor brought news of changes in government thinking almost weekly, and this complicated tasks already underway. Some critics were deeply depressed by the apparent intervention of the government in a matter which they felt should be 'democratically' decided by professionals. But democracy is capable of several interpretations; the government defined it as including the views of parents, employers and school governors, as well as teachers. The test was to see how much weight long-held educational views could muster in relation to the opinions of an intelligent and concerned laity and a task-oriented officialdom. Rhetoric and ideology interestingly jousted with scepticism from time to time with varying results. The Group members were not 'pawns' but in the end they had to work within the realms of the possible.

THE BUTCHER AT WORK …

The Final Report of the Working Group was published in June 1990. It was a document conceived from much discussion and many late-night sessions when, as the Secretary once aptly remarked, 'there had been blood on the floor'. All the members of the Group signed the Report. Alongside its proposals for seven Attainment Targets and 183 Statements of Attainment was a closely argued rationale for the changes proposed, a rationale which provided a focus for discussion in its own right.

A consultation exercise, handled by the National Curriculum Council (NCC), then began; the NCC was the sister to SEAC, and, like SEAC, a descendant from the old Schools Council. (Both were, in practice, never quite able to quite establish themselves, and they were abolished and replaced by the Schools Curriculum and Assessment Authority (SCAA) in 1994. SCAA in turn became the Qualifications and Curriculum Authority (QCA) in 1998.)

The NCC set up a 'Task Force' to examine the Report and propose possible amendments, but the fact that the Geography Working Group was now disbanded meant that there was little or no contact between the authors of the original Report and the body now considering it. The matter was made even more complex by the fact that within the NCC itself there was a power struggle going on between committees and the Chief Executive, later to lead to the resignation of the latter. In addition, the extent of the NCC's own competence and influence on curriculum matters was being called into question by another new Secretary of State for Education, Kenneth Clarke (John McGregor had been speedily removed by Mrs Thatcher on the suspicion that he might be 'cosying up' to teachers too much). Clarke, whilst at the Ministry of Health, had been involved in bruising battles with the doctors; there was expectation that he would take up a similar stance at Education.

The NCC report (November 1990),[14] compiled in a matter of weeks, made marginal amendments to the Final Report; some, although well intentioned, disturbed balances carefully created through months of work by the original Working Group. The NCC examining group seemed less aware of the political context in which such proposals would eventually be scrutinised.

Following this interlude, the Draft Statutory Orders for both geography and history were at the top of his in-tray as the new Minister settled down to examine National Curriculum proposals over the 1990 Christmas and 1991 New Year holiday period. He was aided by his personal political adviser, Tessa Keswick (but significantly no adviser from his civil service team, or from the Inspectorate). The assumption, widely held, that the Draft Order for Parliament would be little different from the version of the proposals agreed by the National Curriculum Council proved unfounded. The Minister, already in ill humour with that body, was disposed to take his red pencil to some of the proposals. He effectively assumed the role of butcher.

When the Draft Orders were published in January 1991, they were accompanied by an explanatory paragraph that demonstrated Clarke's strong 'hands-on' approach:

> (The Secretary of State) considers that the attainment targets should emphasise more strongly knowledge and understanding of aspects of geography, and put less emphasis on assessment of skills – which, however desirable, are not particular to geography – and less emphasis on the assessment of attitudes and values. He also considers that in primary schools, the number of different places to be studied should be reduced. Some other minor changes have been made.

This revealed a clear dislike for some of the more controversial matters with political and economic overtones (such as planning, development and environmental issues) that had so far been included. The Working Group had hoped that, by agreeing to a conspicuous and reassuring base of specified 'factual knowledge', a trade-off had been negotiated, allowing some more ambitious and controversial topics to stay discreetly embedded in the Statements of Attainment. But, unlike Odysseus in the cave, these failed to reach safety through clinging on inconspicuously amidst the passing traffic; the eye of the Ministerial Cyclops proved too sharp, and the plan was rumbled.

Anguish from all quarters of the geographical community was expressed at these late changes, and a further consultation exercise was beseiged by requests (couched in varying degrees of politeness) for material to be restored. This had some small effect, but the Ministerial knife certainly reshaped the Final Orders put before Parliament in May 1991, as a National Geography Curriculum was laid down for the first time.

THE CURRICULUM-FUDGE MAKER

In the event, it was a nugatory battle, since, the high-water mark of geography's place in the National Curriculum had been reached (see Figure 7.1). At a later stage, the requirement for all pupils to study geography at Key Stage 4 was removed and the possibility of a mature study of controversial issues now depends on whether or not students opt for the subject post-Key Stage 3 and which GCSE examination their schools choose to take.

Clarke did not stay long at the Ministry of Education but moved onwards and upwards to the Chancellorship of the Exchequer. Geography teachers expected to be happier with his successor, John Patten, since he had been a geography don at Oxford before entering Parliament, and the editor of one of the discipline's major academic journals, the *Journal of Historical Geography*. Patten had a number of interesting and quite radical ideas but quickly ran into heavy storms in his inability to temporise either with teachers' unions (who were complaining about overloaded timetables and mounting National Curriculum bureaucracy) or with parents (whose representatives he injudiciously accused of holding 'Neanderthal views' early in his ministerial career).

Thus, the possibility of successful compromise and adjustment soon disappeared and Patten had to call in an industrialist as a 'fixer' for the mounting pile of National Curriculum disputes before he relinquished office in 1994. The person in question was Sir Ron Dearing, who had formerly run the Post Office, but whose knowledge of education was avowedly as a layman. Patten had been driven to finding a solution to curriculum issues irrespective of what it might be.

Dearing duly obliged and produced his report within six months, addressing the perceived problem of overload both in the curriculum as a whole, and in the Orders for particular subjects, as well as prescribing a severe curtailment of the national testing programme.[15] He was hailed as a hero by many as seen to be returning calm and stability to the educational scene; but he was also the creator of a curriculum-fudge of classic proportions, dismantling the original vision of the 'broad and balanced curriculum' for which Kenneth Baker had fought so hard in Cabinet.

Professional bodies such as the Geographical Association, supportive of the need for some of the revisions, aware that some of their members were among the 'overload' complainers, and wearied by the hyper-activity of the previous few years, offered only subdued resistance to some of the counter-moves in areas where earlier they had won key battles.

Dearing's solution was to both reduce the number of compulsory subjects in Key Stage 4 and to slim down the content of all non-core subjects in all Key Stages. Hurriedly, subject-groups were convened to do this within a limited time-scale of six weeks. Detailed prescriptions of content (Statements of Attainment) were replaced by single paragraph 'Level descriptors'. Though this tactic reduced the amount of material within the specification for each subject, it has yet to be proved that level descriptors are any easier to understand, unpack or assess.

The number of Attainment Targets was reduced in most subjects, and geography's original seven (reduced to five by the NCC) became one. The number of standard national tests to be taken was reduced, and these were now restricted to the three 'core' subjects. The general view quickly emerged that those subjects (including geography) without a national testing programme have less 'status' than those which are annually examined in this way. This view has been buttressed by a similar concentration of emphasis on 'core subjects' in the inspection and reporting programmes of the Office for Standards in Education (OFSTED). OFSTED came into being in 1994, as part of a drive to strengthen the monitoring of educational standards and now employs former HMI and LEA Inspectors to do its work.

An additional Dearing proposal was to open up the possibility of separate pathways for academic, vocational and occupational education post-14 years of age, a proposal which had startling echoes of the tripartite system of education espoused in the 1944 Education Act and abandoned in the 1960s. Eric Bolton, former Chief of Her Majesty's Inspectors, and key adviser when Kenneth Baker introduced the concept of a 'broad and balanced curriculum' which underpinned the 1988 Act, remonstrated in vain.[16]

Most significantly of all, the balance of the original ten-subject curriculum was dismantled. In the interests of providing more time for the core subjects, the compulsory post-14 curriculum was whittled down to English, maths and science, and short courses in a modern foreign language and in design and technology. Everything else became optional. The level of justification for this was vacuous:

> History and geography are absorbing and valuable subjects. But I cannot see a reason, either nationally or in terms of the individual student, why these subjects should, as a matter of law, be given priority in this key stage over others such as the creative arts, a second foreign language, home economics, the classics [*sic*], religious studies, business studies or economics.

Geography and history sought not priority but parity with the creative arts, and religious studies; all these potential contributors to a post-14 curriculum were diminished in importance by the Dearing decision. The avoidance of the broad curriculum issue (expressed in the artless 'I cannot see a reason why …') would have been disarming in its frankness, had it not been for the fact that English, maths and science were justified elsewhere by Dearing solely on utilitarian grounds. Getting an education as a means of getting a job became the sole justification of the proposals – precisely what Prime Minister James Callaghan had warned against in 1976.

Similarly, the pragmatism of the 'fix' was apparent in the way in which the idea of cross-curricular themes – a recurring issue in early discussions and promoted by Kenneth Baker as an integrating force – was rendered quite invisible in the Dearing review proposals.

It was in vain that some schools were showing that a little ingenuity could deliver a satisfactory broad curriculum in which all students could follow all GCSE courses in all core and foundation subjects.[17] Dearing's aim was the delivery of a report to quell the disquiet between the Ministry and the barons of the teachers' unions. The relief at the reduction of content was immediate, but the dismantling of the Baker vision occasioned much less comment. Dearing's report was topped off by a promise that there would be a period of 'calm' and that any changes made to the National Curriculum at the next review (1999–2000) would be minimal.

In future years any deficiencies in the Dearing 'solution' can, of course, be laid at the door of 'the teachers', to whose complaints he was anxious to be seen to respond. In the last phase of the implementation of a National Curriculum, the industrial-style arbitration of a dispute came to take precedence over measured discussion and consideration of the issues.

THE SAME? OR NOT THE SAME?

Thus, at the end of a decade of great curriculum turbulence the position of geography in schools might appear to have returned largely to where it was before the Education Act of 1988 was ever mooted. And yet it is not quite the same. Many older teachers, exhausted by the mounting piles of documents with which they have been confronted, have chosen to leave the profession. Their complaint, and it is a reasonable one, is that, for at least a decade, there has been little time to focus on the teaching of the subject itself in the midst of all the bureaucratic paperstorms.

Younger teachers are aware that the need to follow a prescribed National Curriculum, to test regularly, to be aware of their school's need to gain good examination results, because of league tables, and to pass regular OFSTED inspections with a clean bill of health is now paramount. It has yet to be shown that the prescription, in helping their planning, does not also inhibit their flair.

Yet on the positive side, the work and the Report of the Geography Working Group created far-reaching discussion about the general nature of the subject, as well as about points of detail. A framework was worked through and put in place and it is already taken as axiomatic in many places. The equality of physical geography was reasserted, the base of place knowledge re-established in a more balanced way, and the importance of environmental themes given new prominence. These things survived across the Final Orders and the Dearing Review. The very act of reformulating the subject for pupils between 5 and 16 years kick-started a debate[18] which may, with benefit, at some time in the future, permeate higher levels of education.

A generation of primary school teachers were prompted to rediscover the enjoyment and stimulus of geography following decades when it had been absorbed into amorphous 'topic' work (sometimes to its benefit, but usually, through superficiality, to its disadvantage). This, however, proved to be a short-lived advantage. In 1998, pressed to remedy deficiencies in reading and number work, and to find time for a proposed 'literacy hour' and 'numeracy hour' the Secretary of State for Education withdrew the statuory force of the detailed geography and history curriculum for primary schools. The withdrawal is intended, it is said, to be temporary, but the effect was discouraging to the renaissance of primary school history and geography which had begun to take place following the 1988 Act.

CLASSROOM RESOURCES

In both primary and secondary work there has been a development of new materials for the classroom in the 1990s, inspired or impelled by National Curriculum considerations. Some teachers have seen the new era as a golden opportunity to rethink whole courses and units of work; others have, at least, welcomed the injections of funds to requip their classrooms with new series of textbooks – and geography has done better than many subjects with the amount and quality of provision in this sphere.

In particular, the textbooks of David Waugh, a former head of geography in a Carlisle comprehensive school, and his co-authors, have made a great impact on schools since the advent of the National Curriculum (see Figure 11.2). Meticulously planned and researched, and given high design values, they have quickly achieved popularity and market-penetration in schools. Surveys suggest that in the late 1990s over 75 per cent of English secondary schools used Waugh's books, a figure which certainly equals and probably surpasses the dominance of the texts of Fairgrieve and Young, Dudley Stamp, or Thomas Pickles in previous generations. Waugh's versatile output ranges from a ubiquitous KS 3 series written with Tony Bushell, to a major A-level text, which appears to be seen as geographical salvation by every perplexed sixth-form student.[19]

Waugh's own modest and thoughtful assessment of how his books should be used includes a belief that textbooks must be supplemented

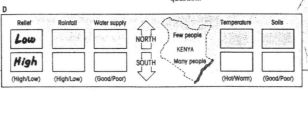

Figure 11.2:
Page from *Interactions* by
David Waugh and Tony
Bushell, 1994 (reduced in size)
(*Source*: Stanley Thornes)

with other materials in the classroom; there are signs, however, that (perhaps exhausted with curriculum bureaucracy) an over-reliance on the textbook has become more frequent in the 1990s than in previous decades.

Recent OFSTED reports on the national state of geography teaching suggest that at Key Stage 3 (11–14 years) the national curriculum has stimulated a return to 'safer' textbook-oriented learning, and that though the proportion of 'unsatisfactory' lessons is low compared with other subjects, geography does not have so many 'good' or 'exceptional' lessons.[20] There is some evidence, that safe, 'bread-and-butter' teaching is predominant over inspirational or imaginative geography as the

Table 11.1(a): Numbers of GCSE Candidates 1988–94

	1988	1989	1990	(90–91) % Change	1991	1992	(91–92) % Change	1993	(92–93) % Change	1994
1. Science	155,713(13)	171,883(12)	262,704 (6)	37.20	374,454 (4)	572,327 (2)	53.11	593,887 (2)	3.76	777,446 (1)
2. Maths	670,128 (1)	651,951 (2)	606,631 (1)	–5.90	570,878 (2)	556,199 (3)	–2.57	547,983 (3)	–1.48	601,613 (2)
3. English	666,962 (2)	653,821 (1)	659,386 (2)	–2.50	642,911 (1)	641,937 (1)	–0.15	630,087 (1)	–1.85	596,206 (3)
4. English Lit.	394,818 (3)	389,323 (3)	423,663 (3)	4.80	444,158 (3)	450,282 (4)	1.36	448,554 (4)	–0.39	425,117 (4)
5. Tech/CDT	157,747(12)	156,832(13)	156,246(12)	3.30	161,511 (9)	149,448 (9)	–7.53	144,467 (9)	–3.34	143,016 (9)
6. French	265,317 (6)	265,239 (5)	270,243 (5)	8.20	292,497 (5)	300,876 (5)	2.86	286,138 (5)	–4.90	289,901 (5)
7. Geography	305,575 (4)	276,740 (4)	273,624 (4)	–2.30	267,931 (6)	268,235 (6)	0.31	265,123 (6)	–1.17	264,224 (6)
8. History	256,309 (7)	232,476 (7)	219,922 (7)	–10.50	196,755 (8)	207,395 (8)	5.40	215,922 (7)	4.11	227,395 (7)
9. Art/Design	227,981 (9)	224,308 (8)	218,196 (9)	–5.10	209,469 (7)	214,425 (7)	2.36	198,023 (8)	–7.65	212,082 (8)
10. German	75,684	77,067	82,728	8.71	89,909	94,361	4.92	106,420(11)	12.80	110,517(10)
11. Religious Studies	104,512	93,972	94,696	3.90	98,033	95,846(13)	–2.23	95,748(13)	–0.11	102,031(13)
12. Bus. Studies	47,365	28,957	59,177	44	82,918	97,282(12)	17.32	99,236(12)	2.00	106,942(11)
13. Biology	304,675 (5)	249,749 (6)	219,085 (8)	–27.00	160,040(10)	103,247(11)	–35.49	90,622	–12.23	75,235
14. Chemistry	217,638(10)	201,799(10)	173,025(11)	–29.10	122,923(13)	72,214	–41.25	62,363	–13.60	52,167
15. Physics	254,107 (8)	224,052 (9)	190,040(10)	–30.30	132,385(11)	78,275	–40.87	65,438	–16.40	53,746
16. Music	29,113	32,343	32,409	–1.00	32,058	32,712	2.04	34,083	4.19	36,471
17. Home Econ.	184,883(11)	174,070(11)	149,133(13)	–12.50	129,067(12)	116,446(10)	9.78	108,041(10)	–7.22	104,488(12)
18. Economics	33,715	29,883	28,168	–15.10	24,231	19,787	(–22.46)	16,701	–15.60	13,985
Total GCSE Candidates										

Note: Figures in parentheses represent rank order.

Table 11.1(b): Numbers of GCSE Candidates, 1995–2000

	(93–94) % Change	1995	(94–95) % Change	1996	(95–96) % Change	1997	(96–97) % Change	1998	(97–98) % Change	1999	(98–99) % Change	2000	(99–00) % Change
1.	30.90	976,642 (1)	25.62	997,442 (1)	2.10	1,007,140 (1)	1.00	1,006,151 (1)	-0.10	1,017,486 (1)	1.20	1,040,139 (1)	2.23
2.	9.80	667,908 (2)	11.01	691,111 (2)	3.50	681,265 (2)	-1.00	670,141 (2)	-1.60	672,950 (2)	0.42	673,056 (2)	0.02
3.	-5.40	646,460 (3)	8.42	663,009 (3)	2.60	649,559 (3)	-1.00	637,748 (3)	-1.80	638,018 (3)	0.04	647,436 (3)	1.48
4.	-5.30	475,297 (4)	11.80	491,850 (4)	3.50	492,678 (4)	0.20	490,845 (4)	-0.40	501,951 (4)	2.26	512,572 (4)	2.12
5.	-1.00	347,904 (5)	143.26	245,132 (7)	-30.00	235,877 (7)	-3.90	385,057 (5)	63.20	407,348 (5)	5.79	424,468 (5)	4.20
6.	1.30	340,155 (6)	17.33	342,751 (5)	0.80	328,299 (5)	-5.00	335,698 (6)	2.20	335,816 (6)	0.03	341,004 (6)	1.55
7.	-0.30	295,229 (7)	11.73	302,298 (6)	2.40	290,201 (6)	-4.00	265,573 (7)	-8.50	257,294 (7)	-3.12	251,005 (7)	2.21
8.	5.30	239,524 (8)	5.33	226,808 (9)	-5.30	227,447 (8)	-2.00	209,789 (8)	-7.80	210,113 (8)	0.15	213,346 (8)	1.54
9.	7.10	212,478 (9)	0.18	228,882 (8)	7.70	221,543 (9)	-3.20	206,781 (9)	-6.70	199,208 (9)	-3.66	201,296 (9)	1.05
10.	3.80	126,848 (10)	14.77	132,212 (10)	4.20	132,615 (10)	-0.40	133,683 (10)	0.80	135,158 (10)	1.10	133,659 (10)	-1.11
11.	6.60	106,223 (11)	4.11	116,549 (11)	7.90	118,545 (11)	1.90	113,381 (11)	-4.40	115,679 (11)	2.03	116,234 (11)	0.48
12.	7.80	85,516	-20.03	114,119 (12)	33.90	115,498 (12)	1.10	103,262 (12)	-10.60	98,787 (12)	-4.34	100,962 (13)	2.20
13.	-17.00	53,984	-28.25	48,276	5.90	47,743	-1.10	47,523	-0.50	47,957	0.09	48,715 (17)	1.58
14.	-17.40	43,846	-15.95	46,885	6.90	45,797	-2.31	46,025	0.50	46,968	2.04	46,917 (18)	-0.12
15.	-18.90	43,784	-18.53	46,446	6.10	44,892	-3.37	45,319	0.90	46,685	3.01	46,627 (19)	0.12
16.	7.80	37,606	3.11	41,801	11.20	43,430	3.10	42,069	-3.30	43,002	2.22	45,797 (20)	6.50
17.	-3.30	54,769 (13)	-47.58	97,340 (13)	77.79	104,863 (13)	7.60	52,855	-50.40	48,391	-8.43	45,093 (21)	-6.82
18.	-16.30	11,206	-19.87	11,127	-0.70	9,600	-13.70	7,430 (25)	-22.60	6,584	-11.39	6,220 (29)	-5.53
		4,659,680	10.30	5,057,143	8.50	5,415,187	7.80	5,353,100	-1.20	5,374,751	0.40	5,481,920	2.01

Note: Figures in parentheses represent rank order.

Table 11.2(a): Numbers of A-Level Candidates, 1989–94

	1989	1990	(90–91) % Change	1991	(91–92) % Change	1992	(92–93) % Change	1993	1994
1. English	65,945 (2)	74,182 (2)	+6.00	79,139 (1)	9.53	85,685 (1)	2.37	88,739 (1)	87,896 (1)
2. Gen. Studies	50,265 (4)	51,399 (4)	2.00	52,191 (4)	2.99	53,651 (4)	2.12	54,788 (4)	53,633 (4)
3. Mathematics	82,987 (1)	79,748 (1)	–6.00	75,006 (2)	–3.53	72,357 (2)	–10.62	64,676 (2)	61,728 (2)
4. Biology	42,138 (9)	46,465 (5)	1.90	48,539 (5)	0.34	48,705 (5)	–2.90	47,320 (5)	50,685 (5)
5. Geography	36,632(10)	41,671(10)	2.00	42,446(10)	7.43	45,603 (7)	1.70	46,399 (6)	46,339 (6)
6. Chemistry	47,559 (5)	46,197 (6)	–3.80	44,450 (6)	–3.95	42,695 (8)	–4.51	40,772 (8)	41,226 (8)
7. History	43,049 (8)	43,806 (9)	0.20	44,064 (7)	5.93	46,680 (6)	–1.36	46,096 (7)	44,787 (7)
8. Art & Design	32,205(11)	31,735(11)	–1.50	31,161(11)	7.90	33,644(11)	5.01	35,330(11)	34,117(10)
9. Business Studies									24,920(13)
10. Physics	44,871 (6)	45,334 (7)	–4.30	43,401 (8)	–4.90	41,273 (9)	–9.51	37,349 (9)	35,959 (9)
11. Social Science	52,421 (3)	56,176 (3)	8.00	60,813 (3)	13.50	70,321 (3)	7.67	75,716 (3)	78,525 (2)
12. French	21,508(12)	27,245(12)	13.00	30,801(12)	7.96	33,254(12)	–10.88	29,637(12)	29,101(12)
13. Economics	44,029 (7)	45,330 (8)	–2.10	43,163 (9)	–6.87	40,194 (9)	–9.90	36,217(10)	30,885(11)
Total A-Level Candidates							–0.23	728,574	728,851

Note: Figures in parentheses represent rank order.

Table 11.2(b): Numbers of A-Level Candidates, 1995–2000

	(93–94) % Change	1995	(94–95) % Change	1996	(95–96) % Change	1997	(96–97) % Change	1998	(97–98) % Change	1999	(98–99) % Change	2000	(99–2000) % Change
1.	−0.95	86,382 (1)	−1.72	86,627 (1)	0.30	93,546 (1)	7.98	94,099 (1)	0.60	90,340	−4.00	89,805 (1)	5.24
2.	−2.10	57,468 (3)	7.15	63,454 (3)	10.40	69,142 (3)	2.50	80,570 (2)	16.50	85,338	5.91	86,428 (2)	−4.33
3.	−4.60	62,188 (2)	0.75	67,442 (2)	8.40	73,114 (2)	15.20	70,554 (3)	−3.50	69,945	−0.87	67,036 (3)	−4.16
4.	7.10	51,837 (4)	2.27	51,894 (4)	0.10	58,534 (4)	12.80	58,457 (4)	−0.10	56,036	−4.14	54,814 (4)	−2.18
5.	−0.10	43,426 (5)	−6.29	42,786 (6)	−1.50	43,641 (5)	1.89	44,881 (5)	2.80	42,181	−6.02	40,856 (5)	−2.09
6.	1.10	42,271 (7)	2.53	40,455 (7)	−4.30	42,458 (7)	4.90	43,030 (6)	1.30	41,727	−3.03	38,779 (6)	0.77
7.	−2.80	42,694 (6)	−4.67	43,355 (5)	1.50	42,547 (6)	−1.90	40,495 (7)	−4.80	38,482	−4.98	38,228 (7)	0.79
8.	−3.40	33,907 (9)	−0.61	33,782 (8)	−0.10	35,289 (8)	4.50	37,119 (8)	5.20	37,385	0.71	37,609 (8)	0.59
9.		26,837(12)	7.69	29,100(10)	8.40	33,359(10)	14.60	37,008 (9)	19.90	37,926	2.48	37,112 (9)	−12.02
10.	−3.70	34,761 (8)	−3.33	32,801 (9)	−5.70	33,508 (9)	2.10	34,244(10)	2.20	33,880	−1.07	32,059(10)	−5.38
11.	3.70	30,371(10)	−61.33	27,871(11)	0.30	30,139(11)	8.10	26,242(11)	−12.94	24,749	−5.69	23,901(12)	−3.43
12.	−1.80	27,489(11)	−5.53	27,490(12)	0.00	25,916(12)	−5.70	23,633(11)	−88.0	21,072	−10.84	18,221(14)	−13.53
13.	−14.80	26,584(13)	−13.92	24,580(13)	−7.60	20,873(13)	−15.10	18,670(12)	−10.60	18,377	−1.34	17,113(15)	−6.88
Total	0.30	725,104	−0.51	752,169	1.20	776,115	3.18	794,262	2.30	783,692	−1.34	760,328	−2.34

Note: Figures in parentheses represent rank order.

century turns. Only at the post-16 stage does the quality of geography teaching appear to be superior to that of most other subjects.

GEOGRAPHY IN EXAMINATIONS

In the sphere of school life beyond compulsory geography in the National Curriculum (i.e. Key Stage 4), examination statistics (see Tables 11.1 and 11.2) suggest that geography was highly successful in recruiting candidates to take the subject at GCSE (instituted in 1988) but that current timetable restrictions are now beginning to bite. Given a 'free choice' of subjects, there is little doubt that geography numbers would remain steady, but, because of other statutory requirements, many schools now require pupils to choose between studying geography and history at GCSE level. Even where this system does not operate, there may be considerable restriction on what pupils may choose beyond the 'core subjects'. The playing field for Key Stage 4 is not a level one.

At A-level, where a genuine choice of subjects is made more freely, the figures for geography remain encouragingly high. For many years geography was the junior partner to history, but geography numbers overtook those of history in 1993 and since then the gap has continued to widen until 2000, when parity again occurred. However, depending on circumstances, the picture can change very quickly, as the decline of economics at A-level shows. In 1992 economics had more than 40,000 candidates but the figure had dropped to less than half that number six years later. Would geography suffer the same fate?

NOTES

1. The author was one of the two teacher-educators appointed to the group and so following description and comment is based on that personal experience.
2. Duncan Graham with David Tytler, *A Lesson for Us All: The Making of the National Curriculum* (Routledge, London, 1993), p. 71.
3. Leslie Fielding *et al.*, *Geography for Ages 5 to 16: Final Report of the Geography Working Group* (HMSO, London, 1991).
4. Department of Education and Science, *Draft Orders for the National Curriculum in Geography* (HMSO, London, 1991); Department of Education and Science, *Geography in the National Curriculum: Statutory Orders* (HMSO, London, 1991).
5. A. Goudie, 'The integration of human and physical geography', *Transactions of the Institute of British Geographers* (1987), pp. 454–8. D. Stoddart, 'To claim the high ground: geography for the end of the century', *Transactions of the Institute of British Geographers*, Vol.12 (1987), pp. 327–36.
6. One of the lay members of the group pointed out that his son had managed to pass through school to the age of 16, without ever studying any material about the United States of America.
7. Department of Education and Science, 'An inspection of GCSE Humanities Courses in 20 secondary schools', a report by Her Majesty's Inspectors (HMSO, London, 1989).
8. Kenneth Clarke, 'The Secretary of State's Speech to the Royal Geographical Society on geography in the National Curriculum', reported in *Geographical Journal*, 158 (1) (1992), pp. 75–8. See also pp. 65–74 and 79–83.

9. Growing government concern for this issue and involvement in it was expressed in a White Paper, *This Common Inheritance* (HMSO, London, 1990), and later through participation in the international 'Earth Summits' at Rio de Janeiro (1994) and Kyoto (1998), though few significant policies have yet been fully implemented.

10. These are explored in detail by Eleanor Rawling, another member of the Working Group in E. Rawling, 'The making of a national geography curriculum', *Geography*, 77, 4 (1992), pp. 292–309.

11. A previous attempt by the Schools Council to promote a Working Party on the Whole Curriculum had not been an encouraging model.

12. See, for instance, R. Robinson, 'Facing the future: not the National Curriculum', *Teaching Geography* (1992), pp. 31–2.

13. The quotation comes in an interview given by the Prime Minister in a feature article in the *Sunday Telegraph*, 15 April 1990.

14. National Curriculum Council (NCC), *Consultation Report on Geography* (NCC, London, 1990).

15. R. Dearing, *The National Curriculum and Its Assessment: A Final Report* (SCAA, London, 1994).

16. E. Bolton, 'Divided we fall', *Times Educational Supplement*, 21 January 1994, p. 17.

17. H. Harrison and N. Croft, 'Core geography – Whole Curriculum issues: a case study of an upper school', in R. Walford and P. Machon (eds), *Challenging Times: Implementing the National Curriculum* (Cambridge Publishing Services, Cambridge, 1994); Ann Kenward, 'Options at Key Stage 4', *Teaching Geography*, April (1993), p.81.

18. D. Lambert, 'The National Curriculum: what shall we do with it?', *Geography*, 79 (1) (1994), pp. 65–76.

19. A dissenting voice about one Waugh series is C. Winter, 'Ethnocentric bias in geography textbooks: a framework for reconstruction', in M. Williams and D. Tilbury (eds), *Teaching and Learning Geography* (Routledge, London, 1997), pp. 180–8.

20. The Annual Report of Her Majesty's Chief Inspector for Schools 1996–97 (HMSO, London, 1998) reported the following statistics:

> 30 per cent of the geography teaching at Key Stage 1 was considered good/very good; 64 per cent was considered satisfactory; 6 per cent was considered unsatisfactory/poor. Comparable figures for English were 43, 52, 6; for History, 34, 61, 5; for Maths, 40, 54, 6; for Science 41, 52, 6.

> 32 per cent of the geography teaching at Key Stage 2 was considered good/very good; 61 per cent was considered satisfactory: 8 per cent was considered unsatisfactory/poor. Comparable figures for English were 44, 50, 6; for History, 42, 53, 5; for Maths 43, 50, 7; for Science 44, 49, 7

> 50 per cent of the geography teaching at Key Stage 3 was considered good/very good; 44 per cent was considered satisfactory; 6 per cent was considered unsatisfactory/poor. Comparable figures for English were 57, 39, 4; for History 54, 39, 6; for Maths 49, 44, 8; for Science 51, 42, 7; for modern foreign languages 50, 43, 8.

> 59 per cent of the geography teaching at Key Stage 4 was considered good/very good; 38 per cent was considered satisfactory; 3 per cent was considered poor. Comparable figures for English were 66, 32, 2; for History 63, 34, 3; for Maths 50, 45, 5; for Science 55, 40, 5; for modern foreign languages 48, 44, 8.

> 75 per cent of the geography teaching post-16 was considered good/very good; 24 per cent was considered satisfactory; 1 per cent was considered unsatisfactory/poor. Comparable figures for English were 73, 25, 2; for History 76, 24, 0; for Maths 66, 34, 0; for Science 68, 30, 1; for modern foreign languages 67, 31, 2.

12

Geography – The Way Ahead, 2000–

MUCH HAS HAPPENED ...

The Way Ahead is one of the classic films of the 1940s. It is a Second World War battle film. Its cinematic images are vivid. Soldiers plod through the heat and dust of the desert, largely unaware of the significance of the battles they are fighting, yet determined to advance, as shells whine around their ears. Commanders yell instructions, officers rally their troops, battalions of infantrymen smile grimly, and (mostly) do what they are told whilst keeping up a stream of earthy comment about it.

It may be something like that for geography and geography teachers as we advance into the twenty-first-century, since it seems that various key (?) battles are in the process of being fought, that educational missiles (or missives?) whine around the ears of practitioners at an ever-increasing rate and that in the heat and dust of the day ultimate horizons are glimpsed only fitfully.

As the last chapter indicated, the advent of the National Curriculum provided first hope and then regret for geographers as the Baker vision of a 'broad and balanced curriculum' which included geography, history and arts subjects for all was initiated but then carelessly dismantled by a combination of pragmatism and power politics.

And yet, looking back over the longer term, it is clear that much has happened to enhance geography in schools in the past 150 years. From being a collection of travellers' tales, cosmography and some informational bric-a-brac it has matured into a major school subject at all levels, passing through several intellectual debates on the way, and gaining something of lasting value from each of them. Its place in the curriculum of schools, once unimportant, is now established, though it is not altogether secure.

THE CHANGING WORLD

One of the major challenges for geography teachers through the last 150 years has been to deal with a world changing more rapidly now than at any time in its history. Consider one of the world's most famous locations in the period covered by the central chapters of this book.

At the beginning of the nineteenth century, the Himalayas stood as a remote, majestic, unexplored, unconquered range of mountains. In 1852, Sir Andrew Waugh, working from the lowlands to the south, made the first known scientific calculation of the height of the mountain which topped the range. In true imperial fashion, the Tibetan name for the mountain, Chomolungma ('Goddess Mother of the World'), was supplanted by a tribute to Waugh's predecessor as Surveyor-General of India, Sir George Everest.

In the century following, Mount Everest was approached, reconnoitred, mapped, photographed, written about, tragically attempted (Mallory and Irvine, 1924), and flown over (the Douglas-Hamilton expedition 1933), 'because it was there'. It was eventually climbed successfully (Hillary and Tensing, 1953) by an RGS-sponsored expedition, and the news released to an amazed and delighted Britain as a last glimpse of imperial glory on the morning of Queen Elizabeth II's coronation.

On 5 May 1999, 18 climbers, one of them a 15-year-old boy, reached the summit of Everest within a period of an hour and 45 minutes. The event was reported to the world through global satellite communication technology by the Nepalese Ministry of Tourism. 'Celebrities' now take film crews with them to make TV documentaries about the mountain and are 'disappointed' when they fail to reach the top. A current concern of environmentalists is the amount of debris left on the mountain by the numerous expeditions who traverse it each year.

Over 150 years, the human ability to challenge, to 'master', and to despoil the environment appears to have 'progressed' beyond all recognition. Yet Everest the snow-capped mountain, the classic piece of physical geography, the icon of travellers and explorers, remains as it ever was. The world changes, yet it does not change. Geography teachers have to grapple with the paradox and seek to transmit its meaning to their pupils.

WHICH WAY WILL IT GO?

At the turn of the century, things can go either way for geography. The current National Curriculum (given only minor revision by the 1999/2000 exercise) will be considered for more radical revision in 2005. Will geography's presence be confirmed or challenged? If the former, there is hope for development of new themes and approaches to learning. If the latter, the current flexibility of topic choice built into the geography formulation by the 1993 (Dearing) and the 1999 revisions may turn out to be its Achilles heel. Though such flexibility may be attractive for teachers, it sends a message that at heart little or nothing in the subject is deemed essential for learning. In the light of that, geography will have few cards to play should fundamental questions about curriculum priorities be raised.

In primary schools, the hope must be that the 'literacy hour' and the 'numeracy hour' are passing phenomena or, that if not, their styles are broadened to allow the contribution of other subjects. Otherwise the restoration of interest in geography in primary schools engendered by the 1988 Act will be a false dawn.

In secondary schools, the subject's future beyond Key Stage 3 is uncertain. Will GCSE numbers stabilise, or continue to drift downwards as geography is marginalised by restricted option choices in the Key Stage 4 curriculum? Can A-level geography maintain its numbers if there is a decline in students taking it as an examination subject at lower levels?

Fewer students taking A-level would mean, in all probability, a diminished flow of students for university courses. Fewer undergraduate students would have implications for adequate teacher provision; fewer well-trained specialists would emerge. In consequence, the quality of school geography teaching could be affected adversely – and this would reduce further the number of students who might freely choose the subject for the purposes of examination. In other words, if weakness shows in one part of the system, a cycle of decline may be precipitated, the very reverse of events in the 1920s and 1930s.

THE NEED FOR POLITICS AND PUBLICITY

If geographers wish to see the essence of their subject survive in schools into the twenty-first century, (whether discrete or in an integrated form) they cannot rely on its inherent virtue. In the current world of public relations campaigns, specialist lobbying and spin doctoring they need to be fully aware of all the nuances of curriculum politics which are at work in schools and in government and be active in turning them to their advantage. Not to do so would be folly.

Regular national initiatives such as Geography Action Week (which has been designated and observed each autumn since 1996) and the major surveys organised by the Geographical Association (Land Use-UK 1996: Coastline 2000) are useful vehicles for such broad publicising. There is also the considerable opportunity for geographers to advance understanding of their subject by taking up local and topical opportunities beyond the immediate context of the school curriculum – for example providing informative and imaginative maps for the school prospectus and noticeboards; carrying out surveys and analyses of key local conservation or traffic issues: publicising the work of past pupils who have studied geography at university, or of geographers prominent in public life.

Another vital strategy for survival (or for the justification of survival) is for geography teachers to teach well. Given the wealth and range of lively material available to geography teachers and the richness of life in the real world, it ought to be rare for a geography teacher not to be able to interest or stimulate students in some part of the subject on its own merits. A key element in any truly successful educational enterprise is that it engages the freely given attention and goodwill of the learner; in the last resort, the survival of geography will depend on the day-by-day professional competence and enthusiasm of those who represent it at the chalk-face.

However well geography does in politics and practice, its value and appeal will also need to be demonstrated to those who see the subject from the outside. Parents, school governors, school curriculum committees, employers and especially key national decision-makers need to have an accurate image of what is being taught. They should not be working from some past antique image of the subject.

The need for professional bodies to present an up-to-date image of the subject, to generate informed policy-discussion, to see ahead to issues on the horizon and to represent the interests of their members effectively on major matters is a vital factor in preventing teachers from becoming beleaguered. Hurried, individual, reactive responses to central initiatives are rarely effective. And, over the past 20 years, the amount of central intervention in educational matters has grown by leaps and bounds.

ROLE OF THE PROFESSIONAL BODIES

The Royal Geographical Society (RGS) and the Geographical Association (GA) (helped by sponsorship from the Ordnance Survey) collaborated in April 1998 to run a seminar and dinner-meeting for Government Ministers, key civil servants and executives from a range of quangos and large charitable organisations.[1] The Council of British Geography (COBRIG) brings together key figures in the geographical world for a biennial weekend seminar on current issues in curriculum politics.[2]

Such pro-active lobbying and networking has to be part and parcel of the work of professional organisations in today's world. A close relationship has to be maintained with the Qualifications and Curriculum Authority (QCA), which deals with the detail of curriculum development,[3] as well as with senior civil servants and Ministers at the Department for Education and Employment.

The Geographical Association has been a model for many other subject associations in this respect since its baptism into curriculum politics following the 'Great Debate' of the late 1970s. Its skill in presenting a good case for geography at the time of the National Curriculum formulation was at least a partial influence in shaping the mind of the Minister and it has kept up a steady stream of activity in this sphere since, Most recently, the appointment of its first salaried Chief Executive in December 1998, (after a century of devoted voluntary service from academics in the post of Honorary Secretary) has indicated a further step along the road from service association to professional institute.

The renewed interest and vigour of the RGS in the world of education (following a largely passive role for much of the century) owes something to its recent merger with the Institute of British Geographers (IBG) (the

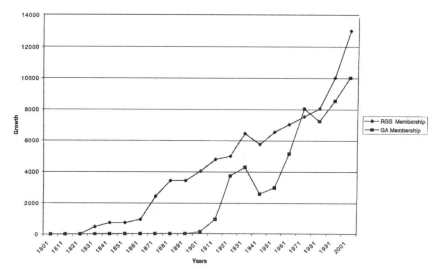

Figure 12.1:
Comparative membership
figures of RGS and GA,
1900–2000
(*Source*: author)

body to which most university geographers have belonged from its founding in 1933) but as much to a recent transformation in the Society's administration and forward planning. The RGS–IBG further strengthened its educational role by appointing its first full-time Education Officer in May 1999.

Both the RGS–IBG and the GA now work with comprehensive strategic plans to guide them, professional management approaches, and a clear perception of the need to be something more than providers of meetings, magazines and services for those who choose to join (see Figure 12.1 and Appendix 1). The present harmonious relationship between the two bodies (with the GA seen as the 'leader' in policy matters concerning schools and the RGS–IBG as the 'leader' in higher education issues) has made geography more agile and energetic than many other subjects in dealing with issues and challenges. There is regular contact between the two professional associations as they negotiate their way through the quickly changing educational landscape. One day, there might even be unity.

Both GA and RGS–IBG in England, aided by COBRIG, (along with their Scottish and Welsh counterparts)[4] are now aware of the need to go beyond the narrow aspiration of servicing the immediate needs of their own members. They are coming to realise that their task is no less than to nurture a geographical consciousness (and a sense of the importance of that consciousness) in the community as a whole. There is some way to go in the present utilitarian climate before that aim can be said to be near achievement.

TAKING THE UTILITARIAN VIEW

It is likely that at least for the next decade, whichever political party is in power in England and Wales, there will be, in essence, a continuation of the post-1988 policies hammered out in the wake of the Education Act and stemming from James Callaghan's Prime Ministerial speech at Ruskin College, Oxford in 1976. This period encompassed long Conservative rule (1979–97), buttressed at either end by Labour governments. The fundamental philosophy of the education policies from both major parties has been commonly utilitarian – education is conceived primarily in terms of 'helping young people to be prepared for the job market'.

The wider concerns of transmitting a cultural heritage, of enabling children to grow into mature self-knowledge through their own active participation in 'discovery learning' and of giving young people the tools to make a critique of their own society (the 'reconstructionist' view) have for the most part been given lesser emphasis, though there was an element of the 'cultural heritage' position emphasised by Kenneth Baker as plans for a subject-centred National Curriculum emerged in the mid-1980s.

It is significant that the most distinctive clashes of opinion in curricular terms have been the ones about the 'broad and balanced curriculum' espoused by Baker, and about the advisability of returning to the idea of separate pathways post-14. These opened up clashes not between the Conservative and Labour parties, but within them. The policies of the Labour government elected in 1997 have been, in most ways, educationally as 'conservative' as those of their Conservative predecessors.

The utilitarian cast of mind has coincided with much greater central intervention than before and so its impact has been greater. Geography's role, as a generalist subject, in such a curriculum is an ambivalent one. In the middle-term, the subject may be valued mostly for whatever 'practical usefulness' it provides for job preparation and creation. There are certainly elements of world knowledge and skill development which can be paraded as geographical contributions to education for the world of work; but these (probably rightly) are not seen as of major importance compared with the knowledge and skills provided in maths and English, neither are they the 'heart' of geography for most people who have studied it.

The contribution which geography makes in a wider context – the understanding of the way the world works spatially and economically, of how landscapes and townscapes come to be the way they are, even more the need to feel wonder and respect for the physical world, are paid lip service but not raised to high priority. There has, for example, been much talk about the need to care for the environment in the last three decades, but little of substance generally has emerged following the hand-wringing of governments at successive earth summits. In Britain, the destruction of valuable natural beauty and habitats goes on almost unabated. Housing continues to eat up 'greenfield sites', roads become daily more congested in the absence of meaningful incentives for people to use other forms of transport, and the problems of increasing pollution, artificial crop modification and urban decay and deprivation have yet to be convincingly addressed. 'Environment' is now freely talked about, but 'environmentalism' is still branded as a policy of unrealistic idealists.

Geography teachers are encouraged to raise such issues in classrooms, but, under National Curriculum guidelines, are sternly warned not to get them out of balance. The presentation of both sides of an argument can be a valuable and democratic exercise; but it can also lead to talk and little else. Lady Bracknell's observation, is still apposite, 'Fortunately, in England, at any rate, education produces no effect whatsoever. If it did it would prove a serious danger to the upper classes and probably lead to acts of violence in Grosvenor Square'.[5]

THE CHALLENGE OF THEMES

In the utilitarian climate, the role of generalist subjects remains uncertain – indeed, the role of subjects themselves may be provisional. The background philosophy to the National Curriculum unfolds only in post-hoc afterthoughts, and the support for subject-formulations is, one suspects, presently based on pragmatism rather than principle.

The Labour government post-1997 has sought to remedy perceived weaknesses in the original formulations and to cater for particular topical matters by setting up working parties on non-subject-specific aspects of education about which there is current concern and debate – citizenship, personal moral and spiritual education, sustainable development.

The handling of the citizenship issue is an interesting case-study, of relevance to geography. Most geography teachers would see their role as already including the inculcation of an element of citizenship. They seek to imbue a sense of national citizenship amongst their pupils as they teach about the United Kingdom and of 'global citizenship' as they teach about other countries and the nature of the world environment. Though their teaching might stretch to covering such matters as the way in which the organisation of the European Union works (or is supposed to work) and what the environmental responsibilities of a local council are they would not usually see themselves as covering such elements of citizenship as understanding the legal system or the constitution.

The assumption would be that this is done in other subjects (notably history or general studies) and that geography makes a contribution to a theme which is, in essence, cross-curricular. Geography teachers would not want geography to be responsible for teaching all aspects of citizenship any more than they would wish geography to be reduced to teaching no aspects of citizenship.

A key question generated by the work of the 1998–99 Citizenship Working Group was : 'Are the rights and responsibilities of citizenship conveyed satisfactorily through the teaching in existing subjects?' The answer to the question was deemed to be 'No' and citizenship outcomes added on to the overall curriculum specification at the wish of the Minister (though not of QCA). If citizenship becomes a separately time-tabled topic in the early years of the twenty-first century, the way will then be open for other bolt-on additions. In which case, the whole notion of a subject-framework for the curriculum may gradually be called into question. The shape of the curriculum in Britain could in time become more like that of the states of Australia or the USA, where particular hybrid formulations (e.g. society and environment, government and community, social studies) form modular-based courses. These, in turn, affect what is offered in universities.[6]

This question (and others which look to the mid-term future) have been lately considered by a new informal gathering of geography teachers and teacher-educators in England , who call themselves the GeoVisions group.[7] In a workshop at a recent major national conference,[8] the question was posed. 'Is geography best seen as a *resource*?; instead of denying its eclecticism and trying to promote from the centre some kind of unified curriculum subject [should we not] delight in it and exploit its propensity for permeable and mobile disciplinary boundaries?' In the next period of curriculum change, this may exactly become the key issue. What has to be weighed in the balance is the benefit of a continuing subject identity, the value of the community which sustains it, and the matter of what is lost if it withers.

WILL THERE BE SCHOOL GEOGRAPHY IN THE LONGER TERM?

What is it about geographical study which might make it deserving of survival in the longer term? Some argue that it will be better in the future to describe the curriculum not by subjects, but by a series of 'entitlements' , targets for particular ages. Others say that modularisation or unitisation of the curriculum is inevitable because there will be pressures for more flexible course arrangements. Still others argue not only for the linkage but the submergence of subjects into wider thematic groupings.

However, by the flow of past educational history, there is a strong subject-identification and subject loyalty which British teachers have developed. On balance, this has been a strength rather than a weakness since it has ensured the development of a sound base of academic knowledge, an evolutionary approach to change and (for the most part) a corporate intellectual integrity. It has also led to a sense of 'belonging' and a focus for study. The existence of an army who assemble under a recognised flag provides coherence and mutual support even if the members of it do not always quite march to the same beat. An understanding of a discipline is more likely to be effective when it is mediated by and through a community of scholars rather than an *ad hoc* pragmatic collection of principles. 'Subjects' are not divine creations – but they have shown themselves to be practical ways of marking out the intellectual landscape.

But do pupils see it that way? The case is sometimes made that subject-boundaries are 'artificial' and that, in reality, learning is a seamless robe which has no divisions. (Such a philosophy prevailed in primary education in the post-war period, though plenty of parents and children were happiest when assured that what they were doing was 'maths' or 'geography'.) The point is rhetorical rather than securely founded in epistemology.

Subjects (whether conceived of philosophically or organically) provide convenient and identifiable segments of learning that help learners to find their way; and they have, on the whole, proved their usefulness as components of an organisational framework from the time that the earliest formal educational institutions were devised. There is no overwhelming reason (or evidence) to believe that what goes on in 'subjects' is any more obscurantist or a deterrent to learning than that which goes on in curriculum innovations conceived in other ways.

The Geography for the Young School Leaver project , begun in 1970, took a fresh line about what was appropriate geographic content for 15-year-olds. It was centred on spatial/geographical ideas but it borrowed freely, using material and insights from other subjects. Its eclectic approaches remain influential with many teachers (and not only geography teachers) and pupils 30 years on. It is a good example of how subject-centred curriculum development can be as open, innovative and relevant as any recasting of material beyond subject-boundaries.

WHAT WILL GEOGRAPHY CONTRIBUTE?

So we return eventually to the question addressed in the first chapter of this book: what is the essence of geography? – but this time to consider it in a future perspective. More, exactly, what, of the generally accepted canon of the school subject that we call geography, will be of interest and relevance to the education of pupils in the twenty-first century? What could justify or will justify the continuation of school geography in the future?

The most fundamental point may be the easiest to overlook. The study of geography deals with a key dimension of life – space and place in the real world : without an understanding of that dimension no young person is properly educated. 'Without geography, you're lost' may be better known as a T-shirt slogan than an educational aphorism but its truth is self-evident. If there is no education about spaces and places, an appreciation of society and environment is unlikely to be developed properly. Concepts such as 'near' and 'far' look as if they are simple and innocent terms, scarcely worthy of any educational consideration, but that is a misapprehension; not understanding them or taking notice of them has sometimes been the undoing of nations, let alone the inconvenience of individuals.

Geographical education is not alone in educating us about the dimensions which enwrap human consciousness, but it is a vital component in doing so. Historical education (dealing primarily with the dimension of time) and religious education (dealing primarily with the dimension of the numinous and the spiritual) have equal claim to be partners in this function. Education about these dimensions broadens, fulfils and matures; schemes which do not appreciate the importance of these dimensions are seriously deficient in their education of the whole person.

Geography is also ordinarily regarded as the guardian of a particular language –the language of maps, which in more recent times has come to be known as 'graphicacy'. Research has shown that the facility to understand maps is independent of linguistic skills and that young children at the age of 3 can be competent map or map-model users.[9] Competence in the use of maps (and diagrams) in the modern world is of increasing significance, as any industrialist or manager will confirm, and all school pupils need to have a grounding in it. It is within geography lessons that this is usually done, though in the future, in Britain, teaching and learning in this sphere will need to go beyond the consideration of particular scales of Ordnance Survey maps and delve extensively into the many other map forms which are used in everyday life. Map-making as well as map-reading needs to be on everyone's basic curriculum.

Just as literacy, numeracy and graphicacy will need to continue to be taught as a base, so too will a knowledge of the planet we inhabit. Starting in primary school, as land and sea are distinguished on the globe, and continents and oceans named and remembered, an expanding mental portfolio of world knowledge is needed for everyday use now more than ever. Not every chance conversation can be conducted with repeated reference to an atlas or an encyclopaedia and so it is vital that future citizens carry around in their heads some general information about the world. A recent survey[10] showed that fewer than half of all schoolchildren could place London correctly on a map of Britain, only 42 per cent could identify Germany on a map of Europe, and only 18 per cent knew that the Acropolis was in Greece. Government advisers admitted that the findings were 'surprising and disturbing'. This, allied to the results from many other similar surveys of the past two decades needs to be acknowledged as a matter of importance: it is not 'the heart' of geography, but it is unwise to dismiss the necessity of the acquisition of a base for future learning with contempt.

The recent work of Hirsch and Bloom in America[11] suggests that some geographic knowledge is an important part of an information base which is vital for underprivileged and minority groups if they are not to be perpetually disadvantaged in their attempts to improve themselves and their own situation in society.[12] As Egan suggests,[13] the acquisition of world knowledge, far from being seen as a bore, is welcomed as an enjoyable task by most pupils, especially when set to work with an atlas or a globe.

A framework of world knowledge is a kind of coathook on which other things may be hung. The mastery of key spatial concepts (such as diffusion, migration, the theory of central places, the connectivity of networks) can then be tied in to the acquisition of understanding about the human and physical environment (such as the agricultural capacity of particular landscapes, patterns of world resources and trade, the growing hole in the ozone layer). It is the two major aspects of geography taken together (knowledge and conceptual understanding) which lead to a realistic appreciation, credible analysis and explanation of real-world situations (such as the limitations to economic development in a region, the impact of pollution, the predicaments of particular nations and peoples).

Thus future citizens may move towards the development of an informed and humane set of values and the tackling of such fundamentally important but apparently intractable twenty-first century questions as: 'Why are there food mountains in some parts of the world, whilst people are starving in others?', 'Are we going to run out of energy?', 'Why don't we colonise the oceans?'

THE IMPORTANCE OF PEDAGOGY

The pedagogy attached to all this is likely to be as important as the content, since no education lastingly takes place without the motivation, co-operation and goodwill of the learner.

One area where school pupils of all ages seem to be well ahead of their teachers is in the use and understanding of information and communications technology. Babes surf the Internet with equanimity, whilst their elders look nervously on from the book-favoured shore. Many geography teachers appear to have embraced innovation with a relatively greater enthusiasm than their colleagues in other subjects (as they have done on many occasions through recent educational history) and the considerable potential of Internet sources, remotely sensed images from satellites, and interactive video technologies is already being explored. ICT in schools is destined to be a growth area in the first quarter of the twenty-first century and it will be relatively well-financed;[14] any subject which grasps the opportunities offered and shows its willingness to explore and experiment will be looked on with favour. Geography is well placed to do this.

But it would be wise not to become too hooked on the VDU; ICT is still in its 'honeymoon' period and much learning is enhanced by human response and sociability. There is still an important place for teacher exposition, and for the guided class viewing of visual material as well as for role-play, discussion, individual and group enquiry learning to help the progress of work; an undue emphasis on one style of teaching and learning (even ICT) is likely to be less productive than a skilful mix of various approaches.

THE ULTIMATE GOAL

Beyond all this lies the necessity to make future generations of school pupils aware of what it is they inherit in the physical and human world, in order that they may be aware of the need to save it from ultimate destruction through human thoughtlessness or malevolence.

Geography teachers should not be ashamed to take the lead in schools in seeking to inspire their pupils about the continuing fascination and beauty of the natural world, as well as making them marvel at the complexity and liveliness of the human one. Not all things on earth are 'problems', as some current geography syllabuses seem to imply. John H. Paterson, was one of the great writers of regional geography in the twentieth century[15] and was as interested in teaching as in the research side of the subject; referring to the needs of both university students and school pupils he once memorably said, 'Let us welcome anything which will increase their opportunities to wonder, as well as to weep, over the world of man.'[16]

Though they have been trained in differing styles, and have been affected by educational and political influences at different periods of its history, geography teachers in Britain have, over the past 150 years, played a not insignificant part in opening the eyes and widening the horizons of those who have sat in their classes. They have sought to explore, explain and enthuse about the world in all its physical and human aspects, in the midst of increasing change.

Now we are aware that we live on a planet ever-more crowded with people, ever-more mobile, ever-more technologically powerful. The 'global village', of which Marshall McLuhan wrote, is now a reality. The physical environment in which we live and travel is revealed as perilously fragile and susceptible to damage and destruction.

In the light of such trends, is it conceivable that, in the twenty-first century, geographical education in British schools might not be made relevant enough or considered not important enough to be taught to future citizens?

SOME FUTURE VISIONS

This book has been largely about the past, with the intention that those who work in the present may be better informed. It began with some personal vignettes of reminiscence so perhaps it is appropriate to end with some personal vignettes of what may lie ahead. These come from a group of Cambridge postgraduates who are just about to start their careers as teachers of geography;[17] to them, the future is entrusted and this is their authentic vision of it:

> As we open the door on the next thousand years, I think geography teaching is poised to offer itself as an atlas of direction in the post-modern eddies of the world in which we find ourselves, I shall tell pupils to open their eyes and look to geography for a view of the bigger picture.

———

I see geography as similar to learning a foreign language.

Geography supplies a person with the tools to look at the wider scheme of things, to look beyond the colloquy of day-to-day existence and to ask how or why. The true value of geography is not quantifiable. It goes beyond locational knowledge or climatic understanding and seeks to help students develop skills and values. In its true form it is unashamedly eclectic. Geography gives pupils the confidence to look out of the window and discuss.

It is frustrating to think that, practically, as a teacher, you may not always be able to teach the geography you want, but it is our task to get pupils interested enough in every topic so that they always want to find out more. I believe that no other school subject is as relevant to the real lives of pupils – to the world that they see and experience. I hope that teaching geography will be a lifetime role for me and that I will learn something new every day.

The lesson begins and with it the voyage of discovery. 'Where will we go today, sir?' 'Can we take another virtual fieldtrip down the Amazon?' But something more challenging is lined up for today. The class will try to solve one of the greatest dilemmas of the age – Who should foot the bill for the on-going attempts to reduce global emissions of greenhouse gases?

We check the Web, gathering fact and fiction from around the world. Then the United Nations Select Committee is called to session. James chairs the meeting. Abi will open the debate, speaking as a representative of the government of the Philippines, a nation now almost completely submerged by rising waters. Rav is a NASA meteorologist; Suzanna a junior environment minister in the British Government, Louise will play a Friends of the Earth activist, fighting her corner as she describes the desperate plight of the coral ecosystems of the south Pacific.

Young minds work on old problems. The meeting draws to a close. One by one the pupils relinquish their characters, returning to their own lives. Everyone has spoken; everyone has listened; everyone has learned.

I think that geography teaching in the twenty-first century must rise to the challenges that come with studying a world that is constantly changing and which is so seemingly full of paradox. Borders shift, environments lose equilibrium, societies simultaneously unify and fragment. We are told we live in a 'global village', yet we do not know our neighbours. By plane we cross continents in a matter of hours, but few of us know much of what lies between destinations. Telecommunications put world facts, figures and images at our fingertips, but we cannot be sure that these are unbiased, undistorted...

Finding our 'place' in this exciting (but uncertain) world is a daunting prospect and children require more than simply knowledge and understanding to do this; they need a survival kit. As geography teachers, we have a key responsibility in equipping pupils with the means to approach and participate in the future.

GEOGRAPHY LESSON

When the jet sprang into the sky
it was clear why the city
had developed the way it had,
seeing it scaled six inches to the mile.
There seemed an inevitability
about what on ground had looked haphazard
unplanned and without style
when the jet sprang into the sky.

When the jet reached ten thousand feet
it was clear why the country
had cities where rivers ran
and why the valleys were populated
The logic of geography –
that land and water attracted man –
was clearly delineated
when the jet reached ten thousand feet.

When the jet rose six miles high
it was clear that the earth was round
and that it had more sea than land.
But it was difficult to understand
that the men on earth found
causes to hate each other, to build
walls across cities and to kill.
From that height it was not clear why.

Zulfikar Ghose
From *Jets from Orange* (Macmillan Education)

NOTES

1. A summary of speeches and points made at the seminar was published jointly by RGS-IBG, GA and OS as 'Education for Life', a well-illustrated glossy pamphlet, which was distributed free to all secondary schools in England and Wales.

2. Biennial COBRIG seminars were organised at Mansfield College, Oxford in 1994, 1996 and 1998 by Eleanor Rawling. See E. Rawling and R. Daugherty (eds), *Geography into the Twenty-First Century* (Wiley, London, 1996) records the 1994 seminar.

3. It has been fortunate for the subject that there have been two experienced and skilful geographic educators, Eleanor Rawling and John Westaway, in post as professional officers at QCA since its inception. The subject was equally well served by the energetic and shrewdly pro-active work of their predecessor at SCAA, Pat Wilson.

4. The Scottish Association of Geography Teachers (SAGT) and the Royal Scottish Geographical Society (RSGS) play, in Scotland, a similar role to the GA and RGS as do in Wales, the Association of Geography Teachers in Wales (AGTW) and the Universities Council for Welsh Geography (UCWG). All belong to the Council of British Geography (COBRIG) and meet regularly to discuss matters of mutual concern.

5. Oscar Wilde, *The Importance of Being Earnest*, Act 1 Scene 1 (1895). The text of the play is available in many editions; for example, in *Plays* by Oscar Wilde (Penguin, London, 1954) – this quotation is on p. 266 of that edition.

6. There is a clear antecedent of this in Scotland, where 'Modern Studies' has been a secondary school course alongside geography and history since the 1950s and is often seen as an alternative to them. It comprises elements of history, geography, sociology, politics and current affairs.

7. 'Co-operative research' in *Teaching Geography*, April 1999, pp. 70–1. See also articles about the Geovisions Group's work in the issues of *Teaching Geography*, October 1998 and January 1999.

8. The workshop was held at the Geographical Association's Annual Conference at Manchester in April 1999. The Geovisions Group can be reached via 998 Bristol Road, Selly Oak, Birmingham, B29 6LE.

9. See, for instance, J. M. Blaut and D. Stea, 'Mapping at the age of three', *Journal of Geography*, 73 (7) (1974) pp. 5–9.

10. The survey was carried out by NOP for Microsoft electronic publishers on 900 children between the ages of 8 and 16. It was reported on page 8 of *The Times* of 23 January 1997. There have been many similar recent surveys which show lack of locational knowledge, e.g. 'Where are we? One in six thick Britons don't know' a survey of 1,000 adults by Mori, reported as the leading front-page story with an eight column-width headline in *Sunday Times*, 7 January 1988: 'British know little about the world and care even less', a report of a major survey of locational knowledge carried out by the Gallup Organisation in 12 countries, in *The Independent*, 29 December 1988. Sweden and Germany came out best.

11. E. D. Hirsch Jr, *Cultural Literacy* (Houghton Mifflin, Boston, MA, 1987); A. A. Bloom, *The Closing of the American Mind* (Penguin, London, 1986).

12. For a thoughtful critique of Hirsch's views and the possible effect on school geography, see P. Dowgill and D. Lambert, 'Cultural literacy and school geography', *Geography*, 77(2) (1992), pp. 143–51.

13. Kieron Egan, *Educational Development* (Oxford University Press, Oxford, 1979).

14. The government has announced plans to link all schools to the Internet before 2001 and also to give every teacher a lap-top computer, though the financial implications of this and the proportion of the cost which will need to be shouldered by the schools themselves remains unclear.

15. J. H. Paterson, *North America* (Heinemann, London, 1965).

16. J. H. Paterson, 'Some dimensions of geography', *Geography*, 64(4) (1979), pp. 268–78.

17. My thanks to Andrew Jennings, Jason Skyrme, Alexandria Moody, Will Abell and Sally Brydon (members of the University of Cambridge Postgraduate Certificate in Education course, 1998–99) for these observations.

Appendix: RGS Fellowship Figures and GA Membership Figures, 1891–1999

Figures for both societies include Associate (student), and corporate members but not reciprocal memberships negotiated with societies overseas.

RGS Figures taken from RGS Council reports and supplemented by personal research: GA figures taken from Appendix B of *The Geographical Association: The First Hundred Years, 1893–1993* by W. G. V. Balchin and supplemented by personal research.

RGS figures calculated as of 31 December in each year; GA figures as of 31 August of each year

	RGS	GA		RGS	GA
1891	3,579	–	1912	4,930	1,000
1892	3,549	–	1913	5,152	1,076
1893	3,646	35	1914	5,191	1,144
1894	3,775	50	1915	5,067	1,107
1895	3,802	60	1916	4,957	1,002
1896	3,829	72	1917	4,834	996
1897	3,854	73	1918	4,778	1,458
1898	3,996	98	1919	4,933	2,379
1899	4,043	105	1920	5,110	3,695
1900	4,026	121	1921	5,324	4,159
1901	3,997	202	1922	5,614	4,462
1902	4,052	287	1923	5,820	4,510
1903	4,136	341	1924	5,990	4,610
1904	4,198	448	1925	6,127	4,585
1905	4,263	503	1926	6,219	4,351
1906	4,367	535	1927	6,318	4,447
1907	4,436	643	1928	6,327	4,449
1908	4,564	793	1929	6,369	4,345
1909	4,681	884	1930	6,452	4,233
1910	4,783	902	1931	6,310	4,293
1911	4,887	962	1932	6,159	4,009

	RGS	GA		RGS	GA
1933	6,039	4,036	1957	6,761	4,366
1934	5,984	4,002	1958	6,884	4,610
1935	5,924	4,001	1959	6,980	4,919
1936	5,990	3,867	1960	7,081	5,110
1937	5,935	3,666	1961	7,210	5,349
1938	5,866	3,646	1962	7,401	5,391
1939	5,667	3,384	1963	7,536	6,177
1940	5,326	2,554	1964	7,466	6,704
1941	5,017	2,261	1965	7,258	7,357
1942	4,831	2,305	1966	7,213	7,883
1943	4,863	2,464	1967	7,203	8,448
1944	4,899	2,747	1968	7,174	8,522
1945	5,010	3,191	1969	7,085	9,138
1925	6,127	4,585	1970	7,103	7,991
1926	6,219	4,351	1971	7,046	8,387
1927	6,318	4,447	1972	6,979	8,301
1928	6,327	4,449	1973	6,847	8,400
1929	6,369	4,345	1974	6,399	8,522
1930	6,452	4,233	1975	6,294	8,470
1931	6,310	4,293	1976	6,642	7,941
1932	6,159	4,009	1977	7,070	7,963
1933	6,039	4,036	1978	7,510	8,049
1934	5,984	4,002	1979	7,703	8,024
1935	5,924	4,001	1980	7,815	7,203
1936	5,990	3,867	1981	7,917	6,635
1937	5,935	3,666	1982	8,707	6,163
1937	5,935	3,666	1983	8,527	6,258
1939	5,667	3,384	1984	8,670	6,463
1940	5,326	2,554	1985	8,433	6,555
1940	5,326	2,554	1986	8,523	6,520
1942	4,831	2,305	1987	8,655	7,191
1943	4,863	2,464	1988	9,134	7,044
1944	4,899	2,747	1989	10,103	6,873
1945	5,010	3,191	1990	10,366	8,499
1946	5,338	4,265	1991	11,005	9,672
1947	5,722	5,200	1992	11,306	10,397
1948	6,043	4,400	1993	11,428	10,844
1949	6,171	4,051	1994	11,457	11,014
1950	6,362	2,944	1995	12,665	11,443
1951	6,417	2,994	1996	12,338	11,462
1952	6,401	3,092	1997	12,456	11,547
1953	6,371	3,383	1998	12,287	10,727
1954	6,528	3,738	1999	12,000	10,000
1955	6,656	3,781		approx.	approx.
1956	6,622	4,109			

Select Bibliography

Note: Unless otherwise stated, all books were published in London.

P. Bailey, *Teaching Geography*, David & Charles, 1972.

W. G. V. Balchin, *The Geographical Association: The First Hundred Years, 1893–1993*, Geographical Association, Sheffield, 1993.

J. Bale, *Geography in the Primary School*, Routledge & Kegan Paul, 1987.

J. Bale, N. J. Graves and R. Walford (eds), *Perspectives in Geographical Education*, Oliver & Boyd, Edinburgh, 1973.

H. C. Barnard, *Principles and Practice of Geography Teaching*, University Tutorial Press, 1948.

J. A. Binns and C. Fisher, *Issues in Geography Teaching*, Routledge, 1999.

P. Boden, *Developments in Geography Teaching*, Open Books, 1976.

D. Boardman (ed.), *New Directions in Geographical Education*, Falmer Press, Brighton, 1985.

I. Cameron, *To the Farthest Ends of the Earth: The History of the Royal Geographical Society 1830–1980*, Macdonald, 1980.

T. H. Dalton, *The Challenge of Curriculum Innovation*, Falmer Press, Brighton, 1988.

J. H. Fairgrieve, *Geography in Schools*, University of London Press, 1926.

L. Fielding *et al.*, *Geography for Ages 5 to 16*, Department of Education and Science and The Welsh Office, 1990.

N. Foskett and W. E. Marsden, *A Bibliography of Geographical Education: 1970–1997*, Geographical Association, 1998.

O. Garnett, *Fundamentals in School Geography*, Harrap, 1934.

A. Geikie, *The Teaching of Geography in Elementary Schools*, Macmillan, 1887.

I. Goodson, *School Subjects and Curriculum Change*, Croom Helm, 1988; republished by Falmer Press, Brighton, 1993.

G. Gopsill, *The Teaching of Geography in Elementary Schools*, Macmillan 1956–73.

P. Gould, *The Geographer at Work*, Routledge & Kegan Paul, 1985.

N. J. Graves, *Geography in Education*, Heinemann, 1975.

N. J. Graves, *Curriculum Planning in Geography*, Heinemann, 1979.

N. J. Graves (ed.), *New Movements in the Study and Teaching of Geography*, Temple-Smith, 1972.

N. J. Graves *et al.* (eds), *Geography in Education Now*, University of London Institute of Education, 1982.

N. J. Graves and C. Lukehurst, *Geography in Education: A Bibliography of British Sources 1870–1970*, Geographical Association, 1972.

E. Hacking, *Geography into Practice*, Longman, 1992.

P. Haggett, *Geography: A Modern Synthesis*, Harper & Row, 1972.

P. Haggett, *The Geographer's Art*, Blackwell, Oxford, 1990.

D. Hall, *Geography and the Geography Teacher*, George Allen & Unwin, 1976.

G. M. Hickman, J. Reynolds and H. Tolley, *A New Professionalism for a*

Changing Geography, Schools Council, 1973.

A. Holt-Jensen, *Geography:History and Concepts*, 3rd edn, Sage, 1999.

L. J. Jay, *Teaching with a Little Latitude*, George Allen & Unwin, 1981.

R. J. Johnston, *Geography and Geographers*, Edward Arnold, 1979.

A. Kent *et al.* (eds), *Geography in Education*, Cambridge University Press, Cambridge 1996.

D. Lambert and D. Balderstone, *Learning to Teach Geography in the Secondary School*, Routledge/Falmer, 2000.

D. Livingstone, *The Geographical Tradition*, Blackwell, Oxford, 1992.

W. E. Marsden, *Evaluating the Geography Curriculum*, Oliver & Boyd, Edinburgh, 1976.

M. Naish (ed.), *Geography and Education: National and International Perspectives*, University of London Institute of Education, 1992.

K. O'Mahony, *Geography and Education*, Educare Press, Seattle, WA, 1988.

E. Rawling and R. Daugherty (eds), *Geography into the Twenty-First Century*, John Wiley, Chichester, 1996.

B. S. Roberson and I. L. M. Long, *Teaching Geography*, Heinemann, 1966.

F. Slater, *Learning Through Geography*, Heinemann, 1982.

R. W. Steel, *The Institute of British Geographers: The First Fifty Years*, Institute of British Geographers, 1984.

D. R. Stoddart, *On Geography and its History*, Blackwell, Oxford, 1986.

D. Tilbury and M. Williams (eds), *Teaching and Learning Geography*, Routledge, 1997.

H. Tolley and K. Orrell, *Geography 14–18: A Handbook for School-Based Curriculum Development*, Macmillan, 1977.

T. Unwin, *The Place of Geography*, Longman, 1992.

R. Walford (ed.), *New Directions in Geography Teaching*, Longman, 1973.

R. Walford (ed.), *Signposts for Geography Teaching*, Longman, 1981.

R. Walford (ed.), *Viewpoints on Geography Teaching*, Longman, 1991.

R. Walford and P. Machon (eds), *Challenging Times: Implementing the National Curriculum in Geography*, Cambridge Publishing Services, Cambridge, 1994.

C. Ward and A. Fyson, *Streetwork*, Routledge & Kegan Paul, 1973.

W. P. Welpton, *The Teaching of Geography*, University Tutorial Press, 1923.

M. Williams (ed.), *Geography and the Integrated Curriculum: A Reader*, Heinemann, 1976.

Issues of the following teachers' journals and magazines:
Classroom Geographer
The Geographical Teacher, later re-titled *Geography*
Geographical Journal
Primary Geographer
Teaching Geography

Issues of the following magazines designed for pupils:
GEO
Geography Review
Wideworld

Various editions of:
Secondary Geography Teachers Handbook, Geographical Association.
Primary Geography Teachers Handbook, Geographical Association.
Post-16 Geography Teachers Handbook, Geographical Association.

See also the plethora of official government documents, reports of HMI, guidance papers etc., especially since 1970.

Index